ADDRESS.

To the Hunters After the Ninety Days' Scout.

The merchant counts over his hard-earned gains,
  The lawyer looks out for his fee,
But the life that the hunter doth lead on the plains
  Is the life that is dearest to me.

How oft in my boyhood I wished that the breeze
  Would waft me to some place of rest,
Away from the cities, away from the seas,
  And into the heart of the West.

And now I am sitting at midnight alone,
  And my dream realistic appears,
Yet I cannot help thinking how poor I have grown
  Within the last four or five years.

But I look to that hour the hunter enjoys
  While the camp-fire is ruddy and bright,
And I very much wonder what all of the boys
  Are planning and plotting tonight.

At this very time I can fancy Bill Kress
  And the firelight shines on his face;
He is plotting some mischief,—God knows what it is,—
  To get square with the whole human race.

There 's Jack and Bill Benson: the latter 's asleep,
  And his dreams do not indicate ease,
For he 's rolling about while he thinks of the scout,
  And the hardship of living on cheese.

Good Hiram and Foley on business are bent;
  The Deacon 's got hold of a pen,
And may I presume that his letter is meant
  For a certain fair one in Cheyenne?

Enough, now, for business matters; besides,
  There are things I will dare to suggest
Concerning the hunters, concerning the hides,
  And the tools which are suited the best.

Next hire a hunter to shoot through the herd;
  Don't hit the old cow in the lead;
Be careful of this.   Now from what I have heard,
  Alt Waite is the man that you need.

Don't put any pegs in your buffalo-hides—
  It is an extravagant trick;
And you never will make a success of your work
  If you hire such skinners as Mick.

With awkward employés there is but one chance—
  Keep the fleshy part on the inside,
Or West will be certain to see at a glance
  All the holes that are cut in the hide.

And now perhaps my readers will think it is strange
  That we find it more difficult, far,
To skin twenty buffalo out on the range
  Than standing at Aikens's bar.

Now, bully George Aikens, his heart is the best,—
  It is twenty degrees over proof;
I must add that his malt is exempt from that fault,
  Having tested it under his roof.

Just look how Tom Sherman is thriving, in spite
  Of a most apoplectic disease;
In Dodge they are reading his burial rite,
  While he smokes a cigar at his ease.

Beware of the pigeon-hole table in town;
  This advice I would give to a few,
Who playing like Sol cannot pocket a ball
  Without knocking the tip off the cue.

Don't steal from your neighbors to furnish yourself,
  Though others have stolen from you;
Better make a clean breast of the matter to West,
  And purchase your outfit anew.

But pray do not run an extravagant bill,
    Unless that you have an estate;
Better follow the track of the warrior black,
    And go it on buffalo straight.

If Cook starts a fierce and political talk,
    To make every nerve in you quiver,
Get Hudson to seat himself down on a rock
    And sing you the "O Roaring River."

Don't fret yourself much 'bout the war—it is best
    For the country's financial career;
Smoky Thompson's ideas will always digest,
    Washed down by his excellent beer.

Now some of the boys since their trip to the plains
    Are not quite so much given to roam,
And I trust when they think of their trials and pains,
    They will live more contented at home.

There are many examples sufficiently strong
    To render them easy to please;
Go talk to Bill Benson, and ask him how long
    He has lived upon cherries and cheese.

And had we all died in this destitute state,
    What a heaven we'd have of our own,
With Squirrel-Eye as warder to watch at the gate
    And old Billy Kress on the throne.

Now, boys, let me tell you what most I admire
    (Excepting fair women, you mind):
'Tis the man who possesses the chivalrous fire
    Of courage and honor combined.

And this is most characteristic of those,
    Whose names it is needless to give,
Yet I doubt not the current of friendship flows
    Betwixt us so long as we live.

Enough for the present, else perhaps you will think
    I have carried my reader too far;
Step over and give Billy Benson the wink,
    And let us stand up at the bar.

Here's a health to our Captain, so courteous and true,
    Here's health to the gallant José;
And though we missed catching the Skinawa crew,
    We shall give them the devil some day.

Thank heaven, my boys, for a land which is blest
    With a frontier so boundless and free,
So drink to the hunters and drink to the West,
    And pass the "red liquor" to me.

REYNOLDS CITY, TEXAS, Sept. 16, 1877.
    [From Dodge City *Times*, Sept. 29, 1877.]

JOHN R. COOK.

THE BORDER AND THE BUFFALO

AN UNTOLD STORY OF THE
SOUTHWEST PLAINS

———

The Bloody Border of Missouri and Kansas.
The Story of the Slaughter of the
Buffalo. Westward among
the Big Game and
Wild Tribes.

A STORY OF MOUNTAIN AND PLAIN

BY

JOHN R. COOK

87077

MONOTYPED AND PRINTED
By CRANE & COMPANY
TOPEKA, KANSAS
1907

THE BORDER AND THE BUFFALO

BY

JOHN R. COOK

Especially dedicated to my crippled wife, who
patiently assisted and encouraged me to write
this book; and to Sol Reese, Mortimer N.
Kress ("Wild Bill"); also, that noble band of
Buffalo hunters who stood shoulder to shoulder
and fought Kiowas, Comanches, and Staked
Plains Apaches, during the summer of 1877 on
the Llano Estacado, or the Staked Plains of
Western Texas and Eastern New Mexico,
whose memories will ever pleasantly abide with

THE AUTHOR

INTRODUCTION.

In presenting these Reminiscences to the reader the author wishes to say that they were written and compiled by an uneducated man, who is now 63 years of age, with no pretensions to literary attainments, having a very meager knowledge of the common-school branches. In placing these recollections in book form there is an endeavor all along the line to state the facts as they occurred to me. The tragic deaths seen by the author in dance-hall and saloon have been omitted, in this work. But to that band of hardy, tireless hunters that helped, as all army officers declared, more to settle the vexed Indian question in the five years of the greatest destruction of wild animals in the history of the world's hunting, the author especially devotes that portion of the book pertaining to the buffaloes. The incidents connected with the tragic death of Marshall Sewall will be appreciated, I trust, by all lovers of fair play. Thomas Lumpkins met his death in a manner that could be expected by all old plainsmen. There were so many tragic incidents that occurred during the author's experience after leaving New Mexico, that it was difficult for him to segregate one event from another, in order to prepare a presentable book,—one that could be read in every home in the land without shocking the finer sensibilities of the reader. And it is the sincere hope and desire of the author that this design and object have been accomplished.

JOHN R. COOK.

CONTENTS.

MISCELLANEOUS STORIES OF BUFFALO LAND.

LIST OF ILLUSTRATIONS.

THE BORDER AND THE BUFFALO.

CHAPTER I.

Boyhood in Territory of Kansas, 1857.—Day Fort Sumter was Fired
On.—First Confederate Army at Independence, Missouri.—Search
for Guns.—Glimpse of Quantrill.—Guerrillas and the Money
Belt.—My Uniform.—Quantrill at Baxter Springs.

I was born in Mount Gilead, Ohio, on the 19th of December, 1844. Father moved his family to Lawrence, Kansas, in the spring of 1857. That summer we occupied the historical log cabin that J. H. Lane and Gaius Jenkins had trouble over,—resulting in the tragic death of the latter. Shortly prior to the killing of Jenkins, we moved to Peru, Indiana, where we remained until the latter part of March, 1861, when the family returned to Kansas. Myself and oldest brother traveled overland by team and wagon. We had three head of horses. We left the State line of Indiana at Danville, and crossed the Mississippi to Hannibal, Missouri, the day that General Beauregard fired on Fort Sumter. And the War of the Rebellion was on. As we were driving up a street, in the evening of that great day, an old gentleman standing at the gate in front of a cottage hailed us and asked where we were going. "To Kansas," was brother's reply.

The old gentleman walked out to where we had stopped, and said: "Boys, you are goin' into a peck of trouble.

(1)

Gineral Buregard cannonaded Fort Sumter to-day, and is at it yit. Boys, I'd turn round and go back to whar ye come frum."

Brother said: "No, Uncle, we could never think of such a thing. Our father and mother are now at Lawrence, Kansas, and we *must* go to them."

He replied: "That place you are going to will be a dangerous place. There has already been a power of trouble out thar whar you are goin', and thar's bound to be a heap more; and all over the nigger, too. I own nineteen of 'em, but if it would stop the spillin' of blood I would free every one of 'em to-night."

This old gentleman had a kind, pleasant-looking face wore the typical planter's hat, and seemed to take a fatherly interest in us; directed us to a certain farm house on our road where we could get accommodations for the night. And we passed on, having for the first time in our lives seen and talked with the owner of human chattels.

Some neighbors came to the house where we stayed that night, and in earnest fireside talk conveyed the idea that there would be no war; for, said they, when the North finds out that we are in earnest they will not fight us.

My brother, being four years older than I, took part in the evening's talk, and told them that it was but fair to leave the negro out of the question, and to consider the Union as our forefathers left it to us, and that he did not think that twenty-odd millions of people would consent to have the Union of our forefathers dismembered.

The next day, as we were passing through a densely timbered region, an old negro came out from behind a large tree near the wagon-track. His wool was white as snow; his head was bared, and, holding in one hand an

apology for a hat, he gave us a courteous bow, and said:
"Please, Mars, is we gwine to be free?" (Their under-
ground telegraph was already bringing word from South
Carolina to Missouri.)

My brother, being more diplomatic than I could or would
have been at the time, said to him, "Why, you surprise
me, Grandpop. You look fat and sleek and I know you
have more freedom this minute than I have."

Passing on up the State road that leads through Independence, in Jackson county, I could not help but notice
the change that had come over my brother. All along the
route we had passed over we would talk about and comment on places we passed, objects we viewed, and anything
amusing he would make the most of, to have the time
pass as pleasantly as we could. But *now* his face had
taken on a more serious look. He seemed at times to be
more concerned than I ever remembered him to be before.
Twelve miles before arriving at Independence, he said to
me:

"John, I will do all of the talking from this on, when we
meet anyone, or when in presence of anybody."

He afterwards told me the reason he had suggested this
to me was, that the man of the house where we had stayed
the night before had told him that a large Confederate
army was being recruited at Independence; that the blockade was in force, and that all people bound for Kansas were
forbidden to pass on through to that State. My brother
did not wish to be caught on any contradictory statements
that I might make.

We had traveled only about three miles after charging
me to not talk, when suddenly five men on horseback rode
up behind us, and, slowing down, engaged in conversation

with my brother. I listened very attentively to the following dialogue:

"Whar you-uns goin' to?"

"To Kansas."

The speaker said: "We air too, purty soon. Me and this feller was out thar four year ago," pointing to one of the party, and meaning the border troubles of 1856. "We're goin' after Jim Lane and a lot more of the Free-State Abolitionists. What place you goin' to?"

"Lawrence."

"Why, that's a Abolition hole. You a Abolition?"

"Abolition? What is that?" my brother asked.

"Why, do you believe in free niggers?"

"I don't know enough about the subject to talk about it."

"Whar did ye come frum?"

"Indiana."

One of the others said, "Thar is whar I come frum."

The first spokesman said: "I come frum Arkansaw ten year ago, to the Sni hills."

Whereupon my brother asked, "What stream is this we are approaching?"

The first spokesman said, "This here crick is the Blue," and added, "you-uns 'll never git to Kansis."

My brother shifted his position in the wagon-seat so as to face the speaker, and asked, "Why do you say that?"

"Oh, because the provost marshal will stop ye when ye git to town," meaning Independence.

My brother's name was Ralph Emerson, the family all calling him "Em" or "Emerson."

I said, "Emerson, I want a drink of water."

Just as he crossed the stream he stopped the team, took a tin cup that we carried along, and got down and handed me up a cup of water; and the five horsemen rode on.

As they were leaving us, the first spokesman said, "We'll see ye up town, boys."

As we were passing up the main street in Independence, we were aware that we were very much observed. This being the very earliest period of the war, there were no Confederate uniforms, but in order to distinguish an en- listed man from a civilian each soldier had a chevron of white muslin sewed diagonally across his left arm. The strip was about two inches wide and five or six inches long. These soldiers were to compose a portion of what was af- terwards known as the famous flower of the Southwestern Army, C. S. A.

When we arrived about the central part of the town, we were halted. The man who halted us had on his left arm, in addition to the white chevron, one of red, just above the white one, on which were some letters, but I do not remem- ber what they were. He had a cavalryman's saber and a Colt's revolver on his person. After halting us, he called to two other men, saying, "Come and search this wagon."

Just as the men were climbing into the wagon we were asked where we were going.

"To Kansas," said my brother.

"Go ahead—search that wagon," said the man who halted us.

Pretty soon one of the searchers said, "Sargent, here is a box of guns on their way to that d—d Abolition country."

I laughed in spite of myself.

To diverge a little: My father had been a cabinet- maker in his earlier life, and he had purchased a nice set of cane-seat chairs while we lived in Indiana. They were put together with dowel pins, and he thought as we boys had no load he would take them apart and pack them in a box, and we would haul them to Kansas. It so happened that the box he made to pack the chairs in did very much resemble a gun box, and I was forcibly reminded of the similarity in October, 1862, when my company was opening some gun boxes at Lawrence to arm ourselves with, when we were now sure-enough soldiers.

The sergeant ordered Emerson to turn the team around. One of the horses was tied behind the wagon. He was a large bay gelding, and as the team swung around on a haw pull, I noticed "Charlie," the horse, had been untied from the wagon and was being led through the crowd. In an instant I was off of the wagon, wound my way through the crowd, jerked the halter-strap out of the fellow's hands that was leading "Charlie," and with a bound I was astride of as fine a horse as was in all Missouri. The crowd set up a yell, but it had more of the cheer in it than that fearful Rebel yell we dreaded to hear in after years.

The crowd was now so dense around the wagon that the way had to be cleared for us to follow the sergeant, who was leading the way to the Provost Marshal's office. I cannot remember of ever being the center of so much attraction as we were that day.

Arriving at the Provost office, we were ordered inside. I tied "Charlie" by one of his mates, and accompanied my brother inside, where we were seated. On the opposite side of a table or desk from where we were was seated a large, florid-faced gentleman about sixty years of age. He had a frank, open countenance, wore gold-rimmed glasses, and was twirling a gold-headed cane in his hands. The sergeant saluted him, and said:

"Colonel, these boys are smuggling guns through to Kansas."

The Colonel replied: "That is a very serious business, indeed."

My brother arose and said: "Colonel, that is all a mistake. That box contains nothing but a set of cane-seat chairs, together with strips of carpet and the necessary wrappings to keep the varnish from being scratched and the furniture from being defaced."

The old Colonel, as they called him, arose, and, walking to the door, asked: "Sergeant, where are those guns?"

"In a box in that wagon by the door," came the answer.

"Have the box put on the sidewalk here and opened," which was done, and found to contain just what Emerson had told them.

The Colonel came close to where we were sitting and asked where we came from, and being answered, he asked to what particular part of Kansas we were going to. Emerson said we were going to Lawrence, but as the Shawnee Indians could now sell their lands we expected to purchase land of them in Johnson county.

"Sergeant," said the Colonel, see that these boys are safely conducted outside of our lines on the road to Kansas City," and said to us, "That is all."

We went to the wagon, my brother driving the team and I bringing up the rear on "Charlie."

Coming around a bend and seeing our flag floating over Kansas City, I hurrahed, when my brother stopped me and made me tie the horse to the wagon and get up on the seat beside him. He said to me very sharply: "Young man, wait until you are out of the woods before you crow. Wait until we get to Lawrence—then we will be all right."

Poor boy! little did I think then what was in store for our country and him, and that he would be the sacrifice our father and mother had laid upon their country's altar.

He barely escaped with his life at the sacking of Olathe, to be finally wholly deceived, surprised and shot down by a volley from Quantrill's bushwhackers at Baxter Springs, Oct. 6, 1863,—twenty-seven bullets crashing through his body. Of this, more extended mention will be made hereafter.

We drove that afternoon and evening through Kansas City and Westport, and arrived at the old Shawnee Mission late in the evening, having crossed the Missouri border in the evening twilight, and were once again on Kansas soil, whose eighty thousand and odd square miles of territory had given, would yet, and did give more lives for liberty and Union than any other State in the Union according to her population.

The next day in the afternoon we drove up Massachusetts street, in Lawrence. We noticed the absence of the circular rifle-pits—one at the south end of the street, the other near the Eldridge House; but we noticed the presence of men in blue uniforms. Then we noticed our father, and in a few moments our family were united. Father and mother had been very solicitous about us. Such men as E. R. Falley, S. N. Wood and others telling father that if we ever got through Missouri at all it would be a miracle, on account of the blockade. All Lawrence was up and preparing to answer back the fatal shot that Beauregard had fired. And the flag we already loved so well took on a new meaning to me.

The next day our family moved down through Eudora and on out to Hesper, where, just over the line in Johnson county, my father purchased two hundred acres of Shawnee Indian land, on Captain's creek. On this land my father, mother, a sister and two little brothers lived during the Slaveholders' Rebellion; and after the Quantrill raiders passed our house that memorable August night in 1863, to do at Lawrence what the world already knows, that mother and sister carried from the house, boxes and trunks so heavily laden with household goods to a cornfield, that when the excitement and danger were over they could not lift them, when they found the ruffians did not return that way.

Before drifting these chapters to the early settlements of southern Kansas, and finally to the mountains and plains of the Southwest, the author deems it pertinent and relevant to follow more or less the Kansas and Missouri border, and on down through Indian Territory and Arkansas, from 1862 to 1865, the final ending of the rebellion, which found me at Little Rock, Arkansas. One incident occurred during the winter of 1861 that gave me my first glimpse of a Missouri guerrilla. My brother Emerson was teaching school at Hesper. One afternoon, one of the scholars left a bright-red shawl on the playground at recess. The road from Lawrence to Olathe ran through this playground. I was seated near a window at the south side of the school-room, in plain view of the road and shawl, when I noticed three men traveling east. One of them dismounted and picked up the shawl, and, mounting his horse, the three rode on. I called my brother's attention to the fact. He went to the door and called to the men, saying, "Bring back that shawl." They looked back and said something to him that he did not understand, and rode on, one of them putting the shawl over his shoulder. My brother dismissed the school, and, going to the nearest house, procured a horse and overtook them at the Bentley ford, on Captain's creek, and brought back the shawl. The words that Turpin of Olathe and his Missouri pals used when my brother overtook them were afterward remembered by one of these desperadoes as he was lying on the floor of a shack on the west side of the public square in Olathe, his life ebbing away from mortal gunshot wounds from Sheriff John Janes Torsey, of Johnson county. My brother, stooping over him, asked the dying bushwhacker if he remembered him. "Yes," came the feeble answer, "and I am sorry I said what I did to you when you came after the shawl last winter."

My next sight of a guerilla was in the summer of 1862, at Eudora. A German named Henry Bausman kept a road-house just north of the Wakarusa bridge, on the Lawrence road. He kept beer, pies, cakes, bologna sausage, and cheese to sell to travelers. His son Henry was about my age, and I thought a good deal of him, and when I would make the seven-mile ride from home to Eudora for the mail, I would cross the bridge and have a few moments chat with young Henry. On this particular occasion we were in the garden, not twenty steps from the road, when we saw a man approaching from the timber from the direction of Lawrence. It was the man that terrorized the border—Charles William Quantrill. But we did not know it at the time. He dismounted, tied his horse to a hitching-rack in front of the house, and went inside. Henry said to me:

"John, I believe that fellow is some kind of a spy. He has passed here several times in the last year, always going the same way. Let's go inside and see him."

When we came into the front part of the house where Bausman kept his beer and eatables, Quantrill was sitting on a bench with his back against the wall. He would look towards the living-room in the house, then toward the front entrance, and two different times he got up and walked to the door, looking up and down the road. He had on two revolvers; his overshirt was red, and he wore a sailor's necktie. After he left and had crossed the bridge going through Eudora, I got on my pony and started for home. When Quantrill got to the old stage line he turned towards Kansas City, I crossing the trail going on southeast to my home.

How did I know it was Quantrill? Only by the general description afterwards.

In the month of August, 1863, at Fort Scott, Kansas, Henry brought me the first published news of the Lawrence massacre. Henry being a poor reader, I read to him the account of the horrible butchery, after which he said:

"Oh if we only knew that that was him at our house last summer how easy we might have saved all this bloody work, for he must have been planning this terrible deed; and just to think my father had two guns loaded leaning against the wall at the head of the bed he and mother sleeps in. We could have killed him so easy and saved the town." Henry was my good German comrade, for we were then both soldiers in the same company.

Early in August, 1862, a gentleman, Booth by name, came into our neighborhood buying steers and oxen to be used in hauling military supplies to New Mexico over the old Santa Fé Trail. The train was being outfitted at the old outfitting post near Westport. My father sold Mr. Booth several head of cattle and he added to this purchase many more in the neighborhood, but could not get near as many as he wanted. He got my father's permission to help him drive the cattle to the outfitting station.

We started the cattle from my father's farm the afternoon of the 16th day of August, 1862, and drove them to Lexington, about four miles from home, on the old Kansas City & Topeka stage line. There was a large hotel there and we put up for the night, turning the cattle in a lot or corral and putting our horses in the stable. We went to the house and were standing on the front porch facing the stage road when suddenly Mr. Booth said: "Johnny, come with me, quick!" and passing through the house and on out and into the barn, and as I followed him in he said "shut the door."

He was nervous and excited. He took off his revolver belt and unbuttoning his clothes as if he was going to disrobe he took from his waist a broad soft belt, saying: "Here, get this around your waist quickly; unbutton your pants and get the belt next to your body." After all was arranged as he wished, he had me take my coat from my saddle and put it on, he saying "I know it is very warm, but please wear it for a while." Then he said: "Now, Johnny, you are a young farmer lad and would not be suspected of having any money. But I would. There is over three thousand dollars in that belt. Now don't say a word about it."

We had no sooner got back to the porch than it was made plain to me what had caused Mr. Booth's quick actions. Looking down the stage line towards Monticello we saw approaching about twenty-five mounted men.

They came up within a hundred and fifty steps of us and halted and for quite a little bit seemed to be holding a council.

Presently three of the party came on up to the hotel. Mr. B. accosted them with "How do you do, gentlemen?" The courtesies of the day passed when one of the three asked "are you the proprietor?" Getting a negative answer, another one asked if he could tell them how far it was to Lanesfield on the Santa Fé trail, and what direction it was. Mr. B. said "perhaps this boy can tell you."

I stepped to the corner of the house and told them it was about twelve miles in this direction, pointing toward the place. They asked "What creek is that we crossed back yonder?" I answered Kill creek. One of them said "I thought so when we crossed it, but was not sure." Another said, "then that is the way we want to go up that west prong;" and saying good-by they rode back to their companions and all turned south and rode over the unsettled prairie toward Lanesfield.

One of the three men I noticed in particular; he had red hair, short scrubby beard and the scar of a recently healed wound under his left ear. I saw this same man's lifeless body in December, 1863, in the Boston Mountains in Arkansas.

That evening after it had become dark Mr. Booth and I took some blankets and went northwest from the house some distance to a swale and lay down in the prairie grass to sleep. Mr. B. told me in the morning he had had a bad night of it and had not been able to sleep but little; but I, a growing husky farmer boy, was sound asleep in a jiffy. Mr. Booth said he would give the world if he could sleep like I did. He awoke me in the early dawn and we went to the house.

After breakfast we saddled our horses, turned the cattle out and grazed them down to Kill creek; then after watering them and grazing them a few moments longer we drove them past Monticello and made our noon stop in some scattering sumac where grass was good and plentiful. We ate our lunch that had been put up at the Lexington hotel and that evening drove to an old Shawnee Indian's on Mill creek and put up for the night.

The next day, when we were about five miles from the outfitting post, we met a second lieutenant with twenty-

five soldiers sent out to look for Mr. Booth. Just at that
period of the war there was an unusual stir along the
border. Lots of the guerrillas from north Missouri had
worked their way south to the Sni hills; those from the
two Blues were active and the troops at Independence
(Union troops now) were kept busy chasing the bushwhackers.

When the lieutenant met us he said "Hello, Mr. Booth!
How are you? We got uneasy about you and they sent
me to look you up."

"What is the news?" asked Mr. B. (It seemed that he
and the officer were former acquaintances.)

"Well," said the lieutenant, "the devil is to pay! We've
been getting the worst of it for the present; the president
has called for more troops; your uncle Jim was killed a
few days ago by the Youngers; Quantrill is going to raise
the black flag. Bill Anderson, Spring River Baker, Pony
Hill, Cy Gordon, and all the guerrilla leaders swear they
will make the people over the border earn the title of
'Bleeding Kansas.'"

That settled the matter for me. I had been importun-
ing my father for the past six months to give his consent
for me to enlist in the army; but he would say, "wait
a bit; let us watch. Maybe we will all have to turn out.
We will see,—you are very young for a soldier." But
this lieutenant's running talk had decided me. I would
go in the army as soon as I got back home.

Mr. Booth told the officer about the mounted men we
saw at Lexington. "Yes," said the lieutenant, "that is
why I was sent this way; those fellows crossed the Missouri at Lee's Summit three nights ago and went west
between Kansas City and Independence; but we never
heard of it until about midnight last night. They were

headed off by Pennick's men from getting to the Sni hills; but I can't see how or why they would go so far west before turning south. But they were thought to be west of here. Some think that George Tod is their leader."

Here Mr. Booth spoke to me, asking, "Johnny, are you afraid to start back home alone?"

I said "No, sir; I don't think anybody would harm a boy." I took the money belt from my waist and handed it to Mr. Booth, who took from a purse in his pocket a ten-dollar bill and a two-dollar Clark and Gruber bill. Handing them to me he said, "you are riding a splendid horse. He is as tough as a pine knot. Now you ride back to the old Shawnee Indian's, have him feed your horse and get you all you want to eat; you can then ride to your father's by 2 o'clock to-night." He bade me good-by, saying, "I hope your folks will come out of this trouble without harm."

Poor Booth! We learned that the gray matter oozed from his brain the following October, in Johnson county, Missouri, he having been shot in the temple by the Youngers.

I arrived home a few minutes after the old Seth Thomas clock struck twelve, August 19th, and on the following 2d day of September I enlisted in what was known in its organization as Company E, Twelfth Kansas Infantry, Charles W. Adams Colonel, son-in-law to Senator James H. Lane.

On the following 24th day of December I was 17 years old. I enlisted at Lawrence, was sworn into the service by James Steele of Emporia, who was my first captain. One of the conditions of oath was that I would accept such bounty, pay, rations and clothing as were or would be by law provided for volunteers. Yet in 1864 I had to skirmish around pretty lively and provide the ration part myself.

After being sworn in I was sent into a room adjoining and put on my first uniform. There was a near-sighted, cross-eyed fellow in this room who had charge of affairs. There was a long table piled with clothing. It was the worst lot of shoddy that ever came from a factory. At this time I was small, even for my age. I had to take a pair of pants that were many sizes too large. Then we hunted over the pile of pea-jackets and got the smallest one, and it was just too much of a fit.

Then my hat! Oh, such a hat! It was black, high crown, about a four-inch rim, a green cord around it, a brass bugle on the front, and it had a large fluffy black feather plume from the band up and angling over the crown.

That day I had a daguerreotype picture of myself taken, and when the artist showed it to me I felt so big that President Lincoln's overcoat would not have made me a pair of mittens.

Shoes came next, and I got a fit. Then came a knap-sack and haversack. The knapsack I loaded up with two suits of underclothes and a fatigue blouse. Then came a pair of dog-hair blankets; and when I strapped the whole outfit on my back I must have looked like Atlas carrying the world.

I now started for home on a three days' leave of absence. That evening I boldly walked into the kitchen where my mother was preparing the evening meal. At sight of me she threw up both of her hands, exclaiming "Great Cæsar!"

I said, "No mother, I am neither Cæsar nor Brutus, but I am a Union soldier."

One could have taken two seamless grain sacks, cut the bottom out and run a gee-string through and made equally as good-fitting a pair of pants as I had on.

On returning to Lawrence I found the recruiting camp up the river a little way from town. It was near the Kansas river and close by a big spring that I remembered of being at many times during the summer of 1857. After staying at this camp a few days we marched south to a block-house on the Osage river, twelve miles north of Fort Scott, Kansas. This block-house was called at the time Fort Lincoln. From there we marched back to Paola, where my regiment was mustered into the service; and a few days afterward the wounded from the Prairie Grove battle passed through Paola to the Leavenworth hospital.

My regiment was formed out along the border by companies and battalions, my company going to Shawnee-town after it had been raided and sacked.

In February we were in Fort Scott. In April I was put on detached duty; was assigned to C Company, Third Wisconsin Cavalry, with headquarters on the Drywood, in Jasper county, Mo., and for months we rode the border from Balltown to Spring river, being in the native heath of Pony Hill, and finally ending his career. Lexington's men suffered in proportion to the killings and robberies they committed, and Cy Gordon made himself scarce.

I was back to my company in August and at 3 A. M., October 7th, 1863. Henry Bausman, our drummer boy, beat the long roll so vigorously that we were in line, some in stocking-feet, some bareheaded. We were ordered to get three days' rations, hard-tack and bacon, and hurry to Baxter Springs, where, the day before, Quantrill with four hundred bushwhackers had surprised and deceived the little garrison and killed 65 soldiers and seven commissioned officers—my brother included in the list.

By daybreak we were *en route* for Baxter Springs, riding in Government wagons drawn by six-mule teams. We

arrived there long after night, and learned that sixty-five
bodies had been buried in one trench, and the bodies of
the commissioned officers we had not met on our road
down were buried separately about fifty feet from the
trench, under some blackjack trees. Henry, a colored
soldier, who had been my brother's cook and camp-keeper,
piloted me out to my brother's grave. My heart for a
time seemed like stone; not a tear, not a sigh, but as I
stood looking down at that mound of fresh earth I realized
that "war is hell" long before I ever heard that General
Sherman said it was.

My brother was in temporary command at Baxter
Springs at the time he was killed, and the circumstances of
his killing were among the most cowardly, brutal, and
treacherous incidents in the annals of a so-called civilized
warfare. The little garrison was composed of the most of
C Company and a portion of L Company of the Third Wisconsin cavalry and A Company of the First regiment of
negro troops that were raised west of the Missouri river.

Baxter was established as a way or change station between Fort Scott, Kansas, and Fort Gibson, I. T. It lies
in the extreme southeast part of Kansas. Here the dispatch bearers and messenger riders changed horses between
points.

My brother had certain trees blazed on the brush and
timbered side of the garrison, and stakes set with little
flags on them on the prairie side, which took in about eight
or ten acres of ground. He had issued an order against
firing guns inside these lines unless so ordered. About
the time this order was made, a Union lady came in from
the Shoal creek country and told my brother that Quantrill was gathering his guerrillas together in the hills of
southern Jasper for the purpose of striking another hard

blow. This time he would capture General Blunt and destroy his escort while the General was *en route* from Fort Scott, Kansas, to Fort Smith, Arkansas, where he was to make his headquarters. This lady said that it was Quantrill's intention to first capture Baxter Springs the day Blunt would arrive. They were to get possession of Baxter before Blunt arrived and attend to him when he came.

My brother at once sent a message to Fort Scott, notifying the authorities of the intent. He also sent a messenger to Carthage, Mo., asking for immediate reinforcements. The messenger that started to Scott was never seen or heard from, and it is only fair to presume that he was captured and taken to some lonely spot and killed. The messenger to Carthage got through, but the next day after my brother was killed the word came back, "No troops to spare."

The fates were at work. The very day this horrible massacre occurred the Neosho river was nearly out of its banks on account of unusually heavy rains to the west. Johnny Fry, a messenger rider, on his way from Fort Gibson to Fort Scott with an important message, was being pursued by Cy Gordon and five Creek Indians. He was some 300 yards in advance of them when he came to the river, and as his horse was taking him ashore on the north side of the stream Gordon and his Creeks had dismounted and were shooting at him from the south bank. He came on into Baxter unharmed, related the incident to my brother and several others, and said in closing that he had gotten his pistols wet when he swam the river, and wanted to shoot them empty, clean and reload them, before going on to Fort Scott. My brother said: "All right, Johnny; after dinner we will go outside the lines and fire them off.

We will shoot at a mark; I'll take my own along, for I want to clean them up too."

They took a Third Wisconsin man along to tally. Blunt was not expected for several days, according to the information this little garrison had received.

The Third Wisconsin man stuck the five-spot of diamonds on a black oak tree just outside the lines and nearly in sight of the water at the Spring river ford. The ground was paced off and the firing at target had proceeded until my brother had one shot left and Johnny two, when like a clap of thunder from a clear sky the guerrillas rode up out of the Spring river ford carrying *our flag* and dressed in our uniforms, stripped from the bodies of Union soldiers they had killed along the border. By this time they were sixty paces from the three men and moving on in column of fours. The tally man, standing where he had a view of the whole line, noticed that only about half of them were dressed in our uniform, and Johnny Frey's suspicions being aroused he said "Run, boys, for your lives; they are guerrillas!" "No," said my brother, "that's the militia from Carthage."

But the Third Wisconsin man took his pistol from its scabbard and threw it on the ground in front of him and begged for his life, and *they* spared it. He told us afterward that they seemed to ignore his presence; but halted, fired a left-oblique volley of about twenty shots at Johnny and my brother. The shots brought both men to the ground. Johnny rose on his knees with both hands gripped to his pistol, and fired. As he did so he fell back, dead. My brother, getting to his feet, fired his last shot, when he too fell forward on his face.

About fifty of these devils incarnate clustered around their bodies. Turning my brother over face upwards one of them called to another that was farther back in the line, saying; "Come here, Storey! Here is your man, by God! We've got him." This fellow came up, dismounted, and drawing a heavy bowie-knife whacked my brother a blow over the front part of the skull, cutting a gash about five inches long.

The Third Wisconsin man had been herded inside this group around these quivering bodies. He saw them rifle Johnny's pockets and take my brother's uniform; then he was ordered to go to the rear and mount one of the extra horses.

Their firing had alarmed the camp, and as they charged up along the northern side of it they were met with a spirited irregular fire from the darkies, and as they swung around the western angle the Third Wisconsin boys took a turn at them and they passed on out of range on the open prairie and marched up the trail, our flag at the head of column in fours dressed as Union soldiers. Is it any wonder that Blunt's advance thought they were the troops from Baxter coming out to give them a fraternal reception?

Blunt had nooned that day at Brushy, four miles from Baxter, and coming down the trail riding in an ambulance and his big gray horse tied behind barebacked, everybody unsuspecting, the Third Wisconsin band getting ready to play a patriotic tune, nearly all of the men that Blunt had being raw recruits, not knowing nor thinking of harm. Is it any wonder, I repeat, that Quantrill made the shambles he did in such an amazing short time? And does it not seem strange that Jack Splain would be lying on the ground badly wounded and Quantrill placing a pistol to his face telling him that when he got to hell he should tell them that Quantrell was the last man he saw, and fired in his face, and that Splain lived to tell it at Grand Army reunions? Was she not a heroine when Mrs. McNary picked up her dead husband's gun that day and killed a bush-whacker at Baxter Springs?

Gen. Blunt's escort was demoralized; but he mounted his horse and with ten men fairly cut his way through the guerrillas and got safely to the garrison, where he estab-lished his headquarters in my brother's tent. When my brother's body was brought in for burial it was found he had received twenty-seven bullets in his body. He had gained a notoriety along the border. Among other things he had killed a guerrilla near Westport who carried a dead list, and among the names not yet crossed out were those of Captain Hoyt, Chief of the Red Legs; John Jones, sheriff of Johnson county, Kansas; Doctor Beech, of Olathe, Kansas; and R. E. Cook, my brother. Unfor-tunately, this list was published at the time, together with the details of the fight between the Border Ruffians and my brother. So he was a particular mark for vengeance and revenge. When it was also known that he was an officer of "nigger" troops, and being recognized when the guerrillas rode onto them, they wreaked their vengeance with revenge.

As I sat by the camp-fire listening to the story of the finding of the body of that brave, generous, kind-hearted and loyal boy, it was then that my pent-up grief came home to me. Those in the garrison were not willing to take chances, that first evening after the attack, to look on the timbered side for dead or wounded friends. So the next morning a strong party went out; they found Johnny's body where it fell, and it was rigid. And, remarkable to say, my brother's body was not yet rigid. He was found in a clump of hazel brush sixty yards from where he had fallen. And the mute evidence of the trails he had made through the blood-stained grass, to where he was found and both hands with broken hazel brush gripped in them, seemed to indicate to those who found the body that life had not been extinct until near morning. Johnny Fry had six wounds, all mortal. But when the soldiers washed my brother's body after bringing him to the garrison, preparatory to dressing him for burial, they found, besides the knife wound, twenty-seven bullet wounds.

Reader, would you call that *war?* No; it was *murder*, pure and simple.

I could not go home and tell this story to my dear little old Irish mother, whose God was the Lord; but I did, if anything, worse. When my brother was killed he was wearing a soft white hat which fitted his head rather tightly, and when the guerrilla turned him face upward and called to Storey, his hat was still on and nearly in the position in which he wore it. So when this fiend delivered the knife-stroke, he cut through the hat a gash nearly six inches long, running from near the center of the crown diagonally across the forehead on the left side.

On the morning of the 10th day of October, I was called to General Blunt's tent, where he informed me he would give me a furlough to take home the effects of my brother. He also gave me an order on the quartermaster at Fort Scott for my brother's horse, that had carried the first messenger to Scott after the disaster.

As I was packing up the things I wished to take home, he handed me a package of papers that had been taken from my brother's desk. At the time, I had the hat alluded to in my hands to put in the box I was packing. He noticed the hat, and said: "Let me see that hat."

I laid it in his hands and he asked me why I wanted to take it. I said, "General, the man that struck that cruel

lick is named Storey, and if he is not killed in this war
the civil law will hang him when peace is restored. And
that hat will be a good witness, and I may want it."

"Y-e-s," he said in a drawling way; "that's all right."

I was not yet eighteen years old, and did not really
foresee the effect it would have on my mother. When
she gazed on the grewsome sight of that blood-stained
and gashed hat, she stood mutely looking for a moment;
then placing both hands over her heart uttered a deep
sigh and was staggering backwards, when I caught her in
my arms and led her to a lounge in another room. She
survived the ordeal and passed on in 1891 to that Beulah
Land she loved so well to sing about, and her last words
were, "I will soon be drinking at the fountain."

It has been said that all is fair in love and war; and that
the end justifies the means. I have an abiding respect
for the Confederate soldier who did his duty in the light
in which he saw it at that time. Yes, I have an admiration for him, He was an American, and did he not
fight on with a dogged perseverance even after the backbone of rebellion broke at Gettysburg, a victim of a hopeless and mistaken course, staying with his forlorn hope
to the end, and as a rule accepting the results? Yes;
all true soldiers have a profound respect for the enemy
that will meet him in the open, his true colors and garb
in evidence, the honest telltale of who and what he is.
This is not only true in a military sense, but it is true in
a moral and political sense. But fiends incarnate, who
respect neither moral, civil, nor military law, should be
hunted like cougars. But, be it said to the credit of the
Confederacy, these border freebooters had no legal status.
Such was the position of Quantrill and his followers. Go
to Aubrey, Olathe, Shawneetown, Lawrence, Centralia,

Mo., Rossville, Ark., and the hundreds of lonely ravines
and hollows along the Missouri border, where death reaped
a greater harvest in the period of four years from '61 to
'65 by murder in guerrilla warfare than any like area
since time began.

The first camp-fires of the slaveholders' rebellion were
kindled on Kansas soil, five years before P. G. T. Beauregard fired the shot on Fort Sumter that was heard around
the world, and saddened every home in our land. The
horde of Border Ruffins that had bent every energy from
1856 and 1857 to fasten the system of human slavery in
Kansas Territory having dismally failed, after leaving a
trail of blood and carnage behind them, "silently folded
their tents" and recrossed the border. But when actual
hostilities came in 1861 on a national scale, the spirit of
revenge came to the front and Kansas must suffer. Men
of desperate character from Kentucky, Mississippi and
Louisiana came out, and up to join the Missourians to
help them even up with Kansans for their failure to make
Kansas a Slave State.

And what a field for operations! At that time the
border on both sides of the line was sparsely settled, from
Kansas City to the Indian Territory and to the Arkansas
line, thus affording many quiet hiding-places between
depredations committed.

After being home a few days I returned to Fort Scott,
to learn that my company had marched to Fort Smith,
Ark. I was placed in a stragglers' camp to await the time
that Colonel Tom Moonlight was to take us down the
western border of Arkansas to Fort Smith. He mounted
us on a fresh supply of horses that were going down to fill
vacancies. There were nearly one hundred of us, ar-
tillerymen, cavalrymen and infantrymen, going to join

our respective commands. Moonlight was given a free lance. The only condition was to keep on and near the left flank of a large transportation train bound for Fort Smith, Ark. It is needless to say that on the trip down the border and over the Boston Mountains several old scores were evened up. We arrived at Fort Smith in late December, and on January 1, 1864, my regiment was reunited, except H Company, and kept so until the close of the war. Its history is briefly written in marches, countermarches, foraging expeditions, the Shreveport campaign and fighting guerrillas—all this was the order of the times.

We were mustered out of service at Little Rock, Ark., June 30th, 1865, and finally discharged, paid off, and disbanded at Lawrence, Kansas, July 20th.

I was not twenty years old, without a scar or scratch, but brought from cypress and alligator swamps of the south a case of malarial fever that tenaciously stayed in my system for four months. I believe I could make a safe two-to-one bet that no mortal on earth ever drank as much boneset tea during that time as I did. My mother, backed by every old lady in the neighborhood, insisted that it was the only remedy to get the bile off my stomach and the ague out of my system.

CHAPTER II.

Early Settlements of Southeast Kansas.—Texas Cattle Fever Trouble.—The Osage Indians and Firewater.—Poor Mrs. Bennett.—How Terwilliger's Cattle Stampeded.—Why the Curtises Moved On.—The Odens Murder Parker.—Parker Was Avenged.—Jane Heaton and Her Smith & Wesson Revolver.—What Became of the Benders.

In 1867 I went to Labette county, and located on 160 acres of land three miles from where the notorious Bender family committed their horrible murders in 1873. Shortly after locating, together with all of the settlers on Timber Hill creek, I got mixed up in the Texas cattle fever trouble that broke out along the Indian Territory border.

At the time the trouble was on an old man and his son who was about 35 years old had taken up a claim on Big Hill creek down near the Montgomery county line, and had established a trading-post and were selling whisky to the Osage Indians, who had recently ceded their lands and were preparing to move south and west to their present reserve.

Milt Adams, James Bennett and myself were delegated to wait on the old man Curtis and son to tell them to quit selling liquor to the Osage Indians. They both denied ever selling them any at all. But we had the indisputable evidence from the best of sources that they had. I said: "Look here, you see that cabin down there on the prairie? That is the extreme frontier cabin that a white man lives in the border. That's John Bennett's home. And that was his wife, who, day before yesterday, was compelled to stand over a hot cook stove, in a little cluttered up

(27)

room, and cook meat and bake nearly half a sack of flour into biscuits for a party of drunken Osage Indians that got their whisky here and went straight from here to Bennett's. You both know that in point of personal valor when sober the Osage is a coward, and cowards have to get drunk to be dangerous. Of course the worst injury Mrs. Bennett received was fright, and now that poor woman is prostrate and the Timber and Big Hill settlements will hold you fellows responsible for it."

A man by the name of Terwilliger had a large corral on Cherry creek near its junction with the Nipawalla, or Drum creek, and on the western border of our settlement. He was grazing about 600 head of long-horned Texas cattle. He had repeatedly been requested to move his cattle farther west, beyond the danger-line, but paid no heed to the wish of the settlers. The day that Mr. Curtis and son were advised "to seek other parts," which they did, that same night, some one rode along the east side of Terwilliger's corral, where 600 steers were lying down chewing their cuds, and threw a big cat over the fence plump on a steer.

Ugh-ee! *Woof!* and the ground fairly trembled. The stampede was on. The eight-rail staked and double-ridered fence was no barrier. Some of the rails were carried 200 feet from the fence. And most of the cattle were twenty-five miles southwest by noon the next day when their herders caught up with them.

It was suspected that the son of a Methodist circuit rider delivered the cat to the steer, his father having supplicated the Sunday before, "that we might be spared from the dreadful scourge of the Texas fever."

This fever was fatal to domestic cattle, but did not seem to affect the native cattle of Texas either at home or on the drive northward. And since the long-horned breeds have become nearly extinct, by crossing and recrossing of breeds, Texas fever is scarcely heard of now. But in early times in southern Kansas eternal vigilance from July to the first killing frost was the price of milk. Had the settlers not been vigilant those days the children along the border would have cried for milk; for Kansas had not yet made any dead-line legislation against Texas cattle.

During the latter part of the winter of 1869, the two Oden brothers killed young Parker over a claim dispute. The killing took place at the house on the disputed claim near the mouth of Onion creek, on the west side of the Verdigris river, in Montgomery county, which was not yet organized. Osage township, the one I lived in in Labette county, was the nearest judicial point to the place of the killing. A mob gathered and surrounded the Oden house near the scene of the murder, as it afterwards proved to be. The mob's purpose was to give the Odens a trial, with Judge Lynch on the bench. But when inky darkness came on, the Odens slipped by the guards and went to, and surrendered to the Justice of the Peace, Wm. H. Carpenter, of Osage township.

I was township constable at the time. Their revolvers, four in number, were handed to me. Subpœnas were given to me to serve on witnesses for the defense, in the neighborhood where the deed was perpetrated. I deputized Henry Waymire to take charge of Bill Oden during my absence; also, Mahlon King, the son of a Methodist minister, to go with me to Onion creek and help to guard and protect Tom Oden, whom we took with us, by his own and also by his brother's request. Tom had told us, which proved to be true, that if he went home alone he might be killed; that his wife was in delicate health, and that he was anxious to see her and allay her fears about him.

We left the residence of the Justice of the Peace about four in the afternoon. It was twenty-five miles southwest to where we were to go. When darkness came on we were on a treeless prairie, taking a course for a trading-post near the mouth of Pumpkin creek, where we arrived about ten o'clock at night. We found about twenty-five men who had congregated there before we reached the post. We had tied a large woolen scarf around the neck, face, and head of our volunteer prisoner, and passed him off for one of my deputies. One of the witnesses that I was to subpœna was a clerk at this trading-post. I dismounted, went inside, and handed a copy of the subpœna to the clerk, took a look at the crowd, and was starting out, when one of the party asked me where the Odens were. My reply was, "Under a strong guard at Timber Hill." I was then asked who the other two fellows were outside. I answered, "Two deputy constables." I was then asked to take a glass of whisky. I replied that "I never drank," which was the second misstatement I had made to them. That was an ominous-looking crowd. I learned afterwards that my first lie had saved Tom Oden's life for a time, and perhaps Mahlon King's and my own. Had the prisoner not given himself up to the majesty of the law? And was he not entitled to a fair trial by the law? And would it not have been inexcusable cowardice had we not defended him to the last?

After leaving the traders we soon came to the Verdigris river, which was more than half bank-full, and was sparsely settled on both sides to the Indian Territory line. Near the mouth of Onion creek we left our horses at an old

negro's on the east bank of the river and called up Mr.
Phelps, who lived on the west bank eighty rods down the
river. At this time I did not know Mr. Phelps was to be
the main witness for the State against the Odens. Tom
Oden said to me, when we arrived opposite Mr. Phelps's,
that "Old Phelps keeps a skiff, and if you will call him
up we can cross here; then it is only a mile down home,
with a plain road all the way." Then he added: "I'd
rather not let the old man know who I am at present, and
if I was to call for him he might recognize my voice."

I hallooed twice, and the response was, "What is
wanted?" I answered, "There are three of us here
from the Timber Hills, and we wish to cross the river."
He remarked: "It is now nearly midnight. Can't you
go to the house a little way down the river and wait till
morning? Then I'll row you over." I told him our
business was urgent, and that "we must cross at once."
He said, "all right; I'll soon be there."

When Mr. Phelps came down the bank he set a lantern
in the bow of the boat. He did not use oars, but sat in
the stern and paddled across, and, as he neared our side,
let the boat drift to the bank, bow up stream.

I caught the gunwale at the bow and said to the prisoner, who yet had his head and face muffled, "Rogers, you
get in first."

Mr. Phelps said, "I can't take but two of you at once."

I said, "Mahlon, you get in here, then, near the bow."

Mr. Phelps then asked me to hold the lantern up high,
as he believed he could make the other bank at a place he
wished to land better than if they took the lantern with
them. The river here was about 200 feet wide, and very
deep, with a strong current.

The boat had not gotten more than ten feet from the

shore, when Oden shifted his position suddenly, which
tilted the boat violently and threw Mr. Phelps into the
river.   I called to Mahlon King to throw me the bow-line,
but he caught up the line and leaped towards shore, the
bank at that place being a gradual slope towards shore.
He made a few strokes, and found footing.

Phelps, being in the stern of the boat when tilted out,
was farther out in the stream; for he had backed out to
swing the bow around; and when pitched out he was in
deep and pretty swift water.   There were some long overhanging limbs just below him, which, on account of the
swollen condition of the stream, nearly reached the water.
Mr. Phelps was calling for help.

I dropped the lantern, jerked both six-shooters out of
their scabbards, dropped them on the ground, ran down
the stream about thirty feet, plunged in, and swam out
under the branches, just in time to catch Mr. Phelps by
his coat-sleeve with my right hand, at the same time
holding on to a sweeping limb with my left hand.   Soon
we were ashore, paddle and all, for he had hung onto it
while struggling in the water.

Here we were, three of us, wet as drowned rats, and Tom
Oden, a cold-blooded murderer, dry as a powder-horn.

I had not the slightest suspicion at the time that Oden
tilted the boat intentionally, hoping to drown Mr. Phelps
in order to get rid of a damaging witness against the Odens.
Replacing my pistols in their holsters, I got in the boat
in front of Mr. Phelps and said, "Now, Rogers, get in and
we will try it again, and be very careful and sit still."

Whether he thought, by my getting in the boat in-
stead of King, that my suspicions were aroused and that
I might shoot him in another attempt to tilt the boat,
I am unable to say.

We went on to Oden's cabin, after crossing, and before a large open fireplace dried our clothing, and got a few cat-naps before daylight. All the time and throughout the entire day until we started back, Tom Oden was in an adjoining room with Mrs. Oden.

I left King at the house, and rode to different cabins that forenoon, hunting for the witnesses I had subpœnas for.

I could not help but notice that a pall had fallen over the people. Expressions of lament, and the high esteem in which Parker had been held by the entire community,—this, together with their outspoken condemnation, from men who had grown to manhood on the frontier, boded no good for the Odens. And I felt that the brand of Cain and the seal of death had been placed upon them.

When I came back to the Oden cabin I got King and Oden together and gave them my impressions; and Oden said, "Yes, there are men in this country that want us put out of the way." Meaning himself and his brother.

I said, "We must still carry out our deception and claim him as belonging in our party." Accordingly, we planned to leave for Timber Hill at four o'clock. I walked up to Mr. Phelps's, and got him to set me back across the river.

From there I went to the old darky's and got the three horses, and went down the river a mile and a half to where the other two men had crossed the river, quite at the mouth of Onion creek.

After mounting I said: "Now, boys, you two keep right up the river, pass the old darky's, and head so as to cross Pumpkin creek half-way between the Verdigris and the trading-post." (Before alluded to.) "I will strike straight from here to the post."

Then I said to King, "You know the course to the mouth of Wild Cat; keep straight on it, and if I am not there by the time you are, go to old Mr. McCarmac's on Big Hill and wait for me."

They started up the river. I rode out of the timber and brush that skirted the river and headed straight across the prairie for the trading-post.

When a little less than a mile from the place I came in sight of it and noticed a large crowd of men outside the store. I put my horse in a lope, galloped up to them and dismounted, saying, "Hello, boys."

This place was known as the Gokey Store. One of the Gokeys came up and shook hands with me (we were quite well acquainted), and he said: "So it was you that passed here last night. I just got in to-day with a load of freight and learned of the trouble just before you came in sight. Where are the other two men?" (He had been told that there were three of us passed his place the night before.)

I told him: "I do not know where they are, but I left them opposite the mouth of Onion creek."

Gokey took me to one side and informed me that there were about twenty of the crowd had provisioned a wagon and were going to Timber Hill to be at the preliminary hearing of the Odens, which was to be held at a log school-house in our township, about one and one-fourth miles south of the justice's residence.

I omitted to state that when the Odens came up to surrender, they brought with them a young man by the name of Powell as witness for the defense. He was the only eye-witness to the killing of Parker, beside the Odens.

When I left the Gokey store, a few minutes after arriving there, the queer feeling of impending danger and trouble came over me, and that serious trouble might yet occur while those two prisoners were still in our charge.

Shortly after crossing the ford at the north and south trail, I struck off across a trackless prairie for the mouth of Wild Cat creek. I found on arriving there that King and Oden had crossed and were only a short distance ahead of me. It had become quite dark when I caught up with them. I said, "Look here, Oden, from this on we will have to use the utmost caution for your safety, while you are in my charge. So when we get to Big Hill you two fellows take the hill road and hurry on to Carpenter's, and I'll keep up the creek bottom trail to the school-house and bring some more deputies with me to Carpenter's;" which I did.

I arrived at Carpenter's after midnight with seven men whom I knew could be depended upon in any emergency. There were now at Justice Carpenter's the two Odens, young Powell, their witness, eight deputies and myself.

The time for the trial had been set for 2 p. m. the next day.

When we arrived at the school-house, just before proceedings commenced, we beheld a motley-looking crowd. There were about thirty of the Timber Hill and about fifteen of the Big Hill settlers. Added to these were the twenty-odd men from near the scene of the murder, twenty-five miles away.

There were men dressed in the garb of homespun butternut, a cloth made on the hand-looms of the day. Some were yet wearing their old army uniforms, the well-known sky-blue trousers, navy-blue blouse, with brass buttons with the American eagle upon them, the blue overcoat with the long or short cape,—a distinction between an ex-cavalryman and ex-infantryman. Others were there togged out in the then up-to-date store clothes and "biled" shirt. The horses were tied to wagons in front of the school-house, on the open prairie and to trees in the rear. Camp-fires were burning in different places, on each side and behind the house.

These men were walking arsenals. Nearly all were each carrying two six-shooters, and among them were rifles of many different patterns. One man could be seen with a long-barreled Hawkins rifle, while his neighbor carried an army Enfield, one a Springfield, and one man an old brass-band American musket. Some had the Gallagher, some the Spencer, and some carried Sharp's carbine.

Not a man was there through idle curiosity, but either to kill the Odens or see fair play. It was learned afterward that the twenty men who had come up from Gokey's had held a council just before they came to the school-house and decided that, in killing the Odens on that trip, they might have to kill others and at the same time sacrifice some of their own lives. They decided not to use one bit of testimony they had for the State. Simply let the whole thing go by default and bide their time.

So the trial came off—or rather, the hearing. Bill Oden, the first witness after young Powell had given his forced-by-threat testimony, stated to the jury that it was very unfortunate that he had killed the young man; that he only intended to disable him so that he could do no harm; had struck with the handspike a harder lick than he had intended.

Tom Oden said that Parker had murder in him when he came to the cabin; that he tried to reason with him, to no purpose; that had his brother not struck him with the spike before he shot the second time,—he claimed Parker had shot at his brother once; but Powell afterward stated that was false; that he, Parker, might have killed all of them. And all this time not a protest; while on the other hand, the Odens had made out a clean case of self-defense. The jury brought in, from under the boughs of an oak tree out in the wood, a verdict, "Guilty of an excusable homicide." Thus closed one of the greatest farces of a trial, in jurisprudence.

A few days after the Odens returned home they were literally bullet-riddled by a determined party of men, some thirty in number, starting from Chetopa and augmenting until Gokey's trading-post was reached.

Unintentionally, in the killing of the Odens, young Powell was shot through the bowels. He then swam the Verdigris river and escaped them, as he thought, at the time. He did not know that they held him blameless for his part in the Oden affair; but the mob, if such it could be called, had heard from his mother his own story to her of the killing of Parker, which was cold-blooded and cruel; also, the threat that if he did not tell the story of the killing as they told him to, they would kill him too. They told him that his mother was a poor woman who could not well spare him. Young Powell was possessed of very ordinary intellect, neither self-assertive nor self-reliant, and just such a subject as Tom Oden's magnetism could control.

Some of the party that came out from Chetopa, not knowing the Odens or Powell personally, fired on Powell as he started to run, when they came up to where he and Bill Oden happened to be as they were together at the time. But as soon as the mistake was noticed he was allowed to get away and the same party rendered him valuable assistance afterward.

I met young Powell in Chetopa, early in 1870. He told

me that, as they were walking over the prairie toward home the next day after the trial, Tom Oden told him he had tried to drown Phelps the night he tilted the boat, but as Phelps had not come forward and testified against him it was just as well that he was not in the Verdigris river for fish-bait.

The following year, Montgomery county was organized, and her legal machinery was set and ready to grind.

That summer, a man by the name of Sam Heaton dropped into our neighborhood; went just over the line and took up a claim that the present site of Cherryvale is on.   Leaving his wife, household goods and some lumber on the claim, Heaton, with four yoke of oxen and a large wagon, started to a saw-mill near Humboldt, about four days' journey, for more lumber.   During his absence the covetous eye of a man named Soaper fell on the claim, and he ordered Mrs. Heaton to move off the land, stating to her that he was the first settler on it, and that his building material was on the ground near the southwest corner.   Mrs. H. did not move.

The next day Soaper and a party of several men came and moved everything they had there at the time, except the tent she was in and what it contained, including herself, just over the line onto the next claim north.   Mrs. Heaton stood in the door of her tent with a Smith & Wesson revolver in her hand, and refused to budge.

The men rode away, telling her they would be back in the morning and move *her*.

She mounted her pony that night and rode to Carpenter's, and stated her case.   Carpenter came to where I was at work, on my own place, the next morning, and informed me what had happened.   We soon gathered ten settlers together, mounted and galloped across that six miles of virgin prairie, laughing and joking like a lot of schoolboys out for a lark, Mrs. Heaton riding along with us in the lead, her Smith & Wesson hanging to its belt around her waist.

In point of real value, for permanent home-making, we, perhaps, had crossed a dozen as good or better claims that could be had for the taking; for they were unoccupied portions of the public domain. But Heaton had selected the particular claim in question and "squatters' rights" was the slogan of the times. The moral law of every frontier settlement is held inviolate and will brook no interference. Besides, custom made propriety. And it was customary for a would-be settler to take any unoccupied piece of the public domain, to the extent of one hundred and sixty acres, that he wanted. Heaton had taken his claim in due form; for the day he located it I was with him. His headquarters were at my house, where he and his wife were camped while he was looking the country over for a home.

Heaton and myself were at every corner of the 160 that day. We were both riding horses fully sixteen hands high. The grass was not over eighteen inches high; the ground was fairly level; the tract was not cut up with ravines or draws. We both had excellent eyesight; there was not at that time a wagon-trail on it. Soaper nor anyone else had a vestige of lumber on the place the day he said he had. He simply lied, as his own conscience compelled him to afterward admit, after he had been the means of bringing two communities to the verge of a feud with bloodshed.

We all galloped to the tent, dismounted, and carried all the things back onto the claim and piled them up neatly by the tent. Then three of the men fell to and helped Mrs. Heaton get a mid-forenoon meal, while the rest of us rode diagonally across the claim to where Soaper had his lumber. We found thirty-two boards, one inch thick, one foot wide and twelve feet long, of native lumber, from a sawmill over on the Neosho river, twenty-eight miles away. We wrote out a trespass notice, fastened it to a board, and returned to the tent, where shortly an early dinner was announced.

On our way down, in crossing a prong of Cherry creek, a two-year-old spike buck white-tail deer jumped up, not more than thirty steps in front of us. John Oliphant whipped out one of his six-shooters and placed a ball in the back of its head where the neck joined on. It was quick action. He claimed he shot more at random than with deliberation. But it got the deer. We drew the carcass and Milt Adamson carried the deer in front of him to the tent.

While we were eating and had nearly finished our meal of fried venison, corn-bread, boiled potatoes and browned gravy, Mrs. Heaton announced that "horsemen were approaching from the south." We all arose from the improvised table, stirred around, gathered up our horses that were grazing around the tent, and awaited developments. There were four of them. They rode quite up to us, when Soaper said:

"How do you do, men?"

"Fine, fi-fi-fine," said Ike Vancel, who had a slight impediment in his speech. "We j-j-jist had a belly-full of d-d-deer meat."

This seemed to put both parties, for the time, in a good humor. Vancel was an acknowledged wit, was a polite and courteous gentleman, a man of sound judgment, and one who liked to see fair play.

Soaper was the next to speak:

"I seen you men here, and thought, me and these friends of mine, that we would come over and tell you that *I* took this claim, and hauled lumber onto it four days before this other party did."

Carpenter said:

"I don't know anything about that part of it, but *we,* that are here, *all do know* that it was a dirty, cowardly deed for you and your gang to come here and hector and threaten just one lone woman that only weighs eighty-nine pounds. You fellows make yourselves scarce, and if this woman is molested again during her husband's absence there will not be enough left of you, Soaper, to make soap-grease."

They rode away, Soaper saying: "We'll settle this in the courts." Two weeks later we were all arrested at our homes, charged with "committing a breach against the peace and dignity of Montgomery county, Kansas." We were all rounded up at Justice Carpenter's house, having been served with warrants, one at a time, by one lone half-Swede Constable. Any one of us could have resisted him with impunity, so far as he was concerned. But the "process" was enough. We were law-abiding citizens.

Just as the last prisoner had arrived at Carpenter's, a lone horseman was seen approaching from the northeast. Our course to where we were going lay to the southwest. We waited for this horseman to come up to where we were, regardless of the protests of the constable, who insisted that "our trial was set for three o'clock that afternoon; that it was about ten miles to where we were to go, and we had no time to lose."

When the rider came up he proved to be a lawyer and a recent arrival from the east, hunting for a place to hang out a shingle. We had a short talk with him, and informed him of the cause of the gathering, whereupon he said:

"Go ahead, boys. I'll follow up and rob the dead."

This man was Bishop W. Perkins, afterward a member of Congress.

When we arrived at the place of trial, we found there a man by the name of Hartshorn, a lawyer, recently from Woodson county, who was to be the prosecuting attorney in the case. We were all a happy-go-lucky lot of prisoners; and when Hartshorn arose with a serious look on his countenance, read the complaint, and had expatiated on the gravity of the offense, we all arose and gave him three cheers.

"Bully for Hartshorn," said Ike Vancel.

The ridiculousness of the whole thing had appealed to the funny side of our natures. We called him "Old Essence of Ammonia," and yelled to him to "Give us another smell."

On the way down to the place, Perkins had volunteered to defend us. He now pitched in and handled a vocabulary of words that took us all by surprise. He juggled words and phrases in such rapid succession that he completely spellbound his hearers. He wound up by painting a word picture of frail little Mrs. Heaton, alone on a desolate prairie, about to be devoured by human wolves. When he closed, Vancel said: "I m-m-move that we adjourn," which we did, by getting on our horses and riding home.

Thus ended the second "legal farce" I had seen during the early settlement of southeastern Kansas.

I was in Denison, Texas, when the news of the Bender murders was heralded throughout the land, and that one

of my old neighbors was in jail at Oswego, under suspicion of being implicated in those crimes. He was the
only man in the neighborhood with whom I had had any
personal trouble, and that was caused by his hogs and my
fence,—his hogs not being allowed to run at large by law,
and my fence not being hog-tight. And over that diffi-
culty we had drifted apart, and seemed to cultivate a
dislike for each other.

He was a Methodist preacher, of the old Peter Cart-
wright school; but had an inordinate love for liquor, and,
periodically, he would get "as full as a goose," and about
as silly. When sobering up he would be struck with the
remorse of a guilty conscience, for the sin he had committed and the example he had set before the people. He
was judged by his neighbors while in these melancholy
moods, as being insincere, hypocritical and mysteriously
secretive. Not *all* of us, for there were those of us who
believed the old gentleman was conscientious in his religious
preachings and teachings.

When I read the news of his arrest, I hastened to his
relief, firmly believing in his innocence. And here the
Golden Rule impressed itself upon my mind more than it
ever did before. I believed that Parson King was as
innocent of the crime as myself; but before I reached
Oswego he had been vindicated and released from custody.

I went up into my old neighborhood where I had been
one of the first settlers and had helped to build the first
hewed log house that was built on the prairies of Labette
county. A blight had been cast on the entire community.
Not two miles from where I helped to build the house
mentioned above, I gazed on the open graves of the Bender's victims. Personally, I think I was better known,
and knew that people better in the first settlement of

western Labette, eastern Montgomery, and southern Woodson, than any other man.

While John Harness, of Ladore, was suspected of being an accomplice of the crime, he undoubtedly was as innocent as his accusers were. 'Twas the same with Brockman, whom the Independence party hung to a tree on Drum creek until life was almost extinct; although Brockman was a cruel and inhuman man to his own family.

No, the Benders had no accomplices. But neighbor had distrusted neighbor, and some were standing aloof from others.

I sold farm machinery in that locality the summer of the spring that the Benders disappeared and the bodies of their victims were found. I was traveling for B. A. Aldrich, a hardware man of Parsons, Kan. I was from house to house, and became familiar with all the neighborhood stories, versions, and suspicions about the Bender murders.

What became of the Benders? Read on in this book under the caption of the "Staked Plains Horror" during the summer of 1877. Listen to the story as told to me, as the narrator and I were lying on our blankets, with our saddles for pillows, the night of the 20th of July, on the border of western Texas and eastern New Mexico. Then let the readers judge for themselves what became of the Benders. Yes, let them decide for themselves as to the truth or falsity of the story. I believed the story *then*, I believe it *now*.

CHAPTER III.

A Trip to New Mexico.—Prospecting Around the Base of Mount
Baldy.—Experience with a Cinnamon Bear.—Wail of the Moun-
tain Lion.—Tattooed Natives, bound for the Texas Panhandle.—
Lanced a Buffalo.—Loaned My Gun and Suffered.

Early in the spring of 1874 I started for Santa Fé, New
Mexico, stopping off at Granada, Colorado, for a short
time. Granada was at that time the end of the Atchison,
Topeka & Santa Fe Railroad. From Granada I went to
Las Animas, and traveled over the Dry Cimarron route,
through Rule cañon, on over the Raton mountains, through
Dick Hooten pass, and on into Las Vegas, New Mexico,
where I arrived in May. There I fell in company with
the Eighth United States regulars, whose commanding
officer was Major Alexander, and who gave me permission
to travel with his command to Santa Fé. At Santa Fé
I met a Dr. Strand, one of the notorious Star Route mail
contractors at the time. We two, with an assayer, H. C.
Justice, formed a company to prospect for gold in the
Saint Mary's range, near the headwaters of the Picorice,
Lumbay, and Bean creeks, all tributaries of the Rio
Grande river.

Leaving Santa Fé, we packed up under the base of Baldy
mountain, and struck camp near timber line, at the head
of the North Picorice. Here we stayed several days,
and prospected out different ways from camp.

It was now past midsummer. The mountains were
grand! The scenery sublime and awe-inspiring! From
our camp, at this place, we had only to climb a short distance to where we could look west and northwest across

(45)

the Rio Grande and behold the San Juan range. Nearly due north of us were the towering Spanish Peaks; and on still further the Greenhorn mountains; and east of us the Pecos river. Still on south, down, over and beyond Santa Fé, the Placer Mountains loomed up as out of a desert. The whole formed a grand and imposing scene. Once this panoramic view is seen, it is never to be forgotten.

We were in a broken, distorted and chopped-up country. I was reminded of the story I had heard of the atheist and some cowboys, which I will here relate. A herd of cattle had been contracted for to be delivered at Taos, New Mexico. They were being driven up the Arkansas river from near where the Great Bend is. The atheist fell in with the outfit near old Fort Dodge. He was an excellent and interesting conversationalist, and after each day's drive, in the evenings around the camp-fire, the boys would get him started; he was always wound up. They gave him respectful hearings, which were always entertaining and interesting to them. He got to injecting his favorite doctrine from time to time in his talks; and finally, as they were approaching the mountains, he gave them a fine discourse upon "The beauties of nature," telling his hearers that "this was a world of chance; that it was an absurd idea that it had been made by Divine hands, as there was no such thing as a Supreme Being," etc.

When they got well up into the mountains they came one day to a place where Nature had seemed to do her best, by way of cañons, storm-scarred peaks, broken and castellated buttes, wild and yawning gorges or chasms; and as they were gazing, far and near, on the grand sublimity of the scene, the atheist remarked: "O, what mag-

nificence! How beautiful! How remarkable! How un-
surpassingly grand and awe-inspiring!" One of the cowboys drawled out—"Yes sir-ee. You've been preachin'
no God to us fellers; but I'm right here to tell you that if
there ain't any God now there has been one, sometime."

Near this camp there was a place where we could gather
mountain dewberries and huckleberries at the same time.
Not more than fifty feet away we could make snowballs
and shy at the saucy magpies. We had grass in abundance
for our saddle-horses and pack-burros. Our camp was at
the margin of a clear, beautiful rivulet bordered with
water-cress and fringed with quaking-asp. At night we
tied our riding-horses to trees, and turned them loose in
the daytime. Mr. Justice's mountain-climber was a free
lance, the doctor's was hobbled, and mine had a bell on.

In the daytime the burros would graze off a hundred
yards or more, but as twilight came on they would edge in
toward camp. And all night long they would stay close
to the camp-fire. This was instinct. They seemed to
act on the principle that caution was the parent of safety.
The loud, piercing, scream of the mountain lion had ter-
rified their ancestry since Cortez had made the conquest
of Mexico.

The second night we were at this camp we were awakened
by the cries of one of these creatures, which appeared not
more than 300 yards south of us. Just north of us was a
sheer, almost perpendicular battlement of decomposed
quartz rising some ten or twelve hundred feet higher than
where we were. This weird, almost human cry would echo
back to us. It was not a roar, but more like a cry of distress, which the brute kept up at intervals for nearly half
an hour, without seeming to change position. At the first
outcry we all got up. I "chunked up" our camp-fire,

replenished it with dry fuel, and soon we had a big blaze. As the flames leaped up and the flitting shadows appeared among the scattering spruce and aspen along the little prong of the Picorice, together with the sound of the water-fall just above us, the neighing of my own horse, the closely huddled burros at the fireside, the long-drawn-out wail of the lion, the superstitious Mexican cook, crossing himself and muttering something about the Virgin Mary, made a show worth going a long ways to see and hear.

At this camp our daily routine was about as follows: Breakfast about 7 A. M.   Old Mr. Justice, the mineralogist, would take his gun and fishing-tackle and start down the cañon to where two other little brooks came into the one on which we were camped.   He, generally, was not absent more than two or three hours, when he would come back with a fine string of mountain trout.   The Doctor and myself would leave camp just after breakfast, each carry-ing a stout tarpaulin pouch about the size of an army haversack hung over our shoulders regulation style.   We carried a stone-hammer, a small pick, a hatchet, our guns, and lunch.   We would take a certain direction for the hunting of specimens.   Neither of us knew anything about mining or minerals.   When we found anything that we thought might contain precious metals, we would take a chunk of it, number it, pasting a piece of paper on it, marking the spot where we found it with a corresponding number.

But it is safe to say that after one of these day cruises, we could not go back and find half the places where we had picked up specimens, especially when we were above tim-ber-line around Old Baldy; for here we would zigzag around minor buttes, cross over gorges, up slopes, and down steep inclines, ever keeping in our mind the way back to camp, and a weather eye out for old Ephraim, or a cinnamon bear, whose territory we were then in. When the afternoon was pretty well gone we would head for camp, and never failed but once to strike it all right.

Arriving at camp, the assayer would mortar and pan out our specimens. The Mexican would soon have our hot coffee, frying-pan bread, some canned fruit, and our daily ration of trout, ready. Then supper was eaten. Mr. Justice would then handle the specimens in mining parlance. He would talk: "Pyrites of iron, porphyry, cinnabar, decomposed quartz, base metal, the mother lode, dips, spurs cross," and the Lord only knows what else,—which to me, a man with scarcely any education at all, was hopeless confusion; for, gold or no gold was the knowledge I was seeking. Then the Doctor would give an account of the day's events, a description of the route we had taken, and wind up with the opinion that "we were in a very rich mineral region." The horses brought in and tied, we would sit around the camp-fire and talk for awhile, then to bed.

Not a mosquito; no fleas; no flies; and such grand nights for sound sleep, under a pair of double blankets, with spruce boughs for a mattress to lie on.

We stayed at this particular place eight days, then broke camp and went to the head-waters of the Lumbay, about three miles away. Here we camped in the edge of a glade, where two branches of the stream proper converged. We were at this camp four days, and while here I shot my first bear, but did not kill him. He was on the opposite side of a cañon from me, and some forty yards away. I was on the brink of the cañon, which would be called a close cañon. It was about sixty feet across, with perpendicular walls, and was fully eighty feet deep at this place. The bear was in an opening of timber, and the ground was covered with a dense growth of mountain dewberries, which were then in their prime. The bear was about twenty yards from the opposite brink from which I was on. He was nearly upright; using his front paws, drawing the tops of the bushes to his mouth, stripping off the berries, leaves, and twigs, eating all ravenously as though he were hungry. His body was slightly quartering to me. He was wholly unconscious of my near presence. I had a 44 center-fire Winchester, the first magazine gun I had owned. I had practiced with it until it had gained my confidence completely as *the* gun. I raised the Winchester, took deliberate aim, thinking to give him a heart shot. At the crack of the gun he threw his right arm across his breast, under his left arm, and seemed to slap his left side, leaped forward, and as I gave him the next shot, he rose straight up, standing on his hind feet, and seemed to be looking straight at me. From that on I worked the breech-block as fast as I could until the magazine was empty.

By this time the bear was not more than ten or twelve feet from the brink of the cañon. I started up the stream on a run, and as I ran I was taking cartridges out of my belt and reloading the magazine. Our camp was less than a quarter of a mile above, and on the same side the bear was on, and the head of the cañon proper was just a little way below the camp. My rapid firing had attracted the attention of my companions in camp, and they were hurrying down the cañon on the opposite side. When we got opposite each other, I said, "Wait; don't go down there or you will get into a fight with a wounded cinnamon." They all turned and came back, and as we met at the head of the cañon, I explained how the situation was when I left.

Mr. Justice said:

"All right. Now let's all get in line and keep abreast and go, step by step, as easy as we can, and look carefully, and if we should meet or find him, we ought surely to be able to down him before he can injure any of us."

I was placed on the side next to the cañon, the same being on my right, Mr. Justice on my left about twenty feet from me, the Mexican next, and Doctor Strand on the extreme left. By this time I had got myself pulled together. That I had "buck ager" and "bear fright" together, goes without saying; for had I taken the second thought I should have known that it was physically impossible for a bear to have crossed that cañon, at or near there, and that I could have stood where I fired my first shot and shot the other thirty-two cartridges at him, if he had stayed in sight, with all impunity. My first shot was a cool, deliberate, dead aim, and I shall always believe that a small berry twig had deflected the bullet.

We started our line of march and search, and had proceeded cautiously about two hundred yards, when Mr. J. stopped and said, "Wope!" His quick eye had noticed some bushes shaking straight ahead of him. "Boys," he said, "we are close onto him; be very careful and make no bad shot; they are desperate creatures when wounded; Doctor, you and the Mexican [whose name was Manuel] stay here and Cook and I will go a little further."

We went about thirty-five yards and came to a large log or fallen tree. Mr. Justice and I were then not above two paces apart. He whispered to me saying, "I'll cautiously get up on this trunk, where I can get a good view." As he straightened himself up, he looked in the direction that he had seen the bushes moving. He raised his rifle, took a deliberate aim and fired. He had killed "my bear," the ball entering the butt of the left ear and going into the brain. Upon examining the carcass it was found that I had made seven hits, but only one that would have proved fatal.

From this camp we moved on down the Lumbay to the mouth of the cañon, some seven or eight miles. We cut our own trail as we went. I generally went ahead on foot and with a squaw-ax lopped off such limbs as would strike our packs. It was a slow, tedious transit. We had to pass through a timber-fall for nearly two miles, where there had been a tornado and the trees had uprooted, and in many places piled one on top of another, crossed and interlocked in such a formidable barricade that we could not pass through; in which case we would zigzag back and work our way around. We met several such obstacles that day, and went only five miles from early morning till late in the evening. We camped on a mountain spur, tired out, arriving at the mouth of the cañon the next day.

About noon we met a party of Greasers, fifteen in number, who lived down in the valley of the Lumbay. Manuel's father was a member of the party. They had not seen each other for more than a year. When they met they hugged and kissed each other, a custom among the peon classes. We learned that a mountain lion had been killing their sheep, and they had gathered together to hunt it to its death, but so far had failed to stalk him, and were going back home.

From this camp, down the cañon, it was fifteen miles to the Mexican town of Lumbay, and a clear open trail all the way except now and then a tree that had fallen across it.

At this camp I saw the evidence of preceding generations of more than 200 years before. It was in the form of an acequia or irrigation ditch, and this ditch, to reach and water the fertile valley of the Lumbay, had followed from just a few rods above the head of the cañon, a sinuous, tortuous course, around the heads of gorges and fairly clinging to the face of perpendicular walls a distance of forty-five miles. This statement about the length of the ditch I want my readers to take as hearsay. But I personally saw enough of it to be convinced that it was a wonderful piece of engineering skill.

We prospected here three days, then broke camp for the valley proper, where we camped near a Catholic church. Here we saw a type of humanity that for downright superstition beats anything I ever heard of. During the season, if a cloud would appear and lightning and thunder accompanied it, they would hang an image of Christ in an exposed place, to appease the wrath of the storm king, hoping to avert a hail-storm. When there was an excessive drought they would fire off old muskets, beat drums and blow horns to bring rain. I saw this same thing done at Las Vegas. Many of the women were tattooed on face, neck, breast and arms, for indiscretions. In the rear of this church were two large piles of crosses. The timbers in them nearly as large as a railroad tie. When doing penance these superstitious beings of the peon class were compelled by their priests to shoulder these crosses and march around the church for a given length of time, according to the gravity of the sin committed. Another mode of punishment was for the penitent to walk bare-kneed on beans strewn on hard ground.

At this place was a water grist-mill of the most primitive kind. Also, was to be seen here the forked wood plow. The mode of grain-threshing was to place the bundles of grain on the ground in a circle and chase a band of goats around over the grain in a circle, until their feet had hulled the grain from the straw. While at this camp we feasted on roasting-ears, melons, string beans, cabbage, onions, and potatoes.

While here we all suddenly recovered from the "gold fever." The Apache Indians had gone on the war-path, and were terrorizing the people south of Santa Fé. We moved down to Santa Fé, sold our burros, and dissolved partnership. I then left Santa Fé, and went to Casa La Glorieta, and early in October I left Casa La Glorieta for the Panhandle of Texas.

In those days it was the custom of the Mexicans to go each fall to border New Mexico and Texas on "meat hunts." They would organize parties consisting of from fifteen to twenty-five men, never taking any women along, and they would take from four to ten wagons with from two to four yoke of oxen to the wagon. There would be from ten to fifteen lance horses, and each lancer would be armed with a lance-blade about fourteen inches long, fastened by sinews to a staff seven to eight feet long.

There was generally some elderly man in charge of each outfit. They were usually gone from six weeks to three months on these hunting trips, and would return with great loads of jerked dried buffalo meat, which found a ready sale.

While at La Glorieta, New Mexico, I became acquainted with Antonio Romero, whose family was among the higher class of Mexicans. He had had some dealing with my uncle, General Robert Mitchell, who had been Territorial Governor of New Mexico. Upon finding out that I was a relative of the general's, Romero invited me to partake of the hospitality of his home. His English was meager, but we could understand each other by engaging in a

tedious conversation. He, upon learning that I wished
to get to Fort Elliott, in the Panhandle of Texas, informed
me that he and his son, two sons-in-law, and some neighbors, were going on a meat hunt and would be glad to have
me accompany them; that we would go as far east as the
"Adobe Walls," in the Panhandle of Texas, and that it
was not far from there to Fort Elliott.

We left Romero's ranch on the 10th of October, 1874.
We followed the old Santa Fé Trail to Bernal Springs, and
from there followed a trail slightly southeastward, and
came to the South Canadian river at old Fort Bascom,
which had recently been abandoned as a military garrison,
and was then being used as the headquarters for a large
cattle ranch. Here we overtook another meat-hunting
party from Galisteo, about eight miles below Bascom.
Four lancers rode out from the Galisteo outfit and lanced
two range steers. Others of their party went to the place
of killing and got the meat.

Our outfit kept straight on to where we camped that
evening, not far from an out-camp of the main ranch. I
asked Romero if such work as I had seen was the custom
of the country. He said:

"No; and them Galisteo people are liable to get us all
into trouble."

"Well," I said, "I am opposed to traveling with them.
Don't let's use any of that meat in our camp, and to-morrow let's separate from them." This we did.

Just before we got to the mouth of Blue Water, we discovered off to our right, and about two miles away, the
first buffalo. They were lying down, and the wind was
nearly straight from them to us. Soon everything was
hurry and excitement. Lances were gotten out, lance
horses saddled, hats discarded, and handkerchiefs tied

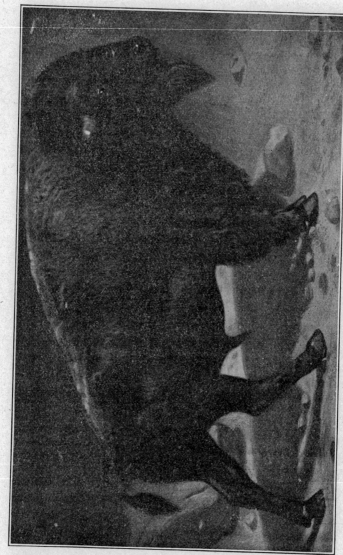

(Copyrighted.—Used by permission of the Union Pacific Railroad Company.)

THE OLDEST INHABITANT.

around the heads like turbans. I was offered a horse and lance, which seemed to surprise the whole party when I readily accepted the offer; for nothing ever pleased me better than a wild, pell-mell ride. One of the party who could talk fairly good English, gave me some instructions, how to do when I came alongside of a buffalo. But I did the opposite, and got the worst of it.

We rode out from the wagons, and getting a mound between us and the herd, we cantered up to the mound and separated, some going around on opposite sides. When we came in view of the herd we were not more than one hundred and seventy yards from them, and we were riding full tilt. Before they could arise and get in full motion we were up to them. There were about thirty-five in all. I was on the left, and the first Mexican on my right was a little in the advance. He gave his horse a quick spurt and was alongside of, and lanced a fat cow. I was close in behind one, and raised my lance to a poise, when my horse veered slightly to the left and with a quick lurch forward I lanced a buffalo. But in doing so I had thrust more backward instead of *vice versa*, as instructed, and in undertaking to withdraw the lance, I lost my balance and was flat on the ground.

Springing to my feet, I saw everybody and everything had passed me. My horse went on a short distance, stopped, and went to grazing. I stood still and took the situation all in. The buffalo I lanced fell on its right side about 200 yards ahead of me with the staff of the lance almost perpendicular. I thought to get my horse, but just then I saw, off to my front and right, a horse and rider fall, and for a few moments witnessed the most thrilling and exciting scene of my life. Buffaloes were reeling and staggering out of line of the run. A lancer would dash up to one that had not been struck yet, make a quick thrust and retrieve, rush on to the next one, and repeat until his horse was winded. Some, whose horses were not as speedy as others, had singled out one certain buffalo and were a mile away before getting to use the lance.

When the chase was over we had sixteen bison for that effort. We dressed the meat and loaded it into empty wagons, and proceeded on to Blue Water, better known in those days as Ona Sula. Here we stayed several days, jerking and drying meat. The lancers were out every day looking for buffalo, but found very few.

From this place we moved about four miles. The lancers that went north that day came in and reported that "we would soon all have plenty of work, as the buffaloes were coming south, in a solid mass as far as they could see, east or west."

The next morning Romero asked me for my Winchester, saying he wished to go north and see if he could see buffaloes. I went to my bed, got the gun and handed it to him. He rode off, and it was many days before I saw him again.

About an hour after he left camp, one of the lancers came in and told me that four Americans were camped about a mile down the Blue Water and on a little stream a half-mile up from the Canadian river. Without taking a second thought, I started for their camp. I had heard scarcely nothing but the Spanish lingo for more than five weeks, and was homesick for my own kind.

CHAPTER IV.

Lost.—Alone at Night in the Wilds.—Quicksanded in the Canadian.
—The Beaver Played in the Water.—Second Day and Night it
Snowed.—Wolves Serenade Me.—Getting Snowblind.—Third
Night Out, Suffered in Body and Mind.—Following Morning,
found Adobe Walls.—And the Good Samaritans Were There.

My earthly possessions at this time consisted of two pairs
of woolen blankets, one large, heavy, water-proof Navajo
blanket, one bright, gaudy serape, a buffalo-hair pillow,
two suits of underclothes, two navy-blue overshirts, an
extra pair of pants, an overcoat, and an undercoat. I told
the Mexican that could speak English that "I would go
and see those men and try to get in with them, and go on
farther east toward Fort Elliott."

I had $96.60 in my purse. I took from the sack that
contained my extra clothing some papers, for my identifi-
cation, wishing to place myself right with the four men at
the start, for on the frontier there were more or less men of
shady repute and some notorious outlaws. Every riding-
horse at this time was out of camp. The English-speaking
Mexican said that I "had better wait until some of the
lancers came in and go on horseback." I said, "No; it
is only a little ways and I would just as soon walk."

The Indians had been subdued the summer before, and
we all felt safe in that one respect, and would continue
to feel so until the next spring. So I struck out. The
Mexican who came in and told me about the four men
being encamped, after describing them and their outfit,
which was interpreted to me, passed on out westward to
look for a chance to lance a buffalo. When I left camp I

(59)

was wearing a half-worn pair of heavy congress gaiters, and a pair of heavy duck leggings. It was not my intention to be gone more than three or four hours. I struck out down the Blue, at a rapid gait. At this time I was in excellent mettle, apparently in perfect health. My muscles were thoroughly toughened by rough, rugged physical exercise, my appetite good and sleep sound.

This was the morning of the 15th of November, 1874. As I walked along I was possessed of hopes of a successful future. I went down Blue Water to where it empties into the South Canadian. I saw a smoke across the river on a little creek that put into the Canadian from the south side. This must be the camp, and the Mexican had said nothing about crossing the river. This smoke was more than a mile away, near a brush thicket. I forded the river and went up the creek, only to find an abandoned camp. The sign was fresh; they had not been gone long. I followed the wagon-trail up the creek to where it crossed, taking up a slope in a southeast direction. I hurried on to the top of the plains, hoping to get a view of the outfit I was looking for.

Standing here and looking over a vast stretch of country, I saw to my left the rugged and irregular breaks of the Canadian; in front of me some two miles or more were the breaks of a cañon coming into the river from the south; and on the opposite side of the cañon saw the outfit.

I was hunting, heading northward toward the Canadian river. They had traveled a southeast course to round the head of the cañon, and were traveling down the eastern side of it when I saw them. Thinking I could yet intercept them, I headed in the direction of the mouth of the cañon. Having short buffalo-grass to walk over and a level, stoneless prairie, without a sign of mesquite or sage-brush, as the cowboys would say, "I fairly rattled my hocks."

Arriving at the mouth of the cañon, there was no one in sight. But, standing on a jutting promontory, I could see scattering bands of antelope, a large flock of wild turkeys, a few straggling buffalo, and one large lobo or timber wolf. I went down into the Canadian river bottom proper, turned east, crossed the ravine below the mouth of the cañon, and skirted along the slope, carefully looking for the wagon-tracks which are always, in the short-grass country, very plain for several days.

I traveled down parallel with the main river about three miles further, and no results. I turned, going up the slope, going on to the table-land, expecting to find the trail going eastward over the bench or table-land. I traveled along this bench and watched the ground closely, occasionally stopping and scanning the country over. In this way I had traveled possibly two miles when I heard the report of a gun to my right front, and, as I judged, a mile away.

From here I could have gone straight back to the camp of Mexicans I had left, not over ten miles at farthest, as I believed. This I should have done. But I reasoned thus: The man who fired that gun was a member of the party I was seeking; I would yet get to them and would offer to pay them well, to go back with me to the Mexican camp for my own gun and outfit, and then work my way to Fort Elliott. Acting upon this reasoning, I started in the direction that the report of the gun came from, walking very rapidly and taking no note of the ground.

I had gone about a mile when I came in sight of another break in the plain by a draw running back from the river. Before going into the draw, or little valley, with a water-course running through it, and standing pools (at that

season the water not running over the riffles), I took a
good look in every direction and could see no sign of humanity. I was dripping wet with perspiration, and could
feel the pangs of hunger keenly, but was not thirsty, as
I had taken a drink of water when crossing the draw below the mouth of the first cañon. I went down to the
nearest pool of water, stripped off, and took a good bath,
and after rubbing my body thoroughly with the outside
of my outer shirt, and dressing, I walked up to the plateau
opposite the way I had come. I sat down on a chalky
point facing the Canadian river.

While resting here and scanning the country over, my
eye fell upon a peculiar-looking object on a flat in front
of me not more than sixty rods away. The grass here
was the short, curly buffalo variety. Not a switch or object of any kind around this lone object. I gazed at it
for some time, but could not make it out. My curiosity
was now aroused; so I started for it, and found upon
arrival that it was a five-gallon water-keg with a gray
woolen blanket sewed around it, the work having been
done with a sacking-needle and twine. It was lying near
the center of a fresh trail made by five or six wagons drawn
by both horses and mules, the tracks pointing southeast.
I followed this trail until near dusk, and, no sign of over-
taking any one being apparent that night, I turned around
and retraced my steps nearly a mile, to where I had passed
at the head of a draw an abandoned camp.

There was quite a pile of wood that had been gathered
and not used. The place was on high ground overlooking
the country to the north and west. There was a thicket
of stunted hackberry and palodura, hard poles of china-
wood, close to where the old camp-fire had been. There
was probably an acre of it all together. It was now quite

dark and the stars were twinkling. I picked up a dry twig and reached into my pocket for my penknife. To my chagrin and discomfiture I found I had left it in my other pocket, when I put on my best trousers that morning. I immediately placed my right hand across my breast to feel for my match-box, which I always carried in my left outside shirt pocket, when to my delight I found my matches were safe and all right. I then gathered some fine twigs, and soon had a rousing fire.

There was a trickling stream of water coming out of the scrubby wood patch, and the campers who had preceded me had dug a hole about two feet deep and thirty inches across for the water to run into. It was full at this time, so I was assured of this and a camp-fire. I was very tired and quite hungry. There was an empty Pierre Lorillard tobacco-box here which the campers had left. This I used for a head-rest, and in a reclining position before my fire I began to think of ways and means. I finally decided to retrace my steps and get back to the Mexican camp. So I folded my hat, tied a handkerchief around my head, placed the hat on the tobacco-box for a pillow, stretched out and went to sleep. Three times during the night I was awakened by the cold. Then I would get up, replenish the fire, get warm, lie down and sleep again.

My last awakening was at daylight, and the sky was overcast with murky clouds; and here I must say that I, for the first time, became somewhat doubtful about making, or finding my way back to the camp I had left. But the trail I had been following was plain, and could be followed no matter how cloudy it might get.

I have been asked many times by various plainsmen, why, from this camp, I did not go north to the Canadian river, take up the south side of it to the mouth of Blue Water, then up Blue Water to the Mexican camp. This thought did occur to me; but what if that camp should be moved? Might I not get so weak from hunger that I would perish before I could reach it?

So I took the trail I turned back on the night before, and traveled over it for about six miles, when it suddenly turned to the right and headed nearly due south. By this time the clouds had grown thicker, the atmosphere warmer and damp. I had not gone to exceed a hundred yards farther when I came to a cross-trail, and noticed that one wagon had turned off into it and followed it in a northeast direction. I dropped down on the grass and pondered in my mind the pros and cons of my predicament; and I reasoned that this one wagon had been the one that I had followed the morning before, and had at all times been on my right; that it had intercepted the trail somewhere along the route from where I had discovered the keg, and while walking along rapidly, looking more ahead than otherwise, I had not noticed it when it came into the one I was on. And as if by impulse I arose to my feet and followed it.

After walking about eight miles, I suddenly came to the breaks of the South Canadian, and walking down a long, gradual draw, gently sloping on each side, I came to the river, and saw that the trail crossed it and that the main channel was hard against the south bank. I got a sounding-stick and noted that the water was about three feet deep ten feet from where the trail entered it. A few rods below I noticed a sandbar projecting far out into the stream, which at this place was about one hundred and twenty-five yards wide from bank to bank.

These southwestern streams are generally very sinuous,

and the channel frequently shifts from side to side, leaving the rest of the stream at common or low stage of water, either in wet sandbars or a thin sheet of water down to this bar.

I went, thinking I would pull off my shoes at the water's edge and wade the river. I had walked out on this bar about sixty yards, when I heard a noise behind me. I instantly stopped, looked around and saw two big raccoons running along the bank, making their peculiar noise.

My feet began sinking the moment I stopped. I raised my left foot, placing my weight on my right, and in drawing my left foot out of the quicksand my foot pulled out of the shoe, so the stockinged foot came down on the sand. I threw all my weight on it, pulled on the right, and yanked, struggled, and floundered in quicksand; but finally extricated myself and hurried back to solid footing, minus my left shoe.

About this time the wind began to rise, coming first from the southeast. I saw, down the river about eighty rods, some large scattering cottonwood trees. I unbuttoned my right legging, took a four-in-hand silk necktie, wrapped the legging around my shoeless foot, tied it as best I could, and went to the clump of trees.

Here I found a large cottonwood log, perfectly dry, that had recently fallen. The top was considerably broken by the fall, and with an abundance of broken limbs I soon had a fire. My feet, and my legs up to my knees, were wet. The sand was gritted into my stockings and drawer-legs, which was very uncomfortable, indeed. I stripped of pants, drawers, and socks; propped up broken limbs for a drying-rack; took off my coat and sat down upon it in front of the fire; rubbed and thor-

oughly dried myself from the knees down. After my
clothing had dried, I beat the sand out of it and rigged up
again.

Here in this sandy river-bottom was tall-stemmed grass.
I got uneasy about my fire; so I went to work to smother
it out, by using my hands for a shovel, and scooping sand
and throwing it on the fire, which had now burnt pretty
well down. The fire had been built in lee of the big log,
and I had taken the precaution to trample the grass down
close around the bare spot of ground I had built the fire
upon. Then I would ignite the edge of the trampled
grass, and, taking both leggings in my right hand, would
beat it out, when I thought it was near the danger-line.

After getting the fire secure from spreading, I got up on
the log and looked down the river, then up stream, and
across; but no sign of mankind. Hunger seemed to be
gnawing at my vitals. I would upbraid myself for lack
of wisdom, and thought how foolishly I had acted in leaving the Mexican camp without my gun and knife. Here
I was, ravenously hungry; and here were deer, turkey,
beaver, coon, buffalo and antelope, a regular hunter's
paradise, and I lost and helpless, perfectly unable to help
myself, with the fat of the land all around me.

I sat down on the log and commenced reasoning, with
this result: I was now in the South Canadian river bottom; the military trail from Fort Dodge, on the Arkansas
river, crossed the Canadian river on its way to Fort Elliott,
which, I had been informed while in Santa Fé, was about
thirty-five miles south of the crossing; that in going down
the Canadian river, from where I now was, one would
have to pass the Adobe Walls before coming to the trail.

I now decided that the sensible thing to do would be
to go down the river; that I was a young, strong man,

and should brush all obstacles aside; should decide on some certain route, follow that and not zigzag on every trail I came to. Then I started and walked out to the foot of the breaks, where the short grass came down to the bottom-lands, then started down the river, hugging the bluffs and crossing the narrow valley of the deeper breaks that ran far back toward the table-land or plain, heading for the nearest and closest headland jutting toward the river. Every mile or so I would have to stop and readjust the legging on my shoeless foot.

I had gone perhaps five miles when I came to a very plain wagon-trail, one that had been traveled considerably. It crossed the river not more than 200 yards from where I came to it, and led up to the mouth of a wide draw in a southeasterly course. I could see, too, that this trail had been recently traveled over and the last outfit that had passed over it had gone up the draw.

Thinking that this trail after getting to the head of the draw might take an eastward trend, more down the river, I vacillated again, and followed it up to the plateau. After getting to the top, this trail followed a hogback for about a mile south, then, rounding the head of another break to the east, it struck straight east, going down the river about two miles from it. This pleased me, as the walking was much better, and I could make better time.

As cloudy as it was, the points of the compass were as clear as a bell, in my mind.

I had not proceeded far on this trail when suddenly the wind shifted to the northwest, blowing quite strong, and soon scattering snowflakes were falling. Traveling on about a mile farther, the trail came to the head of a gradual draw running back toward the Canadian. There were springs here, and here also the trail turned sharply to the southeast, and I started down the draw for the Canadian river. By this time a blinding snow-storm had set in, and I was traveling nearly due north. The storm was pelting me from the northwest.

The only thing that preoccupied my mind now was shelter. Hence, I hurried down the draw, hoping to come to the brakes and find some side-break that would afford me wood and shelter.

Once I thought I was to be run over by a large herd of antelope; they were running at a rapid rate in the wake of the storm crossing the draw right at me, as it were, and before they were aware of my presence they were almost upon me, but discovered me just in time to separate, some jumping high, to left and right, the entire band passing on each side of me. They came and were gone like the wind.

Soon the wind abated, and a steady, heavy fall of snow continued. The flakes were so thick, for a short time, that it was hardly possible to see any distance.

Pretty soon I heard an unusual noise just ahead of me, and all at once I walked almost to the brink of a large pond. It was a "beaver dam," and it was beavers that I had heard. I saw four beavers. They were disporting in the stream, and seemed as delighted as little children could or would be when the first snowflakes of the season came.

After passing on down below the dam, just a little way, I stepped upon a green stick of cottonwood about three feet long and about three inches in diameter. I picked it up, and saw that both ends of the stick had the telltale mark of beaver teeth. This greatly encouraged me; for I knew I could not be far from wood.

Going on still farther, I perceived that the snow was not falling so thick and that I could see quite a distance

ahead, and on either side of me, and also that night was
drawing near.

Soon the hills on each side of me became higher and
more rugged. In a few minutes' walk I saw to my left
a side cañon, or deep ravine, with a heavy growth of
young cottonwood trees. Turning into this gorge-like
place, to my exceeding joy I found an overjutting wall,
and under it had eddied a great pile of leaves from the
cottonwood, hackberry, and stunted elm. I soon found
plenty of dead limbs and poles, which I dragged and carried to the opposite of the projecting wall.

The reader will understand that this side draw faced
and opened into the main draw towards the east; this
overjut was on the north side of the draw, just at the extreme eastern edge of the pole and timber thicket; and
immediately south of the overjut it was not over eighty
feet to the base of the hill, or embankment, which was
some forty feet higher than my night's bed under the
overjut.

I built my fire; turned over two old stumps that the
beaver had cut the trees from some years before; placed
them side by side between the fire and overjut. Then I
sat down; pulled off my shoe and legging, and proceeded
to dry my socks and the bottoms of my pants legs; for
the snowfall was damp and my feet were very wet. The
snow was still falling, and continued to do so all that long
November night.

I now felt the need of fixing my footwear differently;
for I had had trouble all day in keeping it on. I took the
legging that I had not worn on the foot, and placing it
on the ground, put the foot down on it and would fold
it up this way, then would try it that way, and finally
decided that with a hole here, one there, and another at

this place, and then laced this way around the ankle, it could be kept on the foot and not be so bunglesome, and would make a fair moccasin.

I took a dry elm stick, put one end in the fire and got it to burning well; then would hold it on an incline and twirl it around, the charred end on the solid place, on one of the stumps. I repeated this until I got a marlinspike of it. I then took another stick, put the end of it to a live coal, and would hold it on the places, on the improvised moccasin, that had been marked with charcoal where the holes or eyelets were to be. In this way a small eyelet at each place was scorched so that the marlinspike could be worked through, and by reaming it a little, soon had the eyelet-holes all completed.

Then, taking the silk four-in-hand and with good sharp teeth which I then had, I managed to get it started and ripped it through the center from end to end. This gave me two just such lace-strings as I needed.

Everything being dry, I put on the right shoe, laced on the moccasin, crawled into the leaves,—tired, hungry, and sleepy, with not one particle of fear of danger from the elements, which had concerned me so much before I reached this sheltering place.

I was disturbed from my slumber only once during the night. It was some time after darkness had set in when I crawled into and under the leaves, and when I awoke it must have been about three o'clock in the morning. The time is only guesswork with me, as I had no time-piece. The fire was nearly out. I had drawn some of the wood under the overjut, and as there was no snow on it I soon had a bright, cheerful blaze going. I sat on the two stumps a few moments, and, feeling sleepy again, I went to bed. It was then still snowing lightly.

I was awakened by the long-drawn-out howl of wolves, and on rising to a sitting posture I noticed that the sky was clear as crystal, the sun was shining brightly, and two big lobo or timber wolves were sitting on their haunches just across the gorge on the edge of the hill, not more than 130 feet from me, alternating in howling, both facing me and the embers of my fire.

I got up and "chunked up" the fire, and piled on all the remaining wood that I had gathered the evening before. I was well acquainted with the cunning, cowardly wolf, and could only think of him with contempt.

I had read many stories of savage wolves, what they had done and what they could do; but always accepted them with allowance. But here were two of them face to face with me. No gun, no knife. I was not scared. I had read of the effect fire had upon wolves, and, whether it was true or not, resolved to give myself the benefit of the doubt.

Accordingly, I prepared me two strong firebrands. One was about three and the other one four feet long. I worked them partly out of the fire, and by rolling the ends in snow put out the fire to within about one foot of the end of each one; and in walking out of the gorge to the main draw I carried one in each hand, every once in a while flirting them back and forth, to fan them so as to keep the fire on them alive.

The wolves did not followed me, nor did I really think they would, yet, I had made such foolish moves for the past two days that I did not wish to take chances on anything any more.

Instead of keeping on down the valley as I had at first intended to do, I crossed it and ascended the eastern slope to the mesa or plateau, upon coming to the top of which

COOK SERENADED BY WOLVES.

I stopped and scanned the country over, hoping to see a smoke. For on these mornings when the landscape is covered with snow and the air is frosty, smoke can be seen a long way off. But nothing of the kind was visible.

I continued on in a northeasterly direction, aiming to strike the edge of the river-bottom again, and determined now to stick to it when once there, unless I saw a sure-enough camp away from it. The real pangs of hunger had left me, but weakness was creeping on. The old elastic step was gone. The snow was five inches deep. The sun was shining so brightly that my eyes were burning.

Thanks to the wolves, I still had one of the charred sticks in my hands. I pinched off flakes of charcoal with my finger-nails and blackened my cheeks under my eyes. And was it providential that I escaped snow-blindness?

Right here I wish to stop this narrative long enough to say that I will put the Panhandle of Texas against any other 180 miles square of territory in America for spasmodic, erratic weather. Before the sun reached the meridian it was very warm. Not a breath of air seemed to stir. The snow melted rapidly, and before the middle of the afternoon it was a veritable slush; and I slowly spattered through it.

About 3 P. M., as I passed through a gap that separated quite a flat-top from the main plateau I saw, first opposite a bend in the river and off to my left, and fully a mile or more out from the river and on the north side, I being on the south side, what I at first took to be tents. Yes. I was sure I saw tents. That meant to me soldiers and full rations.

Then I felt hungry! Oh, so hungry! The sight seemed

to stimulate me, and I moved on down the river until I came opposite the same objects, but they now ·looked altogether different. I could not make out what I had first seen; but I did see in the north and west a dark-blue cloud near the horizon, rapidly rising.

Here the bluff came down close to the river, dropping down in benches with a narrow sandy bottom. I went down near the river to where there was a rack-heap or pile of driftwood; and, evening coming on, I selected a place between two sand ridges and built a fire. Where I built it it was not more than fifty feet from the water's edge, which was very shallow, just barely a thin sheet of water, the channel running against the north bank. After I had gotten the fire to burning good, I went back up on the bench of land, to where I could see over to the objects that had attracted my attention so much, and just as the sun was disappearing behind the hills the blue cloud had settled back. Not definitely making out what any of the objects were, I went back to the fire.

Just then I heard the sound, as if it were an ax, in the direction I had been looking. It was repeated several times, and then all was silence. Soon it began to turn very cold, and by morning had frozen the river, in the shallow places along the bars. There was no grass where I built the fire. I had made it in a basin between two sand ridges; and when it had burned to a bed of coals I took the end-gate of a wagon, which I found in the driftwood, and separated the coals to right and left, to some little distance from the fire-bed. Then I built two fires and stretched myself out in the original warm fire-bed between the two fires. I was resting, but could not sleep for hours,—or so it seemed to me. I kept turning from side to side, at first on account of the heat in the

sand under me; then I would get up from time to time
and replenish the fires.

Finally I fell into a dreamy slumber, from which I would
suddenly arouse, and at one time in the night, when I
became thoroughly awakened, I was fully five rods from
the fire. This gave me much concern. I had dreamed
that some one wanted my bed and had driven me away
from it, and I must have left my bed while I was asleep.

Here I uttered the first word I had heard since leaving
the camp of the Mexicans. "No," I said; "I am here
alone."

It was very cold, and I judged by the Dipper, that
grand old night clock of the hunter and cowboy, that it
would soon be morning: and to my intense delight it
was but a short time until I heard a rooster crow. The
sound came from the object I had previously seen, and
the place from where I had heard the strokes of the axe.
Again and again that welcome sound came to my ears,
and two miles away, as I soon learned. Then just at good
broad daylight, I heard the bark of a dog.

I picked up a strong cottonwood stick about eight feet
long and three inches in diameter and started for the
river. The ice at the margin for three or four steps bore
my weight. I would use the stick for two purposes:
when the ice would no longer hold me up, I would with
the stick break it ahead until I got to the main channel;
then I would use it for a sounding-pole, step by step reaching ahead and thrusting it to the bottom. The water was
about 100 feet wide from shore to bar, and ran from sheet
water to three feet in depth at the north bank, which was
a cut bank, the top of which was nearly three feet above
the surface of the water. Placing both hands on top of
the bank, I pulled myself up and had both elbows on the

bank, wriggling myself to get one knee up on the bank,
when my hat dropped into the water. In easing back I
let go too soon, and was nearly submerged. I got the
hat, and waded down-stream nearly 200 yards before I
found a place where I could get out.

After getting up on the bank I struck out as rapidly as
my strength would permit. After going about a mile I
saw a horseman coming from the west as fast as his horse
could run. He rode up to the objects that had attracted
my attention the afternoon before, and soon two men on
foot came out, and all ran toward me. I kept my speed
up to the limit until we met. I noticed they all had guns
and were excited. The horseman was the coolest one
of the party. I said, "Don't get uneasy, men; I'm all
right. I've been lost."

The two men afoot handed their guns to the man that
was mounted. Then, getting on either side of me, each
one took a lifting hold under each of my arms to assist
me. I said, "Oh, no, gentlemen—I am not that bad
off;" but they clung to me. "George," said the old
man, "You ride ahead quick and tell Mother to have
the coffee hot."

My first question was, "What place is this?"

"It is the Adobe Walls," came the response.

We were soon inside the walls, and a cup of coffee, one
biscuit, a small piece of fried buffalo-meat, and about
two spoonfuls of gravy were set before me. I had told
them I had eaten nothing since the fourth morning before this morning. I was told to eat slowly and sip my
coffee. The old lady said: "

"Now we want you to have just all you can eat whenever we think you can stand it." And she added: "This
is not new to us; two regular soldiers came to our place on

the Picket Wire [Purgatoire] in Colorado, who had been lost for four days, and it was all we could do to keep them from gorging themselves; but they were both just about crazy, for, after losing their way, and getting completely lost, they lost their heads and one of them never did recover his mind."

After I had eaten everything placed in sight, I was furnished with dry clothing, a large pan of warm water, soap, and towel. A wagon-sheet had been stretched across a part of the room of the stockade that we were in, and before going behind this curtain to bathe and change my clothing I took a look at myself in a looking-glass that was handed to me. I had not washed since taking the bath in the pool the first day out.

And it was no wonder the children, and older ones, too, stared at me as they did; for I really was a fright. My hair was quite thick, and longer than I usually wore it, not having had it cut at the usual time. It was matted, snarled, and shaggy-looking. My mustache was singed; beard was two weeks old, dirty, and full of grit; my face was charcoaled; hands dirty and grimy. My eyes were sunken back in their sockets; and all in all I was a frightful-looking object, and looked like an object of suspicion.

Just then I happened to remember my papers that I had in an inside pocket of my overshirt. Unbuttoning my shirt-front I took out my papers, the bottom ends of which were wet, handed them to the old man and said: "Read those; they will tell you who and what I am; and when I wash and get on dry clothes I will tell you how I came to be here in this fix."

The man who had ridden the horse went back of the curtain with me and said: "Now I'll help you all I can." After disrobing, we both soaped, lathered, and rinsed, and

rubbed, until the glow came all over the body. Then
I put on an entire suit of Buck Wood's clothes, he being
about my size and build.

By the time I got back into the presence of the family,
they had read my papers, and a letter from U. S. Senator
Preston B. Plumb introducing and recommending me to
his cattle partner, Major Hood.

The old gentleman then said to me, "We are the Wood
family, well known down in Arkansaw, Texas and Colorado. Mr. Cook, this is my wife." We shook hands.
"This is my oldest son; Buchanan is his name; this is his
wife; and this is George Simpson, her brother. These
are the two oldest girls, Virginia and Georgia, and these
little ones are all our children. We are on our way from
the Picket Wire [Purgatoire], near Las Animas, to Fort Elliott. We just stopped here until the snow-storms were over,
and had intended to pull out and go about twelve miles
to-day, but as it is we will lie over to-day and give you
a rest."

I said: "I certainly appreciate that, and thank you
ever so much."

Just then George Simpson went back of the curtain and
brought out my wet duds. It was then that I first thought
of my money, since I had gotten so wet and was so long
getting out of the river.

I said: "Mr. Simpson, I am afraid my money is wet.
I never thought of it till now. It's all currency, but a
little change. Let's take it and see the condition it's in."

The purse was of buckskin and opened by twisting two
steel knobs. The bills had to be folded twice for the purse
to contain them, amply. There were two compartments
in the pocket-book. In one there were three twenty-
and two ten-dollar bills. The other contained two five-

dollar bills, a five-dollar gold-piece (the first one I ever had), and one dollar and sixty cents in silver coin.

He handed me the purse, which was sopping wet. I laid it on the dining-table and asked Mrs. Wood to please care for it, adding, "that she could handle the money more deftly than I could." She complied with my request; took out the money and placed each bill separately upon a clean, dry pillow-case. It was all wet through, but the bills were not chafed, and she dried them and the purse so nicely that I had no trouble in using the money. The coin I gave to the little children, in spite of the protests of the parents.

After Mrs. Wood had spread the bills out to dry, she poured out a cup of coffee and gave it to me, together with a biscuit and a slice of meat, all of which I ate ravenously, and asked for more. She said, "N-o! you will have to wait a while." Of course I submitted, but, I do think that at that moment I was hungrier than I had been at any time since I had left the Mexican outfit.

After the money and that portion of my papers that had got wet were dried, Mrs. Wood handed them to me, saying, "These are all right now, and by to-morrow *you* will be yourself again."

I had started in twice before to tell them how I happened to be in such a condition; but they would divert me by making some irrelevant remark about their horses, or "Look out, boys, and see if you can see any buffalo," and wind up by saying they were anxious to hear how it happened, but they wanted to be all together when I related it.

The fact was: I had laughted outright when I sat down to the table, when I first arrived; then again I laughed when putting on Buck's clothes. They mistook the looks of my eyes, and the actions of the two lost soldiers were in their minds; so they thought I was on the border-land of daftness. All this they told me a month later.

At the dinner hour I ate two biscuits, though I could have eaten ten. They said, "Drink all the coffee you want and to-morrow you can have all the bread and meat you can eat."

About 3 o'clock in the afternoon I went to sleep on a bed they had prepared for me early in the forenoon, behind the curtain. Nor did I wake up until seven o'clock the next morning, having slept soundly for sixteen hours. Nor did I know for nearly a month afterward, that the three men had taken turns, time about, all night, watching me. They said they did not know what might happen; for one of the lost soldiers from old Fort Bent, on the Arkansas, had got up in the night, and with a neck-yoke in his hands was striking right and left at imaginary foes, saying, "Come on, you copper-skinned devils; I'm good for the whole Cheyenne tribe!"

When I came out in the presence of the family, Mr. Wood asked me how I felt. I said: "Splendid; I slept good and sound all night, and I could walk forty miles to-day." The breakfast had been over for an hour. My breakfast was awaiting me; and, after taking a good wash I sat down to a plate piled up with biscuits, another with several great slices of tender buffalo-meat, stewed apples, and rich milk gravy (they had three cows with them). Strong coffee completed the "bill of fare." And I could, and I did, eat all I wanted. The women-folks had washed, dried, and ironed my clothes.

CHAPTER V.

We Move.—Acres of Buffalo.—Indian Scare.—Killed Two Bears.—
First Wedding in the Panhandle.—At Last!—Fort Elliott.—Meet
Romero and Son.—The Great Buffalo-slayer.—What Gen. Sheri-
dan Said.—The Great Slaughter Begun.

We moved that day down the river about ten miles.
We camped in a hackberry and elm grove, at the mouth of
a big coulée. This term is used more in the Dakotas than
in Texas, meaning ravine, draw, cañon, arroyo,—all these
terms being nearly synonymous. It was an ideal camping-
ground. Plenty of wood, water, grass, and protection
from storms. I commenced at once to make myself useful. Buck and his father's family camped separately.
Each outfit had a good tent; Buck's tent was ten by twelve
feet, his father's, twelve by fourteen feet. Simpson lived
with Mr. Wood, senior. Buck and his wife lived alone.
Buck invited me to make my home with him, which invitation I gladly accepted.

The first thing in order was unhitching the team; the
harness was hung over each front wheel, collars hung on
the front hounds of the wagon. Then the grass scalped off
where the camp-fire was to be, when not using the cook-
stove. Wood was to be gathered, the camp-fire built,
water brought, the cooking utensils and mess box placed
near the fire, Mrs. Wood getting the meals and Buck and I
putting up the tent, carrying in the bedding, leveling the
rough places, and making down the beds.

This was the universal custom when camping. And the
sun had not yet gone down when supper was eaten. I
walked up onto a little hill, just back of our camp, where I

had a good view back up the coulée, to the north. I was not more than one hundred yards from camp, and after looking a little bit to make sure, I said in a strong voice that "I believed I saw five thousand buffalo." Buck, his father, and George, all came up with their guns; and as they looked and ejaculated I thought my estimate very considerate. The old gent said there were ten thousand in sight, this minute, not counting those in the gulches and ravines that we could not see.

After looking at them a short time we all went down to camp and held a council. Buck said if I would stay with him he would make a killing as long as it would pay to stay; said he would give me 30 cents apiece for all the buffaloes I would skin and peg out. That is to say: after the hides were brought into camp and little holes cut through them around the outer edge and pegs about six inches long, sharpened at one end and driven into the ground through the holes, commencing the work by first driving three pegs at the neck end of the hide, then going to the tail end, and pulling on the hide to a proper degree and driving two pegs, one on each side of the tail, then so on all around it, stretching the hide in a proper and uniform shape. I told him I would stay with him indefinitely if I could get to where I could get some clothes, a gun, and plenty of tobacco.

I omitted, previously, to state that I was an inveterate chewer and smoker at the time; and what made the last day of my pilgrimage to the Adobe Walls worse was, that I ran out of both chewing and smoking tobacco. I told Mr. Wood so the morning that I came to them; told him "how I had missed my tobacco the day before." He gave me a piece, and said they nearly all used it, and had plenty of it. But it did not taste natural to me until this evening.

I now briefly gave the party my antecedents, and when I came to that part, and had related it, of the last few days' experience, they acted toward me more like father, mother, brothers and sisters than mere chance acquaintances.

George Simpson said: "I'll tell you what we will do: let's hunt here a few days until the bulk of these buffalo pass, then you and I will take two of the horses, some coffee, salt, and a little flour, and go back and get your gun and outfit." All of which was agreed to.

That night I slept soundly, and was awakened next morning by the crowing of the roosters. Each family had a coop of chickens. I got up feeling well refreshed.

After building the camp-fire, Buck and his wife came out of the tent. We all helped to get the breakfast, and soon after eating it was light enough to see the horses, which we soon had the harness on. We unloaded the wagon and hitched the team to it. Then, with a steel, a ripping-knife and a skinning-knife, together with an old Enfield rifle, I drove up the coulée behind Buck, who was on horseback, carrying a 50-caliber Sharp's rifle, a belt buckled around his waist containing thirty-two cartridges, besides a dozen loose ones in his coat pocket.

After going about a half-mile he rode down from a little rise he had gone upon, and waited for me to come up to him. When I came up he said: "Now drive on to yonder plum thicket, and go up on the bench to the left of it and wait and watch for me." I did so, and when I got there I saw that the buffaloes were in about the same position as they were the night before, only there were not so many. What breeze there was came from the northeast. I afterward learned much more about buffaloes than I knew then.

I had not waited long until I heard that loud and boom-like report of the "big fifty," that I was to hear more or less of for the next three years. Again I heard it; then about two miles west of where this report came from, pealed out the same deep roar and it came from George Simpson's big fifty. Then from Buck in front of me I heard again the loud detonating sound, and I saw the smoke as it floated away in the air to the southwest, and then for half an hour or more a desultory firing was kept up by both guns. The sound from Buck's gun was much more distinct than from George's, the former being much closer, and more on a line with the air-current.

After about three-quarters of an hour Buck rode up on an eminence in front of me, and waved his hat. I started toward him, and there was not a buffalo in sight; they had all hurried back over the divide toward Wolf creek,—the same creek where seven months after I picked up the brass kettle that verdigris-poisoned me.

Coming up to where Buck was, he informed me that he had killed sixteen buffalo. I was thrilled with delight; whereas, in less than four months I looked upon such things as a matter of course.

Following Buck, and driving nearly half a mile further, we came to the first carcass. One of the horses in the team was so frightened at sight and scent of the dead animal that we had much trouble to manage him. He was flighty and nervous, so much so that we had to unhitch and tie him to the wagon while I skinned the first buffalo. But before we got them all skinned we could drive up to the side of a carcass, and he would pay no attention to it. We thought that the quiet, sedate manner in which his mate acted had made him ashamed of himself.

Buck had skinned a few buffaloes in Colorado, and to me at that time he seemed like an expert. But in four months I could double-discount him. I would not attempt

to tell the different positions and attitudes I placed myself
in that day. Suffice to say, I got the hides off from ten
of them, and when we got to camp, about four o'clock in
the evening, I was so stiff and sore I could hardly get out
of the wagon. While I was skinning the first buffalo,
Buck rode out in the direction where George Simpson had
been shooting and got back a little after I had started in
on the second one.

These carcasses were strung out at even intervals for
half a mile, in the direction that all the others went, viz.,
northeast. Some had turned to right and left of the line of
travel. Buck skinned two of the carcasses while I was
taking the hide from one. He would ride over the breaks
of the coulée and be gone for an hour or so and come back
and skin two more, then off again in some other direction.
And when I was skinning my tenth carcass he came back
and skinned the two remaining ones.

We took the hump from both sides of the hump ribs,
of all the carcasses. In taking out the hump we inserted
the knife at the coupling of the loin, cutting forward down
the lower side, as far forward as the perpendicular ribs
ran; then, starting at the loin again, would cut down on
the upper side; then, taking hold of the end of the piece,
would cut and hold off a little, running the knife as before,
down the upper side,—thus taking out a strip from a
full-grown animal about three feet long and widening and
being thicker as it went forward, and near the front of the
hump ribs it would as a rule be ten or twelve inches wide
and four or five inches thick. When first taken out and
when hung up for a couple of days with the big end down,
it became shrunken, or "set," as we termed it. It also
became tender and brittle, with no taint. The front end

had a streak of lean and fat alternating, and when fried in tallow made a feast for the gods.

I had left the camp that morning without taking any drinking-water with me, and was very thirsty nearly all day, which seemed to contribute toward weakening me. But by quenching my thirst, lying down a few minutes, then eating a hearty meal, with strong coffee, and by stretching and working my arms and lower limbs, I was ready for the pégging-out of the hides, and before it was too dark to see how to strike a peg I had the sixteen hides pegged out and three dollars earned before going to bed, for the ten buffaloes that I had skinned and pegged out.

We reloaded the empty shells from the day's shooting, fifty-one in all, or a little over an average of three shots to the animal. Some were killed with one shot, some two, some three, and one with five shots. Others went off with the herd, carrying lead in their bodies.

Each hunter carried in his ammunition-box a reloading outfit, consisting of bullet molds, primer extractor, swedge, tamper, patch-paper, and lubricator. After reloading the shells we went to bed and to sleep.

I awoke the next morning rested, and eager for the hunt. I had thought when coming in with the hides to the camp the evening before that I would have to give up the job. But if anything I was now more anxious than ever to go on the hunt. Buck and his father went up on the little hill to look the country over, while I was hitching up the team. When they came back they reported that a few buffaloes were in sight, in scattering bands, and that a few were close to camp. Buck advised me to not hitch up at present and said: "I wish you would cut four strong forks and four cross-arms [giving me the dimensions], drive the forks into the ground here [indicating the place],

and when we come into camp to-night I'll fasten a hide inside the frame and we will have a vat to salt the humps in
so we can dry them."

Alas! for plans. Before I had gotten quite through
the work assigned me, I heard shooting up the coulée,
five or six shots in rapid succession.

A short interval and boom! boom! again; and when
he had fired about twenty rounds, at longer or shorter intervals, here there came down and out of the coulée, about
thirty head of old stub-horn bulls, going at their lumbering, nodding gait, passing to within 100 feet of where
our camp was.

I was near the wagon; the Enfield was in the front end
of it, and the cartridge-belt around my waist. I hurried
for the gun, put in a cartridge, and ran out toward them,
dropping my right knee on the ground, took aim at the
leader, and gave him a paunch shot ranging forward.
Then I saw the rear of the herd was being followed by one
with its right front leg broken and flapping. I aimed at
him at the regulation place that I had heard Buck, George
and the old man Wood say was the proper place to hit
a buffalo with a side shot, which would be a place anywhere inside of a circle as large as a cowboy's hat, just
back of the shoulderblade. And here was where I plunked
him, and in much less time than it takes to tell it, the pale,
frothy blood blubbered out of his nostrils, he made a few
lurches and fell over—dead.

By this time the one I had "paunched" fell out to the
left and stopped, while the rest seemed to increase their
speed, with that characteristic motion, loping and bowing
their great foreheads, their chin mops of long hair fairly
sweeping the ground as their heads came down, in their
up-and-down motion. They all passed on out of range

of the Enfield, and the first one I had shot lay down on his hunkers and died in that position.

Soon Buck came riding out of the coulée and reported that he had killed four buffaloes and broken one's leg that had got away.

"Not much he didn't," said his wife; "Mr. Cook killed him with the old needle-gun," which term was used to designate all trap-door breech-blocks, "and another besides," she added. He had not yet seen the carcasses, although they were lying in plain sight on the short grass, the farthest one not more than 200 yards away.

When he saw them and me with the old gun yet in my hands, he said, "Well, I'll be darned! I've threatened to throw that old gun away several times, but I'm glad, now, I didn't."

We took the team and drove up the coulée to where the first bull had been killed, keeping the other three he had killed in sight. As we passed them Buck remarked that "these old stub-horns are harder to skin than cows," which we had the day before, "and I thought I'd help you with them, as I saw that you were pretty near played out yesterday."

Before we got the first hide off, we heard some one calling. Upon looking up we saw the women and children running toward us. We grabbed our guns and ran toward them, they still coming on. When we met them they were badly frightened, and told us that "the camp was full of Indians."

Buck said to me, "You go with the folks back of the wagon in the rough ground and I will try to find out what this means."

I said, "No, I will not; these are your own blood relations. You have the best gun and the most ammunition. You can make a better fight for them than I can. I'll go and see what this means myself."

Accordingly, I started off in the direction of camp, thinking that the women were "panicky." I could not bring myself to believe that there were war parties out at that time of the year.

I had not gone far when I met two soldiers of the Fourth United States cavalry riding rapidly up the coulée. The first thing one of them said, was: "Where are those women and children? Did you see them?"

My answer was, "Yes, boys, they are at such a place about now," pointing in the direction. One of them dismounted, saying, "Here,—you get on this horse, and go with this man and bring them to camp, for there is more danger where they are than in camp."

The other soldier and I hurried on until within about 300 yards of the broken ground, when I pulled up and said:

"Don't let's rush in there; for there is a man with them and he has a fifty-caliber Sharp's and lots of ammunition. They are comparative strangers to me; and if we lope in there one of us might get hurt before they could take us for friends. You stay where you are; I'll ride on slowly a little farther, and halloo and try and attract their attention toward me."

He replied: "All right; that *is* best."

I rode forward about 100 yards and hallooed, "O, Buck, Buck!"

"You-pee!" came back the response. Then he, the women and children, filed out of the broken ground and came on. The soldier then rode up, dismounted, and, walking along beside the whole party, explained the condition of affairs.

By the time we got to where Buck and I had left the team, the soldier who gave me his horse was there. We hitched up, all piled into the wagon, and went to camp. Mr. Wood and Simpson did not get in till near dark, bringing in twenty-one hides.

Arriving at camp, we met a sergeant and six more soldiers, making nine soldiers in all. I then learned from the non-commissioned officer that there had been an order issued from the War Department a few months before, that military escorts would be furnished to all Indian hunting parties in the future.

This was for two purposes: one to see that no overt act would be perpetrated by the Indians against settlers and other hunters, and *vice versa;* and that this was a "Kiowa hunting party," mostly young bloods, old men, and the whole squaw outfit. But some of the worst of the warriors were held as hostages at Fort Sill.

We all knew that the past summer had been a busy one with hunters, soldiers, and Indians.

It was the Indian war of 1874. It was the year that that Spartan band of buffalo hunters, at the Adobe Walls, withstood the siege of all the able-bodied warriors of the Cheyenne, Arapahoe, Kiowa and Comanche tribes. It was that summer, on the Washita divide, that a mere apology, in point of numbers, of an escort and train guard resisted, charge after charge, with blood-curdling yells, more than a thousand of the best warriors of the southern wild Indians. It was that summer that the then Captain, Adna R. Chaffee, who had worked his way up from a private soldier, step by step, for heroic and meritorious conduct, to the position he then held, made his famous battle-field speech, near the breaks of the Red river, when he was confronted with a horde of painted, war-bonneted red-devils under old Nigger Horse. He halted his company, fronted them, right-dressed them, and said:

"Forward, boys! Charge them, and if any of you are killed I'll promote you to corporal."

It was in this country that Lieutenant Elliott was killed, and in whose honor Fort Elliott was named. It was the summer of the first big general slaughter by an army, as it were, of bold, venturesome hunters, making buffalo-hides a specialty for commercial purposes.

Was it any wonder that the Indians were mad? And this same ground that we were camping on was a portion of the Kiowas' favorite hunting-grounds. Here their ancestors had followed the chase for ages gone by.

The sergeant informed us that there was a company of the Fourth Cavalry with these Indians, with two commissioned officers. They had broken camp that morning very early, as they wished to go down the river to the mouth of White Deer that day, and not make two camps. They had crossed the Canadian river that morning about three miles above us, having come in from the south the day before; and that runners had come in the night before, who had been out scouting for good hunting, and had reported that the White Deer country was alive with the game they were hunting. He also said that it was customary in moving the big camp from place to place for a detail of soldiers to go ahead and the main escort to bring up the rear. He and his party had been assigned that duty for that day.

But Quirt Whip and his band of Indians had got ahead of them while they were getting a quicksanded horse out of the river, and when Quirt Whip came along to our camp, so Quirt Whip told him, the women and children all fled. So he sent an interpreter back hastily to tell what had happened, and he and his men had hastened on as fast as they could.

I asked the sergeant why the interpreter did not call out to the women and assure them there was no danger.

"Because," said he, "he was dressed like the rest and is a quarter-breed, three-quarters of it being on the Indian side; and he is totally devoid of intuition, and how in h—l he can talk two languages is beyond my comprehension."

I was silenced. The sergeant sent two men ahead to overtake Quirt Whip and travel with them to the White Deer camp. All the time our conversation was being carried on the Indians were passing our camp, about 100 yards south of it, going in an easterly direction. It was the first travois* (travoy') outfit I had ever seen,—but by no means the last, as I will relate and describe later on.

Just as the last of the Indians were passing by and the other soldiers were near, the sergeant and his men started on and were but a little way off, when suddenly he wheeled around, galloped back to the command, dismounted, and saluted the officers, who were all quite near us. He seemed to be making an oral report, adding many gestures to it, and pointing toward us and in other directions. He then remounted and rode on in the direction his comrades had taken.

The command turned, left-obliqued, came up to within a few steps of Mr. Wood senior's tent, and dismounted where we were all at the time. The first lieutenant was the spokesman. He was as straight as an arrow, well

---

*Travois (from the French). A contrivance of two poles lashed at one end to each side of a pony, the other ends trailing on the ground. A sort of sack made from skins or canvas, is lashed to the cross-bars connecting the two poles. On this travois is carried the camp equipage, and sometimes a sick or wounded person.

proportioned, about six feet high, and about forty-five years old. He commenced by making a courteous bow to the ladies, saying:

"Glad to meet you, ladies, but sorry to find you here. How do you do, men? You people have had quite a shake-up. Where did you come from and where are you intending to go?"

Mrs. Wood, Sr., being a ready talker, briefly told him who they were; where they came from; where they were finally going to; and that the intention was to secure homes for all of them near Fort Elliott, if the country there suited them; and wound up by telling him we were short two men, her husband and her daughter-in-law's brother; that they had gained one man to their party at the Adobe Walls. He had been lost several days, with nothing to eat, and was with them temporarily. She told him that she expected her husband and George any time, and that for her part buffalo-hunting had lost its charms for her; that she would not pass through such a mental strain and physical exertion again, as she had that morning, for all the buffalo-hides on the whole range.

The officer then said, addressing himself more to Buck and myself: "This is no place for these women and children. Strong men can generally come through all right, in an Indian country; and that is what this is at present. The Cheyennes and Arapahoes hunt north of here; the Comanches are hunting south of here; they, or these Kiowas, and a small party of young men, could slip out of their camp, and in the absence of you men murder these women and children, for it is in their hearts to do it. They look upon you as trespassers on their hunting-grounds. I will leave a guard here of five of my troopers; and when the other two men come in I want you all to come with

them to my camp. Be sure and break this camp by to-
morrow morning and follow us."

With that he turned around and said: "Sergeant, detail
five men with their bedding and rations, and instruct them
to remain with these people and bring them to my camp
to-morrow."

Mrs. Wood said, "No, you don't need any rations; we
will do their cooking and furnish the provisions ourselves."

The Lieutenant doffed his hat to her, said "Thank you,
madam," and was gone with his men of blue.

Buck and I went out and skinned our buffaloes; brought
in and pegged out the hides. We helped his father and
George do the same when they came in.

The next morning we all pulled out and went to White
Deer, stopped our wagons close to the soldiers' tents, and
pitched our tents.

The next morning I went to the officer's tent and told
him that the men wished to go back after the hides.

He said: "I'll tell you; I have been thinking about you
people. It is about eight miles from here to the military
trail from Fort Dodge to Fort Elliott. There is less danger
along that trail than where you were. There were several
Kiowas killed and wounded at the old Adobe Walls last
summer. Night before last, where we camped, they held
a kind of mourning powwow, because white hunters had
killed their people. Now you folks unload your wagons
and go back after the hides, take them onto the trail and
spread them out; then come back here and get your outfit. In three more days, I will move down to the Antelope
hills, and camp just over the boundary-line in the Indian
Territory, leaving you people on the military trail, shifting
all responsibility for your welfare."

That being a mandate, we governed ourselves accord-

ingly. After we were in camp a few days near the government trail, and about three miles south of the Canadian
river, we learned that there was a way-station about a
mile and a half north of the river crossing, and that the
proprietor kept hunters' supplies and bought hides.

Buck and I rode over to the place and found we were
at the Springer ranch. It was built on the blockhouse,
stockade, Indian frontier plan. It faced south towards
the river. A square pit six by six feet and six feet deep
had been dug inside the building. Then from it, leading
south, was a trench running outside fifty feet, where was
dug a circular pit ten feet in diameter and five feet deep.
This and the trench were cribbed over and the dirt tamped
down over it. The circular pit was portholed all around.
Also, from the pit inside the blockhouse there was a trench
running to the corral and stable. The stockade being
loopholed made the whole place so impregnable that a
few cool, determined men could make it impossible for the
allied tribes to take it without artillery.

We traded our hides to Springer for provisions, ammunition, etc. Here I was fortunate enough to get me two fair
suits of underwear, stockings, boots, and such necessaries
as I was in need of.

Springer told us he thought there was no danger of the
Indians bothering us before spring; thought we were perfectly safe to go anywhere except to cross the one-hundredth
meridian, which was the line between the Indian Territory
and the Panhandle of Texas. He said: "If you are caught
over the line you will be arrested by some deputy United
States Marshal and put to lots of trouble." But we had
no desire to go that way at the time.

The next day we hauled over to Springer all the hides
we had on hand, receiving $2.50 for the old bull-hides,

$3 for the choice robe cow-hides, and $1.75 each for all the others.

Buck and I found a place four miles southwest of the Springer ranch, about two hundred yards from the river, on the south side, and at the mouth of a dry sand creek, where there was a large grove of cottonwood timber, and in the sand creek at the south end of the grove were several holes of fresh water. Here we decided to build a log cabin, it being the first house built on the South Canadian river, in the Panhandle of Texas, inhabited by a pale-face family. While cutting the logs and building this cabin, we occasionally killed a straggling buffalo, until we had on hand the day we moved into the house (which we were more than two weeks in building), thirty-one hides.

These we hauled to Springer, and while there we met a party of regular buffalo-hunters. They informed us that the great mass of the buffaloes was south of the Red river, and that there would be no profitable buffalo-hunting here until the next May or June. Here I was fortunate enough to buy of one of these hunters a Sharp's 44-caliber rifle, reloading outfit, belt, and 150 shells. The man had used the gun only a short time, and seventy-five of the shells had never been loaded. I got the gun and his interest in the entire buffalo range for thirty-six dollars, he having met with the misfortune of shooting himself seriously, but not fatally, in the right side with the same gun which proved a "hoodoo" to me as the hunters afterwards sometimes remarked. It was an elegant fine-sighted gun, with buckhorn sights.

Wild turkeys were plentiful all about our cabin, and were so tame that it was no trouble at all to kill them in daytime, and in bright moonlight nights one could get up close to their roosts, and by getting them between the

hunter and the moon, they were frequently shot from
the trees.

On the north side of the river from the cabin, and a
half-mile or so from the river, was quite a grove of persimmon trees, some of them twenty-five or thirty feet
high, and some with trunks eight inches in diameter.
About the time we first commenced the building of the
cabin the fruit must have been in its prime, but when we
found them they were nearly gone.

This particular morning that we found it we had crossed
the river on horseback and were riding north toward the
hills to look for chance buffalo, when Buck's attention
was attracted toward the grove, which was on our left
about two hundred yards from us.

"Look! look! See how that tree shakes." We stopped,
and presently saw a violent trembling or shaking of another tree some little distance from the first. "John,"
said he, "that's a 'simmon grove and that's a bear in
there."

We had seen bear-tracks along the river-bars several
times while building the cabin. He told me to keep
around the right of the grove between it and the hills.

Said he: "I'll keep to the left between it and the river;
we will ride slow, and if he breaks out you play it to him.
You can shoot off Barney [the horse I was riding] all right.
He stands good; I've killed many a deer off from him up
on the Picket Wire."

When we parted he said: "Now, John, let's be careful, and don't let's shoot one another."

I rode quartering toward the grove, and on my left I
caught sight of a bear with its head from me. I stopped,
cocked my gun, had my trigger finger inside the trigger-
guard, and was raising the gun to take aim, when old

Barney gave a snort, whirled so quickly that I and the gun both went off, the bullet presumably striking the ground just a little ahead of me, and for the next twenty or more minutes it was the most exciting, busy and laughable hunts for game I ever experienced.

I had fallen forward on my face. The muzzle of the gun struck the ground first and got sand in it. I was on my feet instantly, and picked up the gun; threw down the breech-block, and soon had aim. Then I saw that Buck was riding up rapidly between myself and the grove, and quite close to it. I rushed forward, and, crossing Buck's track in behind his horse, I got a good shot at the bear and broke his back. There was no underbrush in the grove, and what grass there was was literally tramped down, and one could see clear through the grove from any direction.

At report of the gun Buck turned his horse around, and just as I shot the second time he shot at another bear that had broken from cover and was running for the hills. My second shot killed the bear that I was after. Buck's first shot went wild.

Seeing that the first bear was safe, I ran on north through the scattering trees; but before I had gotten to the north end of the persimmon grove, Buck had fired twice more, and when I came in full view of the bear it was nearly three hundred yards away and going north, with Buck a close second. He would stop and shoot about every one hundred yards; but could not get his horse to run onto the bear. Every time he would get up anywise close to it his horse would shy off.

After running and shooting four or five times this way he flanked his horse to the right and put him to his full speed. After passing the bear he circled in toward him.

They were then nearly a mile off, and close to the hills. When he got as close as he thought he could get the horse to the bear, he checked up and dismounted; dropping one knee to the ground, he fired, and as he afterwards told me he was not over eight yards from Bruin.

The moment Buck dismounted his horse bolted, and struck for the cabin. When the horse passed near me he was straining every muscle to its fullest tension. The saddle stirrups were flapping and seeming to keep time to the motion. I only took a hurried glance at "Doc," as the horse was called, as he passed by, then looking toward the bear and Buck, saw they were both coming toward me just behind in the edge of the persimmon grove there was a tree that forked. About six feet from there another one was leaning considerably grown up through the fork. I retreated to this place and got up in the crotch and by leaning my back against one of the forks and with both feet on the leaning tree, which was about five inches in diameter, my weight would press it down solid in the crotch, which gave me fair footing; then by peering out through the small limbs and twigs I could observe all that was going on.

The bear was nearly a quarter of a mile ahead of Buck, and was going along leisurely, and every now and then would look back. Buck was in a kind of dog-trot, and every few rods would stop, shoot, and come on. When the bear was about one hundred and fifty yards from the grove he turned a little to the right, which pleased me, for I had begun to get uneasy for fear a spent ball from the pursurer's gun might hit me. As the animal turned I noticed his tongue was lolling, and that he was badly wounded. I pointed the gun toward him, and, watching to get the best chance, I shot through twigs and all. At the crack of the gun the bear turned east and got on a line between Buck and me.

He had now gained on the wounded animal so much that he was not more than two hundred yards behind it. He called out, "Don't shoot!" I answered back, "Don't you shoot!" The bear was then going very slowly, and Buck now coming as fast as he could trot.

By the time he had come up to within a hundred feet of it it had passed out of line of me, when I said, "Here I am, Buck, in a tree. I think it safe for you to shoot now. The twigs are so thick I can't get a bead on him."

As the report of the gun died away the bear lay down and gave up the struggle. Whether from the last shot or pure exhaustion from loss of blood from its other wounds, we were not able to say. I got down out of my perch and we both met by the dead bear.

Buck asked, "Where is Barney?"

I asked, "Where is Doc?"

Here we were, both afoot and the river between us and the cabin. The sight and scent of the bears had thrown both horses in a panic, and it was sheer fright that had caused them to bolt. We decided to skin the bears, hang the hides and meat up in the trees, go down opposite the cabin, and call for Mrs. Wood to bring the horses over to us.

The bears were the common black species which were frequently found in that region. South of there, in the Brazos river breaks, they were very numerous. The two were in fine condition, a male and female, and would weigh something like six hundred pounds for the male and five hundred pounds for the female.

After dressing them we started for the river. As we were approaching and nearly opposite the camp, we saw

Mrs. Wood riding up to the bank from the home side. She was riding the horse we had left in camp. She crossed over to us, and told us that "Barney" and "Doc" were both scared, and trembled so that she could not lead them. Said she knew where we were all the time by the shooting, and thought she would bring Dave over to us so we could ford the river. Wood and his wife crossed over; then he came back for me, and soon we were at the cabin.

After washing the blood from our hands we went to the saddle-horses, and soon calmed their fears. Then, mounting them, we led Dave, took ropes along to pack with, and went back for our meat and hides. When we again got near the place Doc and Barney snorted and shied and trembled from fear,—so much so that we were compelled to go back toward the river and fasten them to some bushes.

But Dave, good old sensible Dave, had no fear whatever. We led him right up to the carcasses, and packed the hides and such of the meat as we cared to take. Then Buck sent me on ahead to loosen and get on one of the saddle-horses, and to hold the other until he came along.

When I commenced to untie them they snorted, jerked, and trembled violently; but I finally succeeded in getting them both loose. Mounting Barney, I held Doc by the bridle-rein. When they saw Buck, Dave and the pack coming they held their heads high, and stared at the outfit until they came too close for them to stand it any longer when instantly they bolted again. Soon I had to let go of Doc's rein, and away he went for home. I circled Barney around the pack twice, he shying off all the time.

Finally Buck said: "Let me get on him, John; there is no sense in his acting that way. When we get to camp I'll teach him and Doc both to pack bear-hides."

I dismounted and traveled on toward camp with faithful old Dave. Buck struck out for home, and when I and Dave came to the river I led him down the bank and started him across. The water was near three feet deep for about fifty feet; then it shallowed down to a mere nothing on the south side.

The weather was then, and for the past three weeks had been, bright and pleasant. But the water was cold. So I sat down on the bank to wait for Buck to come back. Sensible old Dave went on into camp. The river-bottom from the river to within about five rods of camp was covered with thick buck-brush, plum, and scattering cottonwood. Just as Dave was coming out of this thicket Wood was starting in, and when the horses saw him and the pack they flew the track as usual, and he let them shy off and around, being in a hurry to get me across the river, which was soon done.

I have dwelt at some length on this incident, for two reasons: one is to dispose of the idea that bears hibernate, or go into their holes and cave up in winter and never come out until spring; the other, as I had been told in boyhood, that all horses would tremble and run at sight or scent of bear. We talked of this a good deal at the time. It surprised me when Buck intimated that those trees were being shaken by bears, the time then being after mid-December. Buck informed me that in that climate it was so near spring and the weather being fine, it was only natural for them to be out if they had "holed up" at all; and he doubted that they had done so, saying that "in Arkansas he had known them to be out every month of the year."

We both felt sorry for Barney and Doc, they were so badly frightened and could not help it.

Wood had been feeding his horses a quart of oats apiece every night, as he claimed that would accustom them to camp, so that no matter where he roamed, the horses would always feel at home where the camp was. We spread a bear-hide down on the ground, where we fed the horses and poured out their feed as usual that evening, on a tarpaulin close by the hide; but the two would not come to it. Dave walked up and helped himself to his share. We then took up the rest of the oats and repeated this until the fourth evening, when the other two ventured up and ate their grain. In a few days' time they would both allow us to place the hides on their backs. Seemingly all fear had gone.

At the time we decided to build our cabin Mr. Wood, senior, and Simpson decided that they would pull on to Fort Elliott and get all the information they could about the country in general and the Sweet Water country in particular; and if they could find what they wanted near the garrison they would locate, and consider hunting afterward. We all bade each other a hearty good-by, they taking the trail for the fort.

We heard nothing of or from them until a few days after we killed the bears. The day we heard of them we had all been away from the cabin. All had gone on horseback, and we had ridden south from camp and gone up on the divide between the Canadian and Washita rivers.

We had killed and skinned the only two buffaloes we had seen. I made the remark, as we were on our road home, that I thought that we were "in a poor locality for even stragglers."

Buck said: "Yes; and if fair hunting doesn't show up pretty soon, I'll begin to think that there will be no hunting here until June, as we were told at Springer's; and maybe we'd better put south."

As we came in sight of the cabin, we saw a covered wagon drawn up in front of the door. We were all delighted, excited, and speculated as to whom it could be, and what it meant. We were soon enlightened, for on coming up to the cabin, we were met by George Simpson and Virginia, she that was formerly Virginia Wood, but now Mrs. Simpson.

This couple the day before had been married at Fort Elliott, by the post adjutant. They had taken their wedding tour in a two-horse Bain wagon, over the virgin soil of the Panhandle of Texas, to our humble but hospitable abode, to spend their honeymoon. So I was in the presence of the first couple that was married in the Panhandle.

That evening, around our fireside, I began to get some idea of the magnitude of the slaughter of poor Lo's commissary. George told us of having been at the fort, where there was a large, well-stocked sutler's store, and that at a place called Sweet Water, on the Sweet Water creek, three miles below the fort, Charles Roth and Bob Wright had a large store, carrying all kinds of hunters' supplies, and they had acres of high piles of hides; that it was a wild and woolly place, having a large dance-hall, two restaurants, three saloons, small and large hunting outfits coming and going; generally, from ten to fifteen outfits there nearly every day; that the great masses of buffalo were south of the Red river, fifty miles south of there, and still moving south; that they would keep going gradually south, until by ancient custom they turned north; that they were expected to be back there in May on their way north; that all the hunters were going to follow the herds to Red, Pease, and Brazos rivers.

He said that the story of my being lost was a general subject of talk among the hunters and soldiers, and that

it had been exaggerated and told in different versions so
that he could hardly get them to accept the facts as I had
told them in detail to the Wood family.   One story was,
that I had been gone twenty days, with nothing to eat.
He informed us that old man Wood had located a place
near the head of Gageby creek, ten miles northeast of Fort
Elliott, and was cutting logs to build a house; and that he
wanted Buck and me to come and get land by him, help
build his house, and start the building-up of a community.

So we talked the matter over for two days, and then
pulled out for Gageby, in due time arriving there and
looking the country over for a few days.

George Simpson and myself fitted out to go and find
the Mexican camp, and the people I had come from New
Mexico with.   I was anxious to get a War Department
map before going back to the Owa Sula or Blue Water.
So Buck and I rode to the fort.   As is a rule at military
frontier posts, we reported at the adjutant's office and
registered our names, whence we came, and whither destined.   When I asked for the map the commanding officer,
who was present, asked what I wanted it for.   I told him
"I had made the mistake of being lost between the Blue
Water and the Adobe Walls;" and before I could proceed
with the reason why I wanted the map he called me inside
the railing that partitioned off the office from the waiting-
room, and said:

"Be seated.   Now tell us all about that affair.   We have
heard different stories.   Now I want it at first hand."

After commencing at the time I left my father's house
in Johnson county, Kansas, I detailed my movements
up to the time I was in his presence.   I finished by telling him that so far as the gun, bedding and clothing that
I had at the Mexican camp were concerned, I was not

particular about them. But I had some papers in the outfit that were valuable. He asked me the nature of them. I told him that my grandfather, Jacob Cook, was a soldier in the Mexican War, and for his services was awarded one-third of a league of land; that he had located it in Nueces county, Texas; that he died at Matagorda Bay, of yellow fever, while on his way home after the war with Mexico; that all the papers pertaining to the land belonging to him, consisting of 1496 acres, fell to my father; that he had placed those papers in my hands for my own use.

The commander arose, and stretching himself, said: "A straightforward story, sir; sounds like a book. Adjutant, furnish this man with a map, with instructions to return it as soon as he makes his trip, and to report any water he may find not marked on the map."

Before we left the office an undersized Mexican came in, and in broken English engaged the adjutant in conversation.

The adjutant said: "Oh, by the way, Theodosia [the Mexican's name], your home is at La Glorieta; do you know Anton Romero?"

"Yes, his son Manuel is here now, at the sutler's store."

I stepped up to the Mexican, who was a government scout and guide, and I said: "Come and show him to me."

Theodosia, Buck and I went to the store. At sight of me the young fellow stood for a moment in doubt and amazement; then hurried up to me and gave me the Mexican hug; and how he did unravel his lingo, laughing and crying both at once.

Theodosia interpreted his words to me in this wise: "I am so glad. My father is in distress about you. He would never have let you leave our camp alone. We hunted you for three days; father will be so glad now."

I asked the scout to find out where the camp was now: "En donde es el campo?" (Where is your camp?)

He said it was on the Palo Juan; that we could go and come in two days; that the hunting gave out on the Blue Water; and that they had come on toward the fort, hoping to find better hunting; and also that he had come in the night before to get some ammunition, and to find out if anyone had seen the Americano who left their camp.

To make a long story short, I made arrangements with Manuel to go back and report that he had found me, and for him and his father to come the next day and bring my outfit.

Buck went back to his camp on the Gageby. I rode Doc to the quartermaster's corral; and as I dismounted I recognized the familiar face of Jack Callahan, who had been a six-mule-team wagonmaster during the rebellion, whom I well remembered in Arkansas. It took but a few words for him to remember me. But as I had grown to full manhood, with beard on my face, he did not at first recognize me. I was made welcome and at home.

The next evening after dark, Theodosia came and told me that Romero and son were there, and were going into camp back of the sutler's store. I at once hastened to them, and the joy that Romero expressed at sight of me was genuine. For he had not only been very friendly with me, but he was troubled in mind for my safety. He had my gun, my wardrobe and bedding, and I was missing. He did not know what might have happened. But the saints had been good to him, and the Virgin Mary was smiling. He did not want to be suspected of having murdered me, such an act having been done for less value than a Winchester gun and a few duds. The next morning I had Theodosia go with me to Romero and his son's camp. And after they got my roll of bedding, war-bag and gun out of their wagon, I asked them what I owed them, from the time I came to their place at La Glorieta until this time.

Romero said: "No! No! hombre-man; you owe me nothing. You all the time helped in camp; here are all your things. I shot away all your cartridges but two; how much shall I pay you for them?"

I picked up my Winchester and belt and placed them in his hands, saying, "Romero, these are yours."

"No, no," he said; but when I insisted and told him about my other gun, before spoken of, he thanked me, saying, as he patted the stock of the Winchester, "I'll keep it as long as I live, and it shall never go out of my family." Then, after a general talk of half an hour or so, we each went his way.

I had heard of the professed friendship, the insincerity, the treachery, the thieving propensities of the New-Mexican, until, if I had allowed my prejudices to govern me, as some did, I should be calling them a race of blanketed thieves. Of course there were, and are yet, many of that class among the New-Mexicans, but it was not the rule, according to my experience.

Farewell, Romero! Although your color is cinnamon, and you may have Spanish, Navajo, or even Apache blood in your veins, you treated me white all the same.

After reporting to the post adjutant and handing him the map, I left for Sweet Water, and there I met the real genuine hide-hunters, who followed this as an exclusive business. Several outfits were camped on the creek, and with them I put in the remainder of the day and evening, picking up information, taking items, and asking some questions. Every hunter kept open camp. Hospitality was unbounded. Every man seemed to carry his heart upon his sleeve. It was here this day that I met the greatest of all buffalo-slayers. He was fitting out to make the first southern hunt that had yet been made by the so-called northern hunters in the Pease and Brazos rivers country; and he offered me twenty-five cents per hide for skinning buffaloes. Another man, from northern Kansas, had engaged to go with him. They intended to start in four or five days. I told him I would like to go back to Gageby and talk with the Wood outfit before agreeing to engage with him. Thereupon it was agreed that I would let him know in two or three days what answer to make him.

The next morning I rode over to Gageby, reaching there before noon. I had thought the matter all out, and felt that I was to be a member of that army of hunters that were to exterminate within the next three years the countless herds of the American bison.

We were all camped together at this time, and that night I stated the case something like this: "Now you people are all different from me. You have more of a community interest; mine is a range interest. It is immediate funds that I need, and to get the quickest results it is to my interest to follow the buffaloes." They all agreed with me, but said if I would stay with them till spring I would get all the hunting I wanted, but that I must decide for myself.

So, early the next morning, Buchanan Wood made me a tender of the money for the number of the hides I had skinned, and some I had not, while I had been with him. I told him that I hoped I could not be so ungrateful for the many favors I had received from their hands, and insisted that it was I who owed them money; to which they nearly all in a chorus said: "Oh, no! not to the Woods."

I felt that they were my benefactors. They had treated me just as a member of their family from start to finish. Their hospitality was as broad as the prairies we traveled over; they were kind to one another, and considerate of the stranger within their gates.

They were a common people, of rather rough exterior, but imbued with Christian principles. They were a strong type of the backwoodsman, and had not one personal trait of selfishness among them.

I had arranged with Buck, the night before, to take me to Sweet Water. When we were ready to start I parted from these Good Samaritans of the wilderness with no little reluctance. There were no limpy dishrag handshakes. It was a cordial grasp of the hand and looking me straight in the eyes; from the old man to the least child, it was "Good-by, John."

Mrs. Wood said: "Now, John, if you come back with the buffaloes next summer, you must come and see us; for right here is where we will be if the Indians don't scare us away."

Buck and I went to Elliott first, to get my bedding and clothes to take to Sweet Water. While there I went to the sutler's store and bought a useful present for each member of each family, and sent them back by Buck, as tokens of my regard for them.

Arriving at Sweet Water, James Buchanan Wood and I parted, and I never saw him again. Good-by, Buck; you were one of Nature's noblemen.

I reported to the famous hunter before alluded to. He was a six-footer, built like a greyhound, supple as a cat, a man of unusual vitality, long-winded in the chase, and an unerring shot at game.   His name was Charles Hart. He was a Union ex-soldier, captured at the battle of Shiloh, and lived through the horrors of Andersonville prison. He was in the habit of getting on periodical sprees, at which time his imagination would run riot.

The man from northern Kansas was also a Union ex-soldier, named Warren Dockum.   If the reader will look on the map of Texas, made some few years after this time, he will see marked on a tributary of White Cañon, Dockum's Ranch, where he located in 1877, two years after I first met him.

A man named Hadley was to accompany us with a freight team.   He had six yoke of oxen and a heavy freight wagon.

Then there was Cyrus Reed, and his brother-in-law, Frank Williamson, a green, gawky boy, seventeen years old.   These, with myself, completed the number in our outfit.   We had two two-horse teams hitched to light wagons, on starting out.   One of these teams hauled the provisions and camp outfit, which consisted of one medium and one large-sized Dutch oven, three large frying-pans, two coffee-pots, two camp-kettles, bread-pans, coffee-mill, tin cups, plates, knives, forks, spoons, pot-hooks, a meat-broiler, shovel, spades, axes, mess-box, etc.   The other one hauled our bedding, ammunition, two extra guns, grindstone, war sacks, and what reading-matter we had and could get.

Before leaving, I went to the fort and made the rounds of the garrison, with a sack, and begged and received nearly all the sack would hold of newspapers and magazines.   The soldiers' and officers' wives seemed glad to get rid of them, and we were only too glad to get them.

We left the Sweet Water with enough provisions to last

us three months. We had 250 pounds of St. Louis shot-tower lead in bars done up in 25-pound sacks; 4000 primers, three 25-pound cans of Dupont powder, and one 6-pound can. This description would be the basis for all hunting outfits complete, which would vary in the size of the crew, larger or smaller, and the length of time they expected to be away from supplies.

We left the Sweet Water a few days after New Year's Day, 1875, starting up Graham creek; when at its head, we veered a little southwest until we crossed the north fork of Red river. Here we took and kept as near a due south course as we could get our wagons over. We traveled five days continuously, now and then killing and skinning a few straggling buffaloes that were handy on our route. These hides we put in the freight wagon and every night we spread them on the ground.

The sixth day we lay over in camp, to rest the stock; and the next day we pulled up onto the Pease river divide, and got a view of the rear of the great countless mass of buffaloes.

That night we camped on a tributary of Pease river, where there were five other hunting outfits, which had come from Sweet Water ahead of us, but had kept a few miles east of our route. These outfits can be named in this order, and like our own followed these animals to the last: "Carr & Causey," "Joe Freed's," "John Godey's," "Uncle Joe Horde," "Hiram Bickerdyke." "Hi," as we always afterward called him, was a son of Mother Bicker-dyke, the famous army nurse, during the Civil War, and who was looked upon by the soldiers she campaigned with as a ministering angel.

That evening there was a general discussion in regard to the main subject in hunters' minds. Colorado had passed

stringent laws that were practically prohibitory against
buffalo-killing; the Legislature of Kansas did the same; the
Indian Territory was patrolled by United States marshals.
And all the venturesome hunters from eastern Colorado,
western Kansas, the Platte, Solomon and Republican rivers
country came to Texas to follow the chase for buffalo-hides.

The Texas Legislature, while we were here among the
herds, to destroy them, was in session at Austin, with a
bill drawn up for their protection. General Phil. Sheridan was then in command of the military department of
the Southwest, with headquarters at San Antonio. When
he heard of the nature of the Texas bill for the protection
of the buffaloes, he went to Austin, and, appearing before
the joint assembly of the House and Senate, so the story
goes, told them that they were making a sentimental mistake by legislating in the interest of the buffalo. He told
them that instead of stopping the hunters they ought to
give them a hearty, unanimous vote of thanks, and appro-
priate a sufficient sum of money to strike and present to
each one a medal of bronze, with a dead buffalo on one
side and a discouraged Indian on the other.

He said: "These men have done in the last two years
and will do more in the next year, to settle the vexed Indian question, than the entire regular army has done in the
last thirty years. They are destroying the Indians' commissary; and it is a well-known fact that an army losing
its base of supplies is placed at a great disadvantage.
Send them powder and lead, if you will; but, for the sake
of a lasting peace, let them kill, skin, and sell until the
buffaloes are exterminated. Then your prairies can be
covered with speckled cattle, and the festive cowboy, who
follows the hunter as a second forerunner of an advanced
civilization."

His words had the desired effect, and for the next three years the American bison traveled through a hail of lead.

The next morning our outfit pulled out south, and that day we caught up with and passed through many straggling bands of these solemn-looking but doomed animals. And thus we traveled by easy stages four days more.

Arriving on the breaks of the Salt fork of the Brazos river, we realized that we were in the midst of that vast sea of animals that caused us gladness and sorrow, joy, trouble and anxiety, but independence, for the succeeding three years. We drove down from the divide, and, finding a fresh spring of water, went into camp at this place. We decided to scout the country around for a suitable place for a permanent camp.

About four miles to the west and south we found an ideal hunters' camp: plenty of fresh water, good grass, and wood in abundance. Here we made headquarters until April. This was a broken decomposed "mica" or "isinglass" (gypsum) region, along the breaks of the streams. We were twenty-five miles west of the one-hundredth meridian, in plain view of the Kiowa peak to our east and the Double Mountain to our south. We were in a veritable hunters' paradise. There were buffalo, antelope, deer, and as one of the party remarked, "turkey until further orders."

I had killed wild turkeys in southwest Missouri, also in southeastern Kansas, and had always looked upon them as a wary game bird. But here, turkey, turkey! Manifesting at all times and places a total indifference to our presence. At first we killed some of them, but after cooking and attempting to eat them we gave it up. Their meat was bitter and sickening, from eating china-berries (the fruit of *Sapindus marginatus*, or soapberry trees).

So we passed and repassed them; and they did the same, and paid no attention whatever to us.

Just below our camp there was a large turkey-roost, where they gathered in at night by thousands. They came in droves from all points of the compass.

Deer were simply too easy to find; for they were ever present. The same with antelope, bear, panther, mountain lion or cougar, raccoon, polecat, swift coyotes and wolves—they were all here.

And at times I asked myself: "What would you do, John R. Cook, if you had been a child of this wonderfully prolific game region, your ancestors, back through countless ages, according to traditional history, having roamed these vast solitudes as free as the air they breathed? What would you do if some outside interloper should come in and start a ruthless slaughter upon the very soil you had grown from childhood upon, and that you believed you alone had all the rights by occupancy that could possibly be given one? Yes, what would you do?"

But there are two sides to the question. It is simply a case of the survival of the fittest. Too late to stop and moralize now. And sentiment must have no part in our thoughts from this time on. We must have these 3361 hides that this region is to and did furnish us inside of three months, within a radius of eight miles from this main camp. So at it we went. And Hart, whom we will hereafter call Charlie, started out, and in two hours had killed sixty-three bison.

CHAPTER VI.

Two hundred and three Killed at One Time.—How We Skinned Buf-
falo.—I Saw a Panther.—Cyrus Saw a Bear.—I Killed an Eagle.—
A Great, Moving Mass of Buffalo.—I Kill a Cougar.—Hickey, the
Hide-buyer.—Cyrus Meets a Bear.—The Wounded Panther.—
The Weird Night Watch.—Left Alone.—On Meat Straight, Four-
teen Days.

Dockum and I for the first few days worked together.
We two skinned thirty-three of this killing. Hadley and
Cyrus worked together for a short time. It was now a
busy time. Some days thirty and forty-odd hides, then
a good day with eighty-five, and one day in February,
one hundred and seventy-one; then again the same
month, 203; and these 203 were killed on less than ten
acres of ground.

My experience with the Woods had helped me. In
starting I had learned to keep my knives in good order
and how to handle and manipulate them. But it was
here I learned to simplify, lighten, and speed the work.

We fastened a forked stick to the center of the hind
axle-tree of a wagon, letting the end drag on the ground
on an incline to say 20 degrees; fastened a chain or rope
to the same axle, then we would drive up quartering to
the carcass and hook the loose end of the chain over a
front leg. After skinning the upper side down, then start
the team up and pull the dead animal up a little, and stop.
(The stick prevented the wagon from backing up.) Then
we would skin the belly down mid-sides;. start the team
again, and pull the carcass over, having rolled the first
side of the hide close to the backbone. Then we would
skin down to the backbone, and the hide was separated

(116)

from the carcass. We would then throw the hide in the wagon, and proceed as before until all the hides were skinned from the dead carcasses.

Many times we had in one killing more hides than the two ponies could pull to camp, in which case we spread the hide, flesh side down, by the carcass, in order to get them when there was a slack time in the work.

After the first ten days I went alone with the team, except on the occasion of a big day's killing. Each night Charley got out his memorandum book and I got mine, and we put down the number of hides I had skinned that day. Isolated as we were, we kept track of the days of the week and the month of the year. This was Dockum's work. He was very methodical in everything he did.

He and Frank, the boy, attended to the reloading of the shells, pegged out the hides, and from three to five days after they were pegged out they turned them flesh side down, and every other day turned them back, until they were dried; after which they were stacked one on top of the other until the pile was eight feet high. Then they cut strings from a green hide and tied an end in a peg-hole at each corner of the bottom hide, ran it through the holes of the top one, then drew them down as tight as they could and tie.

The pile was then ready for market. This work, together with cooking and general camp-work, kept them both very busy at times. We classified our hides as we piled them. All bulls to themselves, the cows the same way; the robe hides to themselves, and the younger animals into what was called the kip pile.

Charlie as a rule did the most of his killing from 8 A. M. until noon, but made some good killings in the evening, in which the carcasses would lie all night before being skinned. These would bloat up and the hide would be tight and stiff, which made the work more tedious. We had to be more careful, too; for it was the pride of the skinner to bring in hides free from knife-gashes.

We had good hunting at this camp until the last of February, when all at once the buffaloes were not to be seen.

"Oh, well," said Charley, "we need a little rest and diversion anyhow;" for we made hay while the sun shone.

I thought so, too, for we then had stacked up and drying 2003 hides, 902 of them I had skinned, and was so accredited. This was an average of 22 buffaloes a day for 41 days. At 25 cents per hide I had earned $225.50.

One evening on coming into camp with my day's work in the wagon, I noticed a broken, jagged table-rock disconnected from the mesa, or table-land, to the north of it, and a nearly level space of ground, sixty yards wide, from the rock to the main plateau. All the land for a mile east, west and south, was what would be called second-bottom land. I had gone five miles that day and skinned nineteen buffaloes that had been killed the evening before; and I had lost considerable time in finding the killing, having been misdirected to the place, as I claimed, and "not paying strict enough attention to directions," as Charlie claimed. In a joking way he said: "You've been lost before, have you not?"

It was early twilight as I was passing the table-rock, and about one mile and a half from camp, when I noticed a large panther making leaps toward the rock, coming from the mesa; and I reported this in camp on my arrival there. Cyrus said that he saw a bear that morning, and it was coming out of a gypsum cave near the river. So we thought, now we will hunt for panther first, and bear next.

The second day after the buffaloes disappeared, Charlie, Cyrus and myself went to the rock—all on foot. We climbed up on top of it, and noted that it covered an acre or more of ground, perfectly bare, and was crossed and recrossed by crevices that mostly ran down to the bottom. Some of these were too wide to jump across; some we could step over. On the eastern side we noticed a gradual break from summit to base, and a pretty well beaten pathway in it. There were the skeletons of several deer and buffaloes, calves and yearlings, scattered all around the base of this rocky, caverned and creviced little wonder spot. We peered in and through every nook and crevice, as we thought, but did not find a panther.

Charlie suggested that we leave and go on up the mesa proper, which we did, and after coming up on the summit of it we sat down on a large stone. The west side of this plateau was very precipitous, and irregular and very rugged and was some fifty feet higher than the bottom or plain below. We were seated close to this western edge, when all at once Charlie said, "Look yonder!" at the same time raising the big fifty to his face. At that I caught sight of a large panther, and said, "Don't shoot yet, Charlie; it doesn't see us; let's watch it a little;" for it was coming nearer all the time, along the foot of the escarpment. We all three had our guns at a "ready." It was moving slowly, and stepping methodically, with a soft, velvety step, looking out on the plain to the westward. When it got to within about seventy-five yards of us, Charlie could stand it no longer, and pulled trigger, at which it leaped high in air, and as it struck the ground Cy and I both shot. When we got down to it we found we had all three struck it. We soon had its hide off, and when we got back on the bluff we saw, about a mile to the

west of us, twelve buffalo bulls, in single file, slowly marching toward our camp.

Charlie said: "Now, John, there's your chance. Try
your hand on them now. You've got the wind in your
favor; take a dog-trot toward camp and you can get to
that big ravine just west of camp ahead of them."

I worked my way down off the table-land; and upon
getting down to the plain I took a good sweeping trot,
carrying my "44" in my right hand most of the time,
but changing to the left hand occasionally, for a short
time.

Sure enough, I got to the ravine before they did. I
dropped down to a sitting position, set up my rest-sticks,
placed the muzzle end of the gun in the crotch, and was
ready. By the lay of the ground, and the direction of
the wind, they had not been able to scent or see me; and
when they came in sight they were at the head of the defile that I was upon the slope of.

They were now 200 yards from me, moving along in
an ordinary walk. They would pass to the west of me
about sixty-odd yards. I waited until they got pretty
well opposite to me, and made a good lung shot on the
leader. He crowned up his back, and made a lunge forward and stopped stock-still. The others at crack of
the gun jumped sidewise from me, and started off up the
slope of the ravine. I was reloaded in a jiffy and pulled
down at the one in front, and gave him a quartering shot
that ranged forward into its vital organs.

The others whirled again and started back up the draw.
This gave me a good shot at the one in front, and when I
hit him he turned around and started down the draw in
the direction they were headed at first.

I shot at another and heard the bullet strike; I must

have hit one of his horns, for he whirled around twice and I then saw him run down and hook the first one I had shot, that was down and struggling.

I reloaded, and taking a careful aim at the farthest one from me, which was now about 300 yards, I pulled down on him and fired. In the mean time, the one that had hooked the dying one bolted down the ravine, and I shot at him until he went around a bend a quarter of a mile below.

There were now only three of the twelve in sight, one quite dead, the second one I shot, down and kicking; the third one had come nearly opposite the first one and had lain down, and was weaving his great mop of a head to right and left. I thought he was dying. I rose up and started to go to the head of the draw. Just then he got up on his feet, bowed his back and raised his tail nearly straight up. I shot him twice more, in quick succession. Down he went, never to rise. Then I went to the head of the draw and some two hundred yards west there was one in plain sight, standing with his head from me, and no others in sight. I knew then in all reason I had wounded him.

Sitting down and placing my gun in the rest-sticks, I drew a fine bead on him, holding the muzzle of the gun just at the top of the rump. When I fired it seemed to me that the whole hind part of his body rose clear off the ground. He made a few lumbering, awkward jumps forward, turned sidewise, crouched down on his hunkers, and just as I was getting ready to shoot again he fell over on his left side, kicked up his feet violently for a few seconds and gave up to fate.

I had killed four out of the twelve. By counting my shells I found I had shot thirteen times. I took the tongues from the four and went to camp, boiled tongue being a luxury. Dockum, Hadley and Frank were in camp when I got there. They had heard the shooting, and seemed surprised when they learned that it was I doing it and that I had killed· four out of twelve with only thirteen shots.

When Charlie and Cyrus came in, shortly after I had reached camp, we had the four tongues cooking in a kettle; and when the former heard that I had killed the four buffaloes, he said:

"Cook, I believe if you had had your gun when you were lost on the South Canadian you would have made your living."

I took my hide team and drove out and skinned the four buffaloes I had killed, thus earning one dollar on that holiday.

The next morning Charlie got on his hunting-horse and rode south across the Brazos. He said on leaving us that he would ride until he found good hunting again. Cyrus and I struck out for the place he had seen the bear. After reaching the place, we explored the region pretty thoroughly; found plenty of fresh signs, but we did not see one the entire day. We were both afoot, and roamed at will as thought or fancy pleased us.

Wending our way toward camp, we came to some rough breaks near the Brazos, and saw a large eagle alight on a jutting crag. It had a jack rabbit in its talons, and commenced eating it. It was fully two hundred yards from us, and if it saw us at all it ignored our presence.

"Cyrus," I said, "I would like to have that eagle."

"He is yours if you can get him," he replied.

I then said, "If you will stay where you are and give me a few moments' time I believe I'll get it."

He said, "All right."

I took three or four steps backward, and, bringing a thorn-bush between the eagle and myself, I started across a little valley and came up under the bluff where the eagle was standing on the crag. I scaled the gpysum butte and got up near the summit and peeped over, and there he was, not more than fifty yards from me. I drew a fine bead, and fired. He plunged over the crag and rolled to the bottom—*dead*.

I picked him up and went on into camp. I had heard that eagle-oil was the best kind of gun-oil. He was large, very fat, and had fine plumage. We saved all the oil for our guns, and I bundled the feathers together and kept them until the next summer, when I traded them to a young Cheyenne would-be warrior for a pinto pony that the Quohada Comanches afterward stole from me in the spring of 1877.

When Cyrus and I got to camp we found Charlie, our hunter, there. He brought us good word for more hunting. It was understood that we were to move camp the next morning, cross the Brazos, and go to near the summit of the divide, between it and Croton creek, where he had found a spring of nearly fresh water, with several pools below it. Speaking of Croton creek, it surely was properly named. For a sudden, immediate and effective laxative, it was a whole apothecary shop.

This camp was nearly four miles from the first camp, and here we had fair hunting until the latter part of March. Then one morning on going to our lookout, not a buffalo could be seen. We were all satisfied, for we wanted a rest and change.

At this camp we got 906 hides, and I had skinned 407 of them, thereby earning $101.75.

We had run short of primers a few days previous to this lull in the hunt, and hearing big guns every day in different directions from us, Hadley was delegated to hunt up a camp, in the hope of getting enough primers to tide us over until Hadley could make a trip to Fort Griffin, where there was a supply store. The first camp he found was the Carr and Causey outfit, which had killed 3700 buffaloes. They were out of flour, and were getting low on all kinds of ammunition except primers; but were looking for a man whom they had sent to Griffin to return in a short time.

"Yes, they would divide primers if we would divide flour."

So the exchange was made, they getting fifty pounds of flour, and we getting one thousand primers.

From this camp Dockum and I went with Hadley to our first camp and helped him to load 200 hides. He went to Fort Griffin, and did not get back for seven weeks. Our flour and coffee gave out, and we were three days without bread, when fortunately we heard of John Goff's camp to the southeast of us, and that he had nearly one thousand pounds of flour and would divide with us.

I took my hunting team and went to his camp, which I confess I found by accident more than by design. I had not gone five miles until I saw the great mass of moving creatures, on their annual northern swing. Looking to the east and south as far as the eye could reach, it seemed to me that I saw nothing but a solid mass of bison; and I had to either turn back or go through them. The wind was from the north, and they were heading it and were moving in a quick-step gait. I was supposed to be at this time ten miles from Goff's.

I had heard of stampedes where they ran over everything in their way, and I thought "now should I get out into that big field of animals and they *did* make a run, there would be annihilation." Then I thought "to go back to camp with word that I was turned back by the main herd would be construed as weakness."

Looking to the southwest and west, I saw a moving sea of that one countless host. I decided that I was just as safe going ahead as turning back. So, taking the landmark in view that I was to go to, I started on, and was soon among them. Of course there were intervals of bare ground; but they were small in comparison to the ground actually covered by the buffaloes. As I drove on, they would veer to my right in front and to my left in rear; the others following on behind them, would hardly seem to vary their course.

I had gone perhaps five miles in this way, when all fear from them seemingly disappeared; and, looking that day at that most wonderful sight, I thought it would take the standing army of the United States years to exterminate them. In fact, it was the opinion of conservative hunters as late as the New Year of 1877 that the present army of hunters were not killing the original herds, but only the natural increase.

When I had arrived at the landmark that I started for, I was only two miles from Goff's camp. I was directed to turn a northeast course, and by going half a mile farther I would come to the head of a ravine that his camp was on. I had not gone more than half the distance when, boom! boom! came the sound of death-dealing shots, off the northwest. And not more than half a mile from me it was boom! boom! boom! in such quick succession that it sounded more like a skirmish than a hunt. It was then that the buffaloes filed to the right and commenced running, jamming, and crowding one another, and were crossing the route ahead of me, going eastward pretty rapidly.

I turned east and traveled more than a mile with a compact mass of fleeing, wild, frantic, ferocious-looking beasts. On each side of me and soon ahead of me I heard the same deep-toned notes of the big fifty. Then it was that I saw a large mass of the herd east of me wheel to the right and make a run to the south. Those that were north of my route of travel passed on northward to the Salt Fork of the Brazos breaks.; and the prairie was clear in front of me.

On looking ahead I saw a horseman approaching, and meeting him he proved to one of the Quinn Brothers. He informed me that his camp was still four miles east, and that I would find John Goff's camp about three miles northwest. So I turned northwest and started for the camp, and had not gone far until all the buffaloes in sight were again moving northward. When I had traveled as far as I thought I ought to have gone, I came up to a steep gully, thirty feet wide and fully forty feet deep, with steep-cut banks on both sides. I stopped and craned my neck in every direction, but saw no sign of a camp. Thinking I had gone far enough, I turned to the south to head the gully. I was along close to the bank when I saw down in the gully and ahead of me a cougar, feeding on the carcass of a buffalo. I got out of the wagon; unhitched the team; tied it to the wagon; took my 44, and stooping low, stole up to nearly opposite the cougar, in plain sight of it, not more than sixty yards from where it was feeding. The tawny, dirty-yellow-looking brute appeared to be totally oblivious of my presence. I stretched out on my belly, and, placing a large buffalo-chip in front of me, let the muzzle end of the gun rest on it, and then watched him for a minute or more.   He would get hold of the flesh and try to gnaw and pull until he got a mouthful; then would raise his head and gulp down what flesh he had torn loose, and dive in again.   After he had done this way twice and was busy getting another mouthful, I shot him, pulling for the butt of the left ear.   He never knew what hurt him. I went down, to where it and the buffalo lay, and, taking my ripping-knife out of the scabbard, I scalped the cougar, taking both ears and the frontal hide down to the lower end of the upper jaw, including the lips.   Then I also amputated one of the forelegs at the knee, and hurried back to the wagon.

As I was hitching up, John Goff himself rode up and asked me how in the world I happened to be here.   At first sight I formed an unfavorable impression of him.   He had long hair and was the dirtiest, greasiest and smokiest looking mortal I had ever seen, as he sat there on a fleet-looking horse, holding in his hands a 44 Sharp's rather carelessly.

I replied that I was hunting John Goff's camp, and had been drifted out of my way by the buffaloes, and had seen a cougar down in the gully and killed it, and was going on to find a crossing of the gully and continue my hunt for the camp.

"What do you want to see Goff about?" he asked.

I told him I wanted to get some flour of him; had heard that he had quite a lot on hand.

"All right; I'm John Goff; turn round and follow me," which I did, and found his camp two miles from where I supposed it was, and in a different direction.

After we reached his camp he treated me like a nobleman. Said when he first saw me he "felt a little suspicious, on account of one of the hunters north of him having some hides stolen a few days before; and he did not know but I might be the same party." He added that he was "not particularly given to suspicion; but having only heard of the theft the evening before, and seeing me on his hunting-grounds the next day, led him to be somewhat suspicious." He said the northern hunters were just north of him, and the Quinn boys east of him; but that he thought the parties that had stolen the hides were meat-hunters from the edge of the settlement on the Clear fork of the Brazos.

I told him that I belonged to one of the northern outfits, and stated the facts of our case just as they existed, whereupon, he let me have 300 pounds of flour, stating to me that the buffaloes would soon pass north, and he would break up his camp as soon as the bulk of the herd had passed.

From him I learned that a man named Hickey was at Fort Griffin as agent for Loganstein & Company, of Leavenworth, Kansas, with instructions to buy all the buffalo-hides offered for sale; to pay for them on the range and haul them to Fort Worth, Texas, with freight teams. He also gave me the price-list that Hickey was paying. I stayed all night at Goff's, and at daylight the next morning Goff piloted me out a near way to the open plain, where I called his attention to a landmark near our camp. We parted with the usual parting salutation, "so-long," a phrase common on the frontier for "good-by."

At 2 P. M. I was in our own camp, and not a soul there to greet me. Upon looking around I soon satisfied myself that all were busy skinning buffaloes. Charlie's hunting-horse was close hobbled near camp, his saddle lying by the tepee that we slept in, and a big pile of empty shells were lying by the ammunition-box.

I unhitched and turned out my team; built a fire, and pitched into bread-making. We had been living on sour-dough bread for the last month, and the boys had now gone five days without any bread. So I got of Goff a five-pound can of baking-powder; and I had an agreeable surprise and a bountiful supply of baking-powder biscuits for the boys when they came into camp, which was just as the sun went down.

It did seem to me that if I had been gone a year there could not have been a more joyful meeting. They all agreed that the old saying that "bread is the staff of life" was true, and that I was indeed fortunate both in going and coming through that apparently endless mass of buf-faloes; for as I came back through them there seemed to be but little difference in the solidity of the herd from the day before; and within gunshot of camp as I drove in there were hundreds of them moving northward. Charlie had killed 197 the afternoon before, and took his knives and went early the next morning with the boys about one and one-half miles to help skin those buffaloes. Cyrus, Frank and Dockum had skinned forty-six the same evening they were killed.

All night long these ill-fated creatures passed our camp in silent tread, save the rattling of their dewclaws. We were all up early the next morning; and after breakfast Charlie went up over the slope toward Croton creek. Soon the work of death began; and by the time I had hitched up and driven on to the divide he had killed thirty-eight, mostly bulls.

I saw when I drove up on the ridge that the great mass of the buffaloes had passed by. But looking as far south as my point of view extended, I could see scattering bands of from five to twenty straggling along bringing up the rear.

After killing the thirty-eight, Charlie came to meet me, and said:

"John, it will soon be mighty poor hunting around here. The bulk of the buffaloes have passed; and I have been thinking, from what you told me last night about that man Hickey and his prices, that I would better sell this hunt to him, and let him receive them in camp. Now will you take my hunting-horse to-morrow, go to Fort Griffin, and make a deal with him for me? I'll pay you five dollars a day for what time you are gone; and I believe that is more than you'll make skinning buffaloes from this on."

I said: "All right, Charlie; I'll go."

He passed on up the divide, and I down to the thirty-eight carcasses, and went to work. There were twenty old stub-horned bulls in this killing; two of this lot were smooth, sharp-horned six-year-olds; the remainder were spikes, excepting three cows. The spikes were two- and three-year-olds, which skinned nearly as easily as cows.

I began work about 8 o'clock, and did not get them all skinned till sundown. I did not hear the hunters' guns during the day and wondered why; and I kept looking for Cyrus to come and skin a portion of the thirty-eight. It was dark when I got to camp, bringing half of the hides; and it was all the ponies could pull to the top of the divide.

On arriving at camp I found all there but Cyrus Reed. Charlie had killed eighteen head near where he had made the big killing two days before; and Cyrus had gone to skin them about 11 A. M. It was thought he had ample time to get to camp before I did.

I unhitched and ate my supper, and no Cyrus. We were all a little concerned about him, and were talking of going out to look after him, when we heard the sound of a gun not far from camp. Charlie picked up his gun and fired it off in the air. Then we heard Cyrus answer as he gave the Comanche yell, which I will attempt to describe later on.

He had finished his work and started for camp along what is called a hogback—a narrow ridge between two deep ravines—when he met a bear strolling down the ridge as he was driving up, and his ponies getting scent of it, they whirled suddenly, and team, wagon and hides went plunging, tumbling and rolling off the hogback.

In the scramble, both ponies got loose from the wagon, thanks to an old, half-rotten and toggled-up set of harness. The horses bolted back down the cañon; the bear in the meantime shambling off down the other side; and Cyrus had only time enough, after the near line broke, to grab his gun and hop out of the wagon before it upset.

He had followed the ponies to where the gully came out on the flat, and seeing they had turned north toward the river, he followed them until dusk; then, not coming in sight of them, he took a course for camp, and was not certain where he was until we had answered his shot. He said he never had had such a reckless abandon of the common civilities of life as those two cayuses manifested on this occasion.

The next morning Charlie started on his hunting-horse for the runaways; and Cyrus and I took my team to bring in the wreck. With a hatchet, rawhide, and a few nails, we patched up the tongue and reach of the wagon; got it back upon the hogback by driving to the mouth of the gully. The hides had all rolled out when the wagon first upset, near the summit of the ridge, but we soon had all in as good order as before; and when we drove into camp we found Charlie with the runaway ponies.

I then said to him that "I could ride to Quinn's camp yet that day; I would go by Goff's and get from him or his camp man a landmark to go by, and thought I would have no trouble in making it; that Goff had told me there was an old military trail from Quinn's to Griffin."

Well, I started, with my 44 in front of me, a bootleg for a holster, fastened to the pommel of my saddle. I was at Goff's by 3 P. M., and saw only three small bands of bison on the way. How unlike the three days previous! It seemed to me like Sunday!

I then thought: What fertile soil! And what profitable and beautiful homes this region would make if only moisture were assured! How seemingly ruthless this slaughter of the thousands of tons of meat, one of the most wholesome and nutritious diets, as a rule, in the world! Who ever heard of an epidemic or any contagious disease among the American bison? How many of those of whom Christ said, "These ye shall always have with ye," whose wan features and lusterless eyes would brighten and sparkle at the opportunity of feasting upon the choice selections of this choice meat? Yes, even to crack the marrow-bones and eat with his scant allowance of bread, this choicest and richest of butterine from everybody's herd, with neither brand nor earmark made and recorded.

Then a slight feeling of remorse would come over me for the part I was taking in this greatest of all "hunts to the death." Then I would justify myself with the recollection of what General Sheridan had said; and I pictured to myself a white school-house on that knoll yonder where a mild maid was teaching future generals and statesmen the necessity of becoming familiar with the three R's. Back there on that plateau I could see the court-house of a thriving county seat. On ahead is a good site for a church of any Christian denomination. Down there where those two ravines come together would be a good

place for a country store and postoffice. Some of these
days we will hear the whistle and shriek of a locomotive
as she comes through the gap near the Double Mountain
fork of the Brazos. And not long until we can hear in this
great southwest the lowing of the kine, the bleating sheep,
and the morning crow of the barnyard Chanticleer, instead of the blood-curdling war-whoop of the Kiowas
and the hideous yell of the merciless Comanches.

I reached Goff's camp, and found him there. After half
an hour's talk with him, he directed me how to find Quinn's.

He said: "Now, you travel this course," pointing southeast. About six miles will take you to the McKinzie trail.
It is very plain. You could not cross it in daylight without observing it. When you get to it, take the eastern
trend of it; go on about five miles; on coming up on a
ridge you'll see Quinn's camp straight ahead of you about
two miles, just on the right-hand side of the trail." The
way was so plain and the lay of the land so even that I
was at Quinn's just at sundown.

Here I found Mr. Hickey, the hide-buyer, whom I had
expected to find in Fort Griffin. There were twelve
thousand hides piled here, two thousand of them that the
two Quinn Brothers had killed and traded for. The
rest belonged to different outfits, who had made the entire winter's hunt within a radius of twenty-five miles of
here. Hickey met the owners of these hides that day.
and purchased them.

After talking with three of the hunters who were camped
there for the night, and getting from them some pointers
on Hickey's ideas of classification and his general methods
of dealing, I approached him the next morning, by saying,
"Mr. Hickey, I understand you are from Leavenworth,
Kansas."

He said: "Yes; do you know anything about the place?"
I told him, "Not since the Rebellion."

This brought all those present into nearly an hour's conversation about the past and down to the present. All agreed that there was a hopeful and bright future for our country.

Hickey asked me where my hide camp was and how many hides I had. I told him I was working for Charles Hart; that we were the so-called northern hunters; that we had about 3000 prime hides; that we were assured by Rath & Wright, of Dodge City, that they would come after our hides and give us top prices, no matter how far south we hunted.

He was a quick, impulsive, genial Irishman, who did not want Rath & Wright to get a hide south of the Red river. He asked me if I would pilot him to our camp. I told him I would; and that there were several other camps within gun-hearing of ours.

In a few moments we were saddled up and off. I found him to be a good conversationalist, well informed, and in possession of knowledge upon the latest current events. He said all of Loganstein & Co.'s hides went to Europe; that the English army accouterments of a leather kind were being replaced with buffalo leather, on account of its being more pliant and having more elasticity than cowhide; that buffalo leather was not fit for harness, shoes, or belting; but for leather buffers it could not be excelled. As we were passing a place where lay eighty-odd carcasses, he halted, and for the space of five or more minutes, rapidly reeled off in that rich clarion Irish brogue, as my recollection serves me now, something like this:

"Well: the howly smoke! Did I iver see such wanton distruction? No regard whativer to economy! What

beautiful combs and other ornaments thim horns would
make for the ladies! The money, mon alive, in the glue!
What a harvest for an upholsterer in that hair on their
heads! Ivery pound of that mate could and should be
utilized at a fine commercial advantage. The very bones
have a good money value for compost and sugar-refining.
More than one thousand dollars going to waste before our
eyes." "Mon alive," he said, turning to me, "this will
amount to multiplied millions between the Arkansas and
Rio Grande rivers. It is all right and all wrong; right to
kill and get the hides; wrong to waste the carcass!"

But all was not wasted. When the army of hunters
had annihilated those massive, sturdy creatures, the hair
and bone scavengers followed them up with four- and
six-horse, mule, or ox teams. They gathered up and
hauled to the nearest railroad station every vestige of
buffalo hair and bones that could be found.

I saw in 1874, the year before the great buffalo slaughter
began in earnest, a rick of buffalo bones, on the Santa
Fe railroad right-of-way, and twenty miles ahead of the
track from Granada, Colorado, piled twelve feet high,
nearly that wide at the base, and one-half mile long.
Seven, eight, nine, and ten dollars per ton was realized
from them alone.

So, friend Hickey, after all it was not *all* waste. It was
claimed that during the year 1876 one hundred and fifty-
five thousand hides went down the Missouri river on steam-
boats from Montana; that one hundred and seventy
thousand went East over the Santa Fe, and that two
hundred thousand were shipped from Fort Worth, Texas.

Now I do not vouch for the accuracy of these figures;
but I believe the shipping bills from all these points for

that year would be but little short of that number, and might exceed it.

I do know from personal observation that for every hide they got to a market one and a half hides were destroyed on the range from various causes. Some of the inexperienced hunters failed to poison their buffalo-hides in summer and they were rendered unmarketable by the hide-bugs, which soon made them worthless.

All hunters agree that a large percentage of all buffaloes were badly wounded, and walked from the field of slaughter to some isolated ravine, or brush thicket, and died a lingering death. And when found, if they were, the hide was unsalable. Go to Laguna Sabinas, Laguna Plata, Double Lakes, Mustang Lake, on the Staked Plains, and note the tens of thousands of buffaloes that were mired down and perished in a miry, muddy loblolly, to say nothing of the many thousands quicksanded in the Canadian, North and South Red rivers, the Pease, and the many tributaries of the Brazos river.

And the reason so many perished in this way was because for the last few years of their existence, there were multiplied numbers of big and little outfits camped at the most available fresh-water places, ready to bombard them wherever and whenever they came in sight. They were kept on the go; and when they would find a place that was free from a fusillade of lead from the big long-range guns, they would rush and crowd in pell-mell, crowding, jamming, and trampling down both the weak and the strong, to quench a burning thirst. Many of them were rendered insane from their intolerable, unbearable thirst.

Mr. Hickey arrived at our camp late in the afternoon, and found everybody present. Not a buffalo had been seen that day.

The next morning Charley and Hickey went to the first camp. Mr. Hickey made some little examination of the hides, and they returned. A satisfactory deal had been made between them. He gave Charlie a check for two thousand dollars, and agreed to pay the balance as soon as the hides reached Fort Griffin. It was agreed that each was to bear equally the expense of keeping a man to watch the hides until Hickey could get a freight train to come and get them.

Charlie said he would move the present camp about three miles southeast, below the mouth of Croton creek, and at the head of the south breaks of the Brazos, where the buffaloes had not trampled and destroyed the range for our horses, and he had found a splendid spring of water there, and close by it was a high peak, that overlooked the surrounding country. "And," he added, "that will be our camp until the hides are moved from the range. All the hunting I care for now is just to make expenses until then. Then I will pull north and make a summer hunt in the Canadian country."

I now felt that I'd better ask for the job of watching the two old hide camps. So I said: "You, gentlemen, make me an offer, by the day, to look after those hides until the freight teams come."

Charlie said: "I was just going to offer you the job. Reed said he would like the job himself. We will fix some way between this and morning. Mr. Hickey is going to stay all night, and that will give us plenty of time to arrange matters."

From that on, Reed was not the same Cyrus. He noted to Dockum that Charlie had made it a point to show favors to me, giving me, whenever he could, the skinning of the buffaloes closest to camp, and generally the best ground to drive over, and that I had never skinned but one killing of buffaloes that lay overnight; which all had a grain of truth in it. Dockum assured him that there was no intentional affront given or meant. The fact was there *was* a comradeship that existed between us, on account of our both being Union ex-soldiers, that Cyrus was a stranger to. When Dockum informed me of Cyrus's feelings, I went to him and told him that I was sorry he had misconstrued Charlie's actions; admitted to him that I had, by the lay of the ground and advantage of teams, been able to bring in a few more hides than he. One of his ponies would balk at the most unseasonable times, and frequently delay and fret him. But Cyrus never was the same as of yore.

The next morning, Hickey and Charlie employed me to look after the hide camps. We moved that day to the place before mentioned; I took Hickey out of the breaks and pointed out to him a landmark. We separated, and I came back to camp. The next day I made a pad and rigged me up a pair of rope stirrups, rode one of the ponies I had used in the team, and made a trip to both of the old camps. It was stipulated that I was to be at each once every day.

On my return to camp the third day, Frank, being alone in camp, informed me that he "seed a animal" go in a gulch close by and he took old "Once-in-a-while." This was the name of an old army needle-gun whose firing-pin was so worn that one would have to snap it three or four times before it would explode the primer. Some shells it would not fire at all, and again others would go at first trial. Hence, we named that gun "Once-in-a-while."

"Yes," he said, "I went there, and it was in under the overjut in the head of the gulch, and I bent down and could see it, and it snarled at me. I snapped three or four times, and the thing lashed its tail and had red eyes."

I said: "Why, Frank, you ought not to have gone there with that gun. That is either a panther or a cougar; you might have been killed or badly hurt."

He said: "I did get skeart, and ran back to camp."

From what he told me, and his description of the place, I thought I would not tackle it myself. It might have kittens in the cave, or washout proper, and unless it was given an unerring shot there might be a bad mix-up.

I said: "You make me some coffee; I'll watch from the lookout; and when you get everything ready, come up and watch while I come down and eat." He came up in about twenty minutes; I handed him my gun and went to camp, which was one hundred paces off.

While I was eating, Charlie and a stranger rode into camp. I briefly stated the situation, when the stranger unbuttoned his shirt-collar and said:

"This is what I got from a painter in Arkansaw."

And a horrible-looking wound it had been. Commencing at the collar-bone, and running to the lower end of his ribs, were unmistakable marks of all the claws of one foot of the animal he had battled with.

This man was the much-known Jack Greathouse. I had just finished my meal when Frank fired and at the same time called out, "There it goes!"

And sure enough: out on the plain open ground it was making the most wonderful leaps I have ever before or since seen a wild animal make. It was heading uphill, between where Frank was and ourselves. Charlie and Greathouse both drew their guns on it, but withheld their fire until it had passed by far enough so there was no possible danger of a glancing bullet striking Frank. They both fired at about the same time.

The animal turned and circled around the lookout Frank

was on, and he broke down the hill on a run for camp. I met him, and having my cartridge-belt still on me, I took the gun from him, threw in a cartridge and hurried on to the western slope of the lookout just in time to see it was one of the largest of panthers, as I thought, that ever was. Its entrails were dragging on the ground as it went over the bank and into the same cover it had broken from before. I could not get a bead on it.

Charlie, Greathouse and I were soon at the place where it took to cover; but, peer over the escarpment as we would, from either side, or by going down along the edge of the bank, we could not get a glimpse of it. We could hear it sigh, and whine, and every once in a while it would make a noise like a long-drawn-out yawn. We decided that the best way to do was to place a night-watch at the entrance to the place where the panther was.

Dockum and Cyrus had now come to camp; and evening coming on, we divided into parties by twos, and kept a constant watch. Charlie and I took first watch. We all carried and dragged up dry brush and wood, from just below where a cross-break came down.

As darkness approached, we took a pile of brush, wound some green thongs around it securely, set this afire and dropped it down over the escarpment. Then we tossed sticks and brush down upon this from time to time. The flames leaped up, making fantastic and weird-looking all the objects around. Shaggy-haired and rough-dressed hunters passed backward and forward.

A beautiful calm starlight night! The almost constant whining and yowling of the wounded panther; now and again the distant howl of the gray wolf; the yelping ventriloquism of the snapping coyote, a few seemingly trying to make one believe there were thousands of them; the occasional swish of the night-hawk; and the flapping around and overhead of the numerous bats we had disturbed and started from dark recesses in cracks or crevices, their favorite hiding-places,—all this was as entertaining as going to a theater or some other place of amusement.

And to us it was a diversion from the constant rush and hard work of the preceding six weeks or more, with just enough excitement to make it exhilarating.

Our watch ended long before anyone thought of sleep. We had brought up from camp the most of our bedding and spread it down by twos close to the escarpment. Dockum and Greathouse took the second watch, leaving the last watch for Cyrus and Frank.

I had just got to sleep, and it was just at the close of the second watch, when I was awakened by a never-to-be-forgotten ear-piercing scream, sounding like a woman in distress. We were all on our feet instantly, when, flop, flounder and cry; and finally, the panther had worked itself out to the edge of the opening. Lying flat on its right side and in a wheezy, gasping, guttural noise, as if it were trying to talk, it "gave up the ghost." We all then gathered up our blankets and went to camp and to sleep.

The next morning Frank went down to the gulch and tied a rope around the dead panther, and we pulled it up hand over hand to the cut bank. We skinned the panther "shot-pouch fashion," as the term is mostly applied, and stuffed the hide as tight as we could tamp it with buffalo hair. We placed it on its all-fours, and what time we kept it we had some fun.

This man Greathouse, who was afterward universally known as "Arkansaw Jack," told me that at his camp he had a good saddle-horse which he would sell me, and would loan me his partner's saddle until I could get one. I made arrangements for him to bring the horse over, and if it suited me I would buy it. He said it was only about six miles to his camp; and he would bring the horse over the next day, which he did, and I bought it.

Cyrus seemed to want to get away; and Charlie sold to him the team and wagon I had used.

Just then, Dockum took a notion that he wanted to go home to his family in Kansas.

So it was arranged that they would all go to Fort Griffin, where Charlie could get his check cashed and settle up in full with all of them. They were to start in three more days. Charlie and I settled up before they left, and I had to my credit, including the two days I was credited with when I went to find Hickey, the hide-buyer, $345.75.

Charlie found a few straggling bands of buffalo, and killed quite a number from them.

The morning they all pulled out for Griffin I was left alone, in charge of 3363 hides, less the 200 Hadley had started with, in three different camps.

It was now the early part of April.

As Charlie bade me "good-by," he being the last one to leave the camp, he said he would be back in six days. I had just three quarts of flour (for we had loaned "Arkansaw Jack" a portion of the flour we got from Goff) and about one-half pound of coffee. Out of the twelve pounds of coffee we got from Goff we had used all but what was left with me.

I saddled up and made the rounds of the other camps and was back by midday. After frying some choice meat and making a cup of coffee, I ate my dinner and went upon the lookout.

While there I determined at the first opportunity to be

the owner of a pair of good field-glasses. Looking to the southwest, some five or six miles miles away, I saw what I took to be a team traveling in an easterly direction. I looked so long and so intently that my eyes watered, and for a little time everything blurred. I made up my mind to find out for sure what it was. I brought "Keno," my horse, in, and saddled up. Before starting I cut a china-wood pole, about twelve feet long, sharpened. one end, tied an old red shirt on the other end, went up on the lookout, and, like a discoverer, planted my standard. There were two other round-tops, one about three miles west, and the other about two miles northeast of this one. They all had a similarity, and I wished to be sure to not get misled, in case I might be at times in some place where I could not distinguish one from another of the three. Taking a good look again south and west, I was satisfied now it was a team I saw. So I decided to travel south toward the McKinzie trail. Coming down and mounting "Keno," off we started in a little fox-trot. After going about five miles I came to a well-beaten trail, turned west on it, and soon met the team in a depression of the land. The driver was none other than Hi. Bickerdyke. He told me it was about ten miles back to his camp; that he and the two men with him had 1700 hides, all in one camp; that the farthest carcass from camp was not over one and one-half miles; that his camp was on a tributary of the Salt Fork, coming in from the south side. He had heard of our success through "Arkansaw Jack," who was at his camp a few days before. Said he was "crazy for a chew of tobacco." I had about one-third of a plug of Lorillard with me, and plenty in camp. I cut enough from the piece to do me and gave him the rest; whereupon he said, "My troubles have come to an end."

We talked for some minutes, and down the trail he went, going after supplies, and I back to camp. My standard could plainly be seen for three or four miles in any direction, at that time of the year, for the atmosphere was not hazy.

How different this first night alone in this camp from the ones I spent alone a few months before! I now had blankets, a good gun, and a horse to ride.

I was awakened the next morning by the gobbling of turkeys, and for the next three weeks there was an incessant gobble! gobble! gobble! The fifth day, as I was going from the second to the first camp, I came to and crossed a travois trail going in a southwest course. This trail was made sometime between the time I had passed here coming back the day before and the time I discovered it.

Indians? Yes, sure enough! I looked all around me, but moved on until I came in sight of the old first camp, and saw that it looked all right. I turned back and rode to the travois trail, followed it about three miles, and decided that there might be two or three families in the outfit. I had learned enough about wild Indians to know that they did not drag lodge-poles when on plunder raids. That when you saw a travois trail they were moving and had their women, children, and dogs along. Was it a visiting party going to see the Staked Plains Apaches? If so, they had a pass from the commanding officer at Fort Sill. If not, then they had secretly stolen away from the agency at Fort Sill. I felt I must know more about it; but how was I to find out?

While I was pondering, I happened to think of the red shirt and how I had advertised myself. I followed the trail about a quarter of a mile farther, where it turned down a long narrow draw, then turned "Keno" to the left and rode to my own camp. After dismounting I threw the bridle-rein on the ground, went up on the lookout, pushed the flag-pole over, and scanned the country over, but saw no unusual sign.

I had some cold meat left over from breakfast, and four biscuits. I put the biscuits in my coat pockets, took the meat in one hand and the gun in the other, and went up on the lookout again and sat down and ate my lunch, surveying the surrounding country as I ate. After a short time I went down and carried my powder, lead, and all the shells and reloading tools out of camp, and cached* them about one hundred and fifty yards away; then I got on "Keno" and rode nearly due west about two miles. Coming to some excellent buffalo-grass, I dismounted and let "Keno" graze for nearly half an hour. When I remounted I said, "Now, Keno, for Arkansaw Jack's camp, if we can find it." I thought from what he had told us that a little more north and west, about four miles, would strike it.

Keno and I struck out. We had gone about one mile and a half when we struck the travois trail again, heading southwest. About a mile farther on I came to a place where eighteen buffaloes had been skinned, close to a slight ravine. On the west of the carcasses, by looking closely, I found the tracks of the wagon that had hauled the hides to camp. I followed it up. It took me down the ravine; but in another mile I was at his camp.

There were four men in camp and all were sitting under an awning, which they had made of poles covered with buffalo-hides. They were playing draw poker, using cartridges to ante with. Each was trying to win the others'

---

* CACHE (French; pronounced *cash*).   A hole in the ground used as a hiding-place for provisions or other articles.

interest in the piles of buffalo-hides they had stacked up around camp. This I learned afterward.

'At sight of me, and before I had yet dismounted, through courtesy to a visitor, the game abruptly closed. Arkansaw Jack recognized me instantly; and remembering my name sang out, "Hello, Cook! glad to see you; light and unsaddle."

As I dismounted they all came forward, and Arkansaw introduced me to the other three men. After which I said, "Gentlemen, there is a fresh travois trail; the Indians are going southwest, and they passed about two miles from here."

Jack said, "Get the horses, boys, quick!"

The horses were soon saddled up and one of the boys, Charles Emory, who was known only as "Squirrel-eye" on the range, said, "Now, look here, boys, let's have an understanding; what are we going to do?"

I said: "By all means let's understand one another."

"Yes," said George Cornett, "we don't want to bulge in on a band of peaceable Tonkaways and play the devil before we know it."

Squirrel-eye said: "Tonks don't travois; they are Kiowas or Comanches."

"Well," said Jack, "we ought to find out something about them; so here goes."

We all started for the trail with no better understanding of what we were each one to do than before we began our talk.

After we reached the trail, Cornett took out of their case a large pair of binoculars and said: "Boys, let's ride up on that hill to our right and take a squint over the country." When we arrived at the top of the hill we could see the breaks of the Double Mountain fork of the Brazos. Cornett adjusted his glasses and looked for some time to the south-west, and observing no sign of them we all proceeded along the travois trail. After following it a distance, Cornett said: "I believe they are runaways, and that they passed through here in the night-time. There are no hunters south of here and only one camp west of us. They have a guide. Some renegade from them that lives with the Apaches has sneaked into Fort Sill and he has piloted them through here in the night, in order to keep them from being seen. The next thing we will hear of is soldiers after them."

This fellow was raised on the northern frontier of Texas, near Henrietta; and by that was authorized to speak. We accepted his version of the affair, and went back to Arkansaw's camp, where I stayed all night.

The next morning I rode east to the Indian trail and followed back to where my trail between the two first hide camps crossed it. I had not followed this trail far until I came in sight of a horse ahead of me. I was then in a sag between two higher points of land on each side of me. I rode "Keno" upon top of the one to my right, being the side my own camp was on, but several miles away. Then riding and looking along I came up close to the animal near the edge of a small plain. It was a steel-gray mare, nearly as large as the ordinary American horse, branded O Z on the left shoulder. She was perfectly gentle and as sound as a dollar. And now, I thought, if this doesn't prove to be some hunter's animal, it's mine. I dismounted and by holding out my hat and talking to her, she let me walk up to her, put the end of "Keno's" bridle-rein over her neck, and, holding it with one hand, I loosened my lariat from the saddle with the other, tied the rope around her neck, mounted "Keno," and rode on, the mare leading up nicely and traveling by the side of "Keno."

After going on to the upper hide-pile and seeing that every thing was all right, I pulled back for headquarters camp, arriving there in mid-afternoon. The sixth day had come and gone, and no Charlie. And where was Hadley? He too should have been back long ago.

After I had been on meat straight for five days I broke for Goff's camp, early the next morning, only to find it abandoned, the hides all gone, too. I had agreed to be at all of our hide camps once each day, and not having time to go to Quinn's and return in time to make my rounds, and hoping for Charlie's return, I pulled back and made my regular trip without bread. Two days later I went to Arkansaw Jack's, and found Cornett there alone, on meat straight. I stayed all night with him, and made my pilgrimage to the camps the next day. And to sum it all up— I was on meat straight for fourteen days.

To make a long story short, Charlie was twenty-one days getting back to camp. But he had had a glorious spree. He got his check cashed at the post sutler's; paid all the boys up, and deposited all that was coming to me with the sutler, taking his receipt for it. He had flour, coffee, sugar, and lots of different kinds of delicacies, and a brand-new saddle for me.

He said: "I never intended to get drunk; but what could a fellow do? There were about thirty outfits camped on the Clear fork of the Brazos, under big pecan trees; and we all had a time. Oh, you'll hear about it; and I might just as well tell you. I got drunk one day and went to sleep under a big pecan tree, close to the edge of the river-bank, and some of the fellers set that stuffed panther in front of me. They had put glass marbles in the eye-holes, and when I waked up it took me by surprise, and I jumped back and fell over the bank into ten feet of water. And if they hadn't been there to fish me out I guess I'd have drowned my fool self."

All the time he was talking he was making bread, and flying around, hurrying everything along, demeaning himself and bemoaning his *fate,* as he called it. Said he did not want to get drunk; for he knew what his sufferings with remorse were when sobering up. "Now," said he, "please be as easy on me as you can. I know I have disappointed you; and I'm sorry for it."

Poor fellow! when I told him that I was one among many other unfortunates who could deeply sympathize with him, he broke down and cried like a child.

Charlie said he could not hear a thing of Hadley. And when we did hear from him, it was to learn that he had gotten off the Fort Griffin trail and had gone a long way south to the Phantom Hill country. And as he was a man that never was in a hurry and loved to talk as long as anyone would listen to him, it was no wonder he had taken seven weeks to go to Fort Griffin and back, about seventy-five miles. And when he did come he drove into camp with a four-mule team and new thimble-skein wagon, having traded his oxen and freight wagon for the rig he brought in.

He was by no means profuse in excuses for his long absence. All he said was that he missed his way, and had a chance to trade for the mule outfit and had to wait nearly three weeks for one of the mule teams to come from Fort Worth. After hearing this and how he bragged on his mules, it exasperated me so that I told him he was one man that I would not go to a dog-fight with, let alone trucking up with him on the frontier. He made no reply whatever.

Charlie called upon him for a statement for the hides he

left camp with, and for an invoice for the stuff he brought back. All he could tell was that he got $325 for the hides; that the stuff he brought back cost $150; that he had given $100 of the balance that he got for the hides for boot between teams, and that he intended to make everything come out all right when he got through freighting the hides.

It did not take Charlie and Hadley long to settle up; and Mr. Hadley pulled out. He and Cyrus meeting in Griffin went into partnership in hunting. Charlie, by Hickey's request, had staked a trail from Quinn's to our camp. Every two miles or so he had driven a stake, on the highest places he passed over, with a thin box-lid nailed to it, and the words written on the lid: "To Hart's Camp."

CHAPTER VII.

The freighters were instructed to look for these stakes after leaving Quinn's. Five days after Charlie's arrival, the freight teams arrived in camp. Each wagon had on a big rack, built like hay-racks. The hides were piled in this rack with a lap and boomed down tight like a load of hay. I have seen 200 bull-hides piled on one wagon. A dry bull-hide, as a rule, would weigh about fifty pounds. So the reader may have some idea of a train of six yokes of oxen to the team, lead and trail wagon to each team, the lead wagon hauling nearly 200 hides, and the trail hauling from 100 to 150. In bad places the trail was uncoupled while the lead wagon was drawn to good going. Then the driver would go back and bring up his trail wagon, couple on, and proceed.

It was quite a sight to see an outfit of twenty-five teams, as was frequently the case, weaving its way through the heart of the range. After loading at the camps, I piloted the freighters to our first camp, and my services were rendered to Hart and Hickey. By this time Quinn's was getting to be quite a headquarters for the hunters; so Charlie and I pulled for their place.

When we got there there were not less than twenty outfits, large and small, there. Some were going to the Canadian, up in the Panhandle, others were going west up the McKenzie trail to the Whitefish country and vicinity. Not one there knew or ever heard of the O Z brand. While here, Hart changed his mind about the Canadian hunt, and decided he would go to the Whitefish country. He believed from what he had heard that we were near the line of the second division of the great herds. He argued that the buffaloes were in three grand divisions: those from British America coming south in the summer, as far as the Platte river, and returning north in the fall; those in central western Texas going north to the Platte in summer, and returning south in the fall; and all from the Staked Plains region down to the Rio Grande were located, and they traveled east, west, north and south a certain distance, heading the wind. Part of all of which was fact.

But in six months more I knew more about the buffaloes than I did then. For all buffaloes had their nostrils for their protection. They were keen of scent, and would run quicker from scent than sight or sound.

I remember that in the Wolf creek country north of the Canadian, in July of this same year, the country was full of buffaloes; and there were some of them far north yet of the Arkansas river. The wind, what there was at a certain time, came from the southwest for seven consecutive days, and every buffalo was either traveling or headed that way; and on the eighth day the wind changed to the east about midnight, and blew pretty strong all the next day. And all day long the buffaloes moved eastward. That night there was heavy thunder and sharp lightning in the south; and just before daylight the wind whipped to the south and rain began to fall. As soon as it was light we noticed the buffaloes were headed south, and moving *en masse*.

Then again: In the following November, while hunting on a little tributary of Red river, when they were on their southward swing, there came up a "norther," a common term used in the southwest for a sudden cold spell, with the wind generally coming from the north. For three days they were headed north and northwest. So I, and all hunters of any observation, would be justifiable in saying that when unmolested, as a rule their heads were toward the wind.

Another characteristic about them was the family tie. I have heard old hunters who grew up on the borderland of the last great range declare that, "Where little, isolated and disconnected bands were seen, on either side or rear of the great mass, they were all related, generally having some old cow for a leader."

While here at Quinn's I met a namesake who wanted a partner. He was a tall, sinewy, fine-looking plainsman. Had a family in northern Kansas and a homestead that a succession of drouths had driven him from, to get means to support his family; and the chase had captivated him. He had followed the buffaloes from Sawlog creek, north of the Arkansas river, to the Clear Fork of the Brazos. He had a good heavy team; and with a neighbor boy had done well, from a financial standpoint.

He sold 300 hides at Dodge City, Kansas, and did not know that it was against the law to hunt for the hides in his own State until after he had sold them. That was his midsummer hunt.

He then came south, and made an early fall hunt on the Washita, in the Panhandle of Texas, selling the hunt for $400. Then he made a late fall hunt on the North Fork of Red river, getting $300 worth of hides. Both of these last hunts he sold to Rath & Wright at Fort Elliott.

His winter hunt was made on California creek, between Quinn's and Fort Griffin, together with a few days' hunt on the Clear Fork of the Brazos. All of the last two netted him $471. He was paying the boy $25 per month.

He told me that he had sent most of his money to his family from Dodge City, Fort Elliott and Fort Griffin to their home in Kansas; that he wished to make a summer hunt on Commission creek, and the Wolf creek country, northwest of the Antelope hills and north of the Canadian river, in the Panhandle of Texas; and after making the summer hunt he would retire from the range.

"Now," said he, "I would like to have you for a partner, if you can see your interest that way."

I told him about my land claim in Nueces county; and that I was going to Fort Griffin, and from there to Albany, the county seat of Shackleford county, the county Fort Griffin was in, and from there I intended to commence the establishment of my claim to the land through an attorney; and not being in possession of the original warrant for the land, it would take some time to perfect my claim; that I did not want to be on expense during the time it took to establish the validity of my rights; that I was open to a proposition of hunting, but not of skinning buffaloes as a specialty.

He had injured one of his eyes, and wanted me to do the principal killing. He said he was going to Griffin, then to take the western cow trail, that crossed the North Fork of Red river, in a gap of the Wichita mountains; also the South Canadian at the Antelope hills, and on to Commission creek, where the Fort Dodge and Fort Elliott trail struck it. And would I give him an answer in Griffin?

I told him I would.

I told Charlie of my talk with Cook; and that I believed

I would go with him. He replied that he always said that he never wanted to go partner in any kind of business; but if I would not stay with him any other way, he would take me into full partnership.

I said had I known that before it might have been different; but I had gone so far now that I did not think it right to break square off with the other man. "And I have never mentioned a partnership with you, for I knew your mind in relation to it long ago."

His only reply was that he hoped I would have the best of success. We separated at Quinn's and did not meet again until early in 1877.

Before Cook and I left for Griffin I put my new saddle on the O Z mare, the one I had picked up on the Indian trail. I had not tried to ride her before. Gentle as she seemed to be, I would not take any chances in trying her, for fear she might be a chronic bucker; and there being no crowd around to run her in case I was thrown, I thought to let the trial test go until a favorable opportunity, which this seemed to be, and the first real good one to present itself. She paid no attention to saddling, and when I mounted her she moved off nice and gingerly, and proved to be a camp pet.

The next morning after I arrived at Griffin I met Cyrus Reed. He and Hadley were now in partnership, and were outfitted for a hunt to be made near the head of the Double Mountain Fork of the Brazos. Cyrus read a bill of sale to me that he had in his possession for the steel gray O Z mare I had. It purported to be given to him by a man named Thomas Hubbard. The consideration was a Sharp's rifle and $14 in money. It was dated at Fort Griffin, and gave a complete description of the animal: "dark gray, branded O Z on left shoulder."

On the first impulse I felt that this bill of sale was *bogus*. I asked where Hubbard lived.

"Oh," said he, "he—lives—somewhere—in Kansas." I didn't ask him *where*.

"Well," I said, "is there any reliable person here that knows him?" He didn't know.

I said, "Let me have that paper. Who witnessed it? Who executed it? I must know all about it." He would not hand me the bill of sale.

I said: "Just let the O Z horse alone. I'll lay this case before Johnny Lorin, the sheriff of this county. He is right over there at Jackson's store. I am willing to turn the mare over to him, if you will give him the bill of sale, until we can locate this man Hubbard."

No; he wanted his mare.

I went to camp; led the mare up to Jackson's store, and found the sheriff. He was talking with Captain Millet, of the firm of Millet, Ellison & Deweese, a large cattle outfit. As I laid the case before the sheriff, Captain Millet took in the situation. He believed the bill of sale was a fraud. We all three hunted Reed up, and before we were done with him, he did not seem anxious to get the mare.

The captain and the sheriff both advised me to keep the mare in my possession for want of better proof of the validity of the bill of sale.

The facts were, that Hadley had seen the mare when he came to our camp, after his long absence; heard Charlie tell him how I had found her; he had walked all around her; looked in her mouth and looked her well over; and after he left thought that a bill of sale was a cheap way to get her. But it did not pan out, as the miner would say. He had used Cyrus for a stool-pigeon, and had taken the name of Hubbard in vain, if any such person ever existed.

I now told Cook that I would cast my lot with him for a summer hunt to the north. I bought a new wagon and harness; hitched "Keno" and the O Z mare together, which made me a fair team. Cook and I were to bear share and share alike all the expenses, and the same with the profits. We hired a Mexican called Pedro to skin buffaloes at 20 cents per hide, and we would board him whether at work or idle. The boy, Jimmie Dunlap, continued on at $25 per month, work or play. We bought our flour, groceries and ammunition of Jackson. I laid in a good supply, and after counting out the price of my saddle, wagon, harness, and some clothing, I had just $106 left from all sources. I had received $105 as camp watch and had $12 of the $96 I had brought from New Mexico.

So one fine morning we left the Clear Fork and made good daily drives to Commission creek, some 250 miles, without incident. The Mexican rode mostly with me and Jimmie Dunlap with the other Cook, whose given name was Charles, and whom, hereafter, I will call Charlie, as I did the famous hunter, Hart.

We caught up with the rear of the buffaloes at Red river. We camped one night at the gap of the Wichita Mountains, where the great western cattle trail crossed the North Fork of Red river. This is the trail that 200,000 head of Texas cattle passed over during the summer drive of 1881.

From the summit of one of these western spurs of the beautiful Wichita Mountains, I got a view of an inland empire-to-be. I had purchased an elegant pair of long-range field-glasses of Mr. Conrad, the post sutler at Fort Griffin, and with these I had a view that seldom falls to the lot of mankind for variety of scenery. The great herds of buffalo were in sight from any point of view, east, west, north and south, but the heaviest, thick, dark mass was many miles to the west. Skirting the edge of the table-lands, on the northern line of the Llano Estacado, north-west as far as the vision extended, were to be seen the seemingly countless bison. Looking down the Otter creek way were many scattering bands of antelope; and yonder to the southwest were three big gray wolves following a limping buffalo, whose leg perhaps some hunter had broken.

Coming down off of that mountain, east of me were hundreds of wild turkeys; looking back adown the trail we came over and on still south of Red river, on a big flat as large as two Congressional townships, could be seen the herd of 3000 Texas cattle that we had passed by on the Wichita river. Even the covered cook-wagon was plainly to be seen in the rear of the long-strung-out herd, on its way to Ogalalla, Nebraska, and finally destined to the Wind river country in Montana.

Looking northward, coming down the trail is a covered wagon and a buggy and thirty-two cow-ponies being driven by two men, whom I learned afterward were on their way to Cleburne, Texas, after 2500 head of cattle, to stock a range on the Cimarron in the southwestern part of Kansas.

Yes, Sheridan was right. We hunters were making it possible for this to be done. As I turned away from this inspiring scene I felt that I had witnessed the greatest animal show on earth.

Coming on up the trail to the Antelope hills, we crossed the South Canadian and left the trail, taking a northwest course across a trackless broken country to Commission creek, where we heard the sound of the big fifties and the more rifle-like crack of the 44's. Our first night's camp on this creek was with Wrong-wheel Jones. He had been in this camp ten days and had 600 hides, an average of sixty per day, with three men employed.

There were three Joneses on the range at this time. Buffalo Jones, Dirty-face Jones, and Wrong-wheel Jones. The latter got his nickname the summer before. He had broken down the right hind wheel of his wagon. The Carr & Causey outfit came along by his camp the day the accident happened. They told him they had passed an abandoned wagon just like his in some sand-hills on Red Deer, about eight miles back, and that by following their tracks back he could find it easily. So Jones harnessed up his ponies, rode one, and led the other, taking along a pair of stretchers and a chain, went the eight miles, and found the wagon. And the *left* hind wheel was the only one of the four but what was entirely useless.

He came back to camp and said that "The *right* hind wheel had six spokes broken in it, and that he couldn't use it at all. The left-hand hind wheel would have done first-rate; but it was for the wrong side."

His two men, that were in camp at the time, commenced laughing at him.

"What are you fellers laffin' about?"

One of the men, known on the range as "Morning-star Dan," asked him, "Why he did not bring the left wheel along?"

"What do you reckon I want of two left hind wheels?" he replied.

At this the two men fairly roared with laughter. Jones would look at them and then at his broken wheel. Gradually *the truth dawned upon him,* and he joined in the laughter, and said, "Why, yes, I could turn that other wheel around and make it fit, couldn't I?"

So he made another trip and this time he dragged in the *left* hind wheel. From that time on he was known as "Wrong-wheel Jones."

There were five other outfits, besides Wrong-wheel, on this creek. And, as it was close to the military trail, the hunters would go a long way for hides and bring them in from ten or twelve miles distance, when they could not find them nearer their camp. This was in order to get better freight rates to the railroad at Dodge City.

Charlie Cook and I decided to pull west by a little north for Wolf creek, where we arrived the evening of the day we left Wrong-wheel Jones's camp. Here was fine hunting. We had been at this, our first Wolf creek camp, about twenty days before we heard another hunter's gun in close proximity to our camp. In that twenty days we had secured 500 hides, or an average of twenty-five per day.

I started out to do the killing the next morning after we came to this camp. There were buffaloes in sight in nearly every direction. About three-fourths of a mile east of camp and near the route we come over the day before, there was a band of some 300 head. I chose them on account of the wind and the lay of the ground. I got up quite close and had as fine a first shot as I ever had, before or since. They were headed to the wind, and I had come on to them quartering it. There was a large cow standing somewhat in the lead. I pulled down for the regulation spot, and fired. To my astonishment, I shot her in the jaw. The shot startled the herd, and the cow, raising her head as high as she could and holding it high, off to one side, began turning around and around not knowing or caring where she was going—shaking her head violently as if she had Saint Vitus dance, and all the time coming closer to me each circle she made. I whaled away at her again, this time breaking her right front leg above the knee. At this shot she bolted past me, running in a straight line toward our camp with about fifty head following her. I began pumping lead at them as fast as I could load and fire, until they were over 200 yards from me and not an animal fell.

I straightened up, picked up my rest-sticks, and, in looking around saw that the others, that had not followed the cow, were nearly half a mile away, and walking slowly.

On looking to what had been my rear while I was shooting, I saw a small band slowly moving toward me, about one-fourth of a mile distant. I stooped over, and taking long strides I hurried to cross the wind so that they might not scent me, and I gained a point of vantage about 200 yards from where they were grazing along very slowly.

And here now I would make a killing. Taking the best shot that presented itself, I fired and the bullet went away to the right and kicked up a dust two hundred yards beyond them. They all turned back the way they came from, and I jumped up and ran, following them until they stopped, when I dropped flat upon the ground. Some had turned their heads and were looking back in the direction where I lay.

I gradually rose up into a sitting position as soon as they quit looking, and shot at the nearest one, and off the whole band went. I gave them six parting shots and not a bison fell. What kind of a hunter had Charlie Cook for a partner? Great Scott! here was a golden opportunity, and no results. Then I got fidgety and went to camp. Charlie had been watching me through my field-glasses, and when he saw that the broken-legged cow and the band that followed her would cross the creek a little way below camp, he struck down the creek with a belt full of cartridges and seventy-five extra rounds in a haversack. Just as they all got out a little way from the west bank of the creek and had slowed down to a slow walk, he shot the leader through the lungs, and the next one the same way. Noticing the broken-legged cow about the middle of the band, as it was strung out, he gave her a shot. By this time the first one he had shot lay down and others were hooking her, and the result was he got what is called "a stand," and killed thirty-seven of them, and could easily have exterminated the band, but what were left of them were mostly yearlings and two-year-olds which would be called kip hides, the price of which we were warned would not bring to exceed 75 cents apiece that year, and the buyers claimed they did not want them at all.

I could hear the sound of Charlie's gun as I was on my road to camp. But I did not think of him in connection with it, on account of his affected eye; but on arriving at camp I learned it was he.

The boys had both teams hitched up and were about to start in the direction I had been shooting.

I said, "Boys, I did not kill one; I'm no good."

Jimmie said: "Maybe your gun is no good. Did you look at the sights before you left camp? Charlie did the same thing last fall on the Washita. He shot away about thirty cartridges before he knew what was the matter."

I picked up my gun and looked, and sure enough! the front bead had slipped in the slot on the gun-barrel.

There was a large cottonwood tree about 110 yards from my wagon. I had the Mexican tack a box-lid onto the tree, with a charcoal in the center of it. The circle was eight inches in diameter. I took a rest off of the hind wheel of the wagon, fired, and missed the tree.

Just then Charlie came into camp, and finding out what

my troubles were, he said, "I am glad you found it was not your fault."

We moved the bead block into the slot to where it had slipped from, and I fired again, getting inside the circle this time. Then I was pleased, and confidence in myself was again restored.

We all went to the killing, and were as busy as bees until the thirty-seven were skinned and the hides were in camp. That same evening I killed thirteen more buffaloes, and the next day eighteen more.

After the experience related above I never picked up my gun but what I would see to it that the sights were all right. All that summer I did most of the killing, but mostly with Charlie's gun; for my own gun had hoodooed me. If I made a wild shot, I examined the front sight. Any hunter will make wild shots sometimes. But that particular gun got on my nerves. I would keep thinking of and talking about that lost opportunity.

So after a few days Charlie said: "Now, John, when you do the killing, take my gun and leave me yours;" which I did thereafter.

Jimmie had a condemned army gun, the old Long Tom; and Pedro, the Mexican, had a Remington revolver that he called his pistolie.

Frequently, in a killing, the hunter would leave badly wounded buffaloes when in a hurry to go to another band. In such cases the skinners would give them their last shot, if they were not dead when they arrived on the skinning-ground.

After we had been in this camp about twenty days, the hunting was not as profitable as we liked, and hearing other guns down the creek we decided to hunt for another camp. Charlie and I went up the creek a good half-

day's ride and found fair hunting, to which we moved
our camp the next day, and the day following I made the
biggest killing of all my three years' hunting.

It happened about midday. The weather was quite
hot; for it was now the latter part of June. These buffaloes
were undoubtedly very thirsty, for they came down to the
creek from a broad plain to the northwest, and had probably been bombarded from the Beaver creek waters to
the north when they were in a thirsty condition.

There must have been more than a thousand of them.
They came on to the creek in a wild, pell-mell run. After
drinking they came out on a flat about 150 yards from
the creek, on the opposite side from where they entered
it. There they stopped and commenced lying down. By
the time I got up within good gunshot, perhaps half of them
were lying down. At this time they had all shed their
last year's growth of hair. Some that were standing
seemed to be sound asleep. I was not more 'than eighty
steps away when I began shooting. They were a mixed
herd—very old and young bulls, old and younger cows,
then all ages from red spring calves up. I shot a tremendously large bull first. All he did was to "cringe" a
little. Not half of those lying down arose at the report
of the gun. After making three good dead shots those
closest to me moved off a little toward the creek. Getting
in a good shot at the leader, I stopped him and that stopped
the rest.

I now had, what I had so often heard about but had
never actually seen before, *a stand*. Charlie Hart, while
I was with him, had given me some good pointers how to
manage "a stand," if I ever got one. He told me not to
shoot fast enough to heat the gun-barrel to an over-ex-
pansion; to always try to hit the outside ones; to shoot

at any that started to walk off, unless I thought they were mortally wounded. He said that "with an over-expanded gun-barrel the bullet would go wobbling, and would be liable to break a leg; and that would start a bolt."

After I had killed twenty-five that I knew of, the smoke from the gun commenced to hang low, and was slow in disappearing. So I shifted my position and, in doing so, got still closer. And I know that many of the herd saw me move. I had shot perhaps half a dozen times, when, as I was reloading, I heard a keen whistle behind me. Looking around I saw Charlie Cook. He was on his all-fours, creeping up to me. He said: "Go ahead; take it easy; I am coming with more cartridges." He crawled right up to my side with my gun and an extra sack of ammunition for me, and a canteen of water. He asked if the gun was shooting all right. I told him "Yes; but the barrel is pretty warm." He told me to try my own gun a while and let his gun cool a little. We exchanged guns, and I commenced again.

Even while I was shooting buffaloes that had not been shot at all, some would lie down apparently unconcerned about the destruction going on around them. I fired slowly and deliberately. Charlie poured some water from the canteen down the muzzle of his gun; then pulled down the breech-block and let the water run out. He then ran a greased rag in the eyelet of the wiping-stick and swabbed the barrel out, leaving the breech-block open for a while, thus cooling the barrel, in order to have that gun ready for use when my own gun got too warm.

About this time I shot an old cow that at the crack of the gun bolted down the creek. I shot at her three times in rapid succession. The third shot broke her back just forward of the coupling.

I laid the gun down and said, "Charlie, finish the job."

He said "No, take my gun and go ahead, this is the greatest sight I ever beheld."

I took his gun, and without thinking put in a 44 cartridge and fired. Then he put the cartridge-sack in front of me, saying, "You used one of your 44's that time." And as I pulled the breech-block down to put in another cartridge, a bull, about a six-year-old, started walking toward us, with his ferocious-looking head raised high. Before I could divine his intentions I fired, and he fell almost as suddenly as the cow whose back I had broken.

I would shoot five or six times, wipe the gun, and we would comment, in a low tone, on the apparent stupidity of the herd. Some came back and stood by the dead ones. Some would hook them as they lay dead. I kept this work up for as much as an hour and a quarter, when I changed guns again. And at the first shot from my own gun I broke the left hind leg above the knee of a big bull that was standing on the outer edge of the herd, about ninety yards from me. He commenced "cavorting" around, jamming up against others, and the leg flopping as he hopped about.

He finally broke in through the midst of the band and my *stand*. They all began to follow him, and I with the big 50 that I now took from Charlie, commenced a rear attack, Charlie putting cartridges in his belt which I was wearing; and with the belt about half full and several in one pocket, and a half-dozen or so in my left hand, I moved up to a dead buffalo, and got in several good shots; when I moved again, on through the dead ones, to the farthermost one, and fired three more shots and quit. As I walked back through where the carcasses lay the thickest, I could not help but think that I had done wrong to make such a slaughter for the hides alone.

In counting them just as they lay there, their eyes glassy in death, I had killed *eighty-eight;* and several left the ground with more bad than slight wounds.

Jimmie Dunlap and Pedro Laredo had driven up to within less than a quarter of a mile, and had witnessed more than half the slaughter.

I helped all hands at skinning until an hour from sundown; and, being nearly exhausted, lay down on the buffalo-grass, with a fresh-skinned hide rolled up for a pillow, and stretched myself out for a rest.

My nerves had been at a high tension; the heat of the day had been oppressive; then stooping over so much while taking off the hides I got dizzy; all of which contributed to my utter fatigue. The other three men worked on until it got too dark to see well; then we all went to camp, having skinned, all told, fifty-nine of the eighty-eight carcasses. I had killed bulls principally, on account of their hides being more valuable than the others. Sometimes I had to kill cows that were on the outside, and at times they would obstruct a shot at a bull.

The next morning early, Charlie, Jimmie and the Mexican drove out and finished the skinning; while I reloaded shells. Before noon everybody was in camp and the 88 hides pegged out and drying.

We hunted from this camp with varying success until the middle of July, when we moved south on the Canadian and camped on Red Deer, near where the Wood families and I camped the winter before with the soldiers and Kiowas. About a week before we made this move we went back and poisoned the hides at the first camp. Also, those at the second camp on Wolf creek. The day before we left it, Charlie and I had ridden south from Wolf creek to the edge of the Canadian breaks and saw a few scattering bands. But we thought there would be plenty of buffaloes in that region later on.

The day we moved, the Mexican wanted some antelope-hides to make himself a suit of clothes, and started ahead with my gun and belt, he taking the course that we told him we would take to cross the table-land, between the two streams. If my recollection serves me right, from where we were and the direction we would travel it was about ten or twelve miles. When Pedro handed me his "pistolie" I said, "Now, don't get lost; keep in sight of the wagons." He said he would. The antelopes were plentiful, indeed, along the route we were going; and off he went.

A few days before we moved, I had gone up Wolf creek about six miles from camp, this being very near the head of it, and while there I came across an abandoned Arapaho camp. The Indians had left it so suddenly the summer before—that being the summer of the Indian War of 1874, when they received such a severe punishment from the hunters near the Adobe Walls,—that they did not take time to move all their effects, and the camp for half a mile up and down the creek was strewn with tin cups, plates, stew-pans, camp-kettles or *brass kettles*, and several Dutch ovens, besides axes and hoes. I picked up one of these brass kettles and took it to camp.

We had been cooking our dried apples in a black sheet-iron kettle, and the apple-sauce had a dark, grimy look. I had a vivid recollection of a beautiful well-polished brass kettle that my mother used to cook fruit in, and in which she made fine preserves; but my observation went no farther. Now I thought we will cook our dried apples in this and our sauce will retain its natural dried-fruit color.

It so happened that the evening before we moved we cooked a kettle of dried apples and set them to one side with a lid over them. They were not thought of at the morning meal, nor until we were packing up to move camp. On this particular day I hauled the entire mess-kit. There was a five-gallon keg of water in each wagon, and when all was ready we pulled out of camp, Charlie and Jimmie in the lead.

After traveling about four miles I heard the report of a gun off to my left and rear. Upon bringing my field-glasses to a focus in the direction the report came from I saw it was the Mexican. I said, "Charlie, you and Jimmie might go ahead to camp and maybe you'll get a chance to kill a few buffaloes. I'll mosey along slowly, and keep an eye on the Greaser; for he might get lost."

The two started on, and I watched the Mexican and saw that he was skinning an antelope. After he got through he threw the hide over his shoulder and started on south. When he passed a line east and west of me, I drove on, turning a little left from the route Charlie had taken. This I did in order to get closer to the Mexican; also to gain a high point of land ahead of me. I saw him skinning another antelope. All this was taking time; and as it was late when we left camp, it was now near noon, and I was hungry. I went to the hind end of the wagon, opened the messbox, got some bread, took a spoon and dived into the apple-sauce. Eating out of the brass kettle from one side, I ate several large spoonfuls of it with my bread, then poured a quart cup full of water out of the keg, drank about half of it; then dived into the apple-sauce again, and ate until my appetite was perfectly satisfied.

I then got up on the spring seat and looked for the Mexican, but could not see him. Thinking now that he was acting in a sensible-like way, and that he had gone on south, I started ahead, and had not gone far until a strange sickening feeling came over me. The sun was boiling down and the heat radiating in front of me. I was getting dizzy-headed and "squeamish" in my stomach. I could hardly retain a sitting position, but before it was too late I stopped the team, climbed down and crawled under the wagon. Sick? Yes, unto death, as I then thought.

Whether I had gone to sleep or was unconscious I am unable to say. It was late in the afternoon before I came to a realization of anything. The first I knew was: The Mexican was bathing my face with a wet towel. He spoke fairly good English and said to me, "you are sick."

My sight coming to me, I asked him to get me some strong salt water, which I drank. It was an excellent emetic, for I was soon relieved of all that poisoned apple-sauce and sour-dough bread that I had eaten. Presently I could sit up, and the dizziness had passed; but I was, oh, so weak! Pedro told me he had come to me nearly an hour before. He had loosened the horses from the wagon and taken the wagon-sheet and hung it over the side of the wagon the sun was shining against, and had been washing my face, neck, and arms for some time. He said: "Now let me help you into the wagon and I will hitch up and we will go to camp." He helped me to get a reclining position, and started. After he had started, he asked me if I knew which side of us the other wagon-track was on. I told him, "To the right." When he found it he stopped and asked me how I was feeling. I replied, "Very sick. Don't you eat any of that apple-sauce. It has poisoned me." The fact was, I had been verdigris-poisoned from the brass kettle; and for several days I was an invalid without any appetite. And fifteen years elapsed before I could eat apple-sauce again.

It was now the breeding season of the buffaloes, which was July and August. And there was a constant muttering noise, night and day, made by the bellowing, or, more properly speaking, the roo roo-oo of the bulls, which in the individual case could not be heard in ordinary atmospherical conditions above a half-mile, but when uttered by the thousands has been known to be heard for twenty miles.

The mosquitoes punished our horses so severely at nights, and the green-head flies by day, that we decided to move southeast, to the top of the Washita divide. Charlie's left eye was gradually covering with a film, and he wanted to go home and have it operated on; so after we had moved to the divide, we established our camp on the prairie 200 yards from the water of a big spring that Buck Wood and I found the winter before when living in the cabin we had built. We left Jimmie and the Mexican here to do what they could with Charlie's and my gun. Taking the "pistolie" and Long Tom we went to the White Deer camp, and, loading all the hides on the two wagons, took them to Springer's ranch and sold them. We offered Springer our Wolf creek hunt, but he told us he did not have the money to pay for them; but, said he, "George Aikin's outfit will camp here to-night, going to Fort Elliott, with a load of Government supplies; and maybe you can get him to haul them to Dodge City."

It was nearly night, and while we were talking Aikin rode up. I had met him before, during the past winter, at Sweet Water, when I hired to Hart. I told him how we were situated, and he said that if we gave him the same rates as from Elliott and twenty dollars besides he would take all of the Wolf creek hides to Dodge City. He wanted to lay by and rest and graze up his teams at Commission creek, on his way back; and that he would load the train with hides at Sweet Water, less the number of wagons it required for our hides.

So it was settled that way. It was arranged that Charlie would be at Springer's when Aiken came back and pilot him to the hides. Aiken left us, saying he would be back to Springer's in eight days.

Charlie and I went back to our camp by way of the cabin; but it did not look natural. Nettles had grown up by one side of it ten feet high. A wild gourd vine had climbed over the roof and the wood-rats had piled one corner of the inside high up with chips, bark, sticks, turkey feathers, and pieces of bones that we had cracked to remove the marrow from. The big cottonwood grove was in full leaf; and as we drove on in the direction of camp we saw many flocks of young wild turkeys.

We arrived in camp about the middle of the afternoon; although we could have covered the actual distance the nearest way in less than three hours. The boys were out of camp when we got there, but came in late in the evening, having killed and skinned thirteen buffaloes, while we were gone.

When Charlie and Jimmie drove out the next morning to get the hides, there was a young calf standing by one of the carcasses, its mother being one of the victims of yesterday's work. It still had the reddish color that all buffalo calves have in their infancy, not obtaining their regular blackish brown until in the fall of the year, when they are very fat, plump and stocky, and take on a glossy look. I have watched buffaloes many times during my three years' hunt, not with a covetous eye at the time, but to study the characteristics of the animal; and I do not remember ever seeing buffalo calves frisky, gamboling, and "cavorting" around in playful glee like domestic calves. Perhaps their doom had been transmitted to them! Yes, this was the pathetic side of the question. And thousands of these little creatures literally starved to death, their mothers being killed from the time they were a day old on up to the time they could rustle their own living on the range. Charlie killed this calf and salted the hide to take home for a rug. But, personally, I should want no such reminder of the last buffalo-grounds, especially one gotten in that way. Charlie and I settled up in this camp, I taking over the supplies of all kinds we then had on hand. He was to go to Dodge with the Wolf creek hides, make the sale of them, pay the freight bill, pay Jimmie my half of his salary, and send my share of the hunt in money to Fort Elliott, together with half that was due the Mexican for what hides he had skinned.

The day before Aiken was to be at Springer's, we broke camp, and all pulled for that place. When Aiken came along he informed me that there was fine hunting on the Washita, at the mouth of Gageby creek. Bidding Charlie Cook and young Dunlap good-by, the Mexican and I pulled for the mouth of Gageby by way of the Washita ranch, on the trail to Fort Elliott.

Here I met Rankin Moore, the owner of the place. This is the man who saved my life a little over a year after. Here I learned that my friends, the Woods, just a few days before, had sold and quitclaimed their interest near the mouth of Gageby to the Andersons from the Picket Wire country of southeast Colorado, who were preparing to start a horse-and-cattle ranch. The Woods had gone 200 miles southeast and off from the then last and only remaining frontier of the Old Southwest. I was disappointed in not again meeting these Samaritans of the prairies.

Pedro and I pulled down the Washita on the south side of the stream, and crossed the Gageby near where it flows into the former stream. Here we camped among some large scattering cottonwood trees.

We were now near the one-hundredth meridian, and close to danger-ground. We had been in this camp about ten days and had been going from three to eight miles for what hides we got. Some days we got five hides, and from that up to ten, which was the most we got any one day.

The tenth day, toward evening, as we were pegging out the six hides we got that day, a band of Cheyenne Indians rode into our camp, saying "How, John; heap buffalo." At the same time holding out a long official envelope toward me. We were both down on our hands and knees cutting holes, driving pegs, and stretching the hides. The suddenness of their arrival startled us. My gun was about twenty feet from me. As I rose up I started toward it, whereupon the Indian, holding out the envelope, said, "No, no shoot; heap good," and turning the en- lope toward me, said excitedly: "You see 'em! You see 'em!"—pointing to the envelope and saying, "*Big white man, heap chief.*" I picked up the envelope, which was unsealed, and found out that it contained a pass from the commanding officer at Fort Reno, Indian Territory, "For the bearer and his family to visit James Springer, on the Canadian river, northwest of Springer's. And they must follow the Canadian river, both going and coming, and are not to be absent from their agency but twenty days."

They were then ten miles south of the Canadian, on the Washita. After reading the pass and handing it back, I said, "wayno" (bueno), a Spanish word for *good*, known far and near by hunters, trappers, soldiers, cowboys, and all tribes of Indians from the Rio Grande to British America. But it was more commonly expressed by the word "skookum," by the Crows, Blackfeet, and extreme northern tribes. "Skookum" is Chinook for "good." When I said "wayno," he repeated the word after me; then, pointing just a little way upstream, he said: "Me campa!" Away they went with their travois outfit about 200 yards, and camped. There were twenty-two of them, men, women, and children. Three young bucks lingered at our camp, and examined and talked among themselves about everything that attracted their attention. My bundle of eagle-feathers was in sight and caught their eyes. There was a flour-sack wrapped around them; and one of the young fellows picked up the bundle and brought it to where I was now cooking supper. He talked his own language, whatever that was, and made signs that he wanted me to take the sack off. I did so, and he examined them closely; then he bundled them up and said, "You swap?"

I had learned a good deal of the universal Indian sign-language from the Osages, in southeastern Kansas, and had picked up a little more from the Navajoes that were camped a short time near where I was once in New Mexico.

I now commenced to make use of it; and by signs I told him I would trade. When I gave the sign for "yes," he stepped closer to me and in pantomime he asked, "How much?"

I crooked my right thumb and forefinger so as to bring them in a circle, thus making the Indian sign for dollar. Then I held up both hands, palms toward him, all fingers and thumbs spread out, thus counting *ten;* then I quickly

shut both hands and opened them again, then let them
drop to my sides, indicating that $20 was my price.   I think
he had as good an idea of what $20 really meant as he did
of where the "happy hunting-ground" was located.

They went to their own camp, and the next morning
the one I talked with came back, leading a pinto pony.   He
wanted the feathers, and goodness knows how much sugar,
coffee, tobacco, and powder.   I measured out a pint
of green coffee, and one quart of sugar; placed the eagle-
feathers beside them, and sat down upon my ammunition-
box and assumed a far-off look.

I had traded a good deal with the Osages; so I played
Injun with Injun.   I had looked the pony well over, seeing
he was sound and large enough for a pack-horse, but too
light for a saddle-pony for a man of my weight.   Presently
the Indian called my attention to a half-sack of flour which
we were using from.   It was standing by a tree.   I got up,
and, picking up the bread-pan, I turned it bottom-side
up, placing it over the flour-sack and again sat down on
the ammunition-box.   He stood there a little while, then
went up to a powder-can and made signs for powder.   I
got up, picked up the can, and set it in the hind end of the
wagon, went and sat down again on the ammunition-box.
He stood for a moment, then commenced laughing.   I
looked as sober as a judge and as wise as an owl.   He
picked up the feathers, examined them again, and could
stand the nervous tension no longer.   He motioned me
to get a rope.   I told him I wanted the one on the pony.
He wanted some tobacco.   I made a sign across the fingers
of my left hand, showing how much I would give him.   He
nodded that stoical face and head, and the trade was
made.

He wanted me to go to his camp with him, where he

showed me his father's eagle-feather war-bonnet, and gave me to understand that now he would have one of his own. I judged him to be about 22 or 23 years of age. He was about 5 feet 11 inches tall, straight as an arrow, and withal had a rather pleasant countenance, of a serious look. His face was not hideously, but gaudily, painted with red and yellow vermilion. He wore a bear-claw necklace and the tail of a chapparal bird on the top of his head, just back of the scalp-lock. His wrists were encircled with broad, thin, highly polished steel bands. His breech-clout was nicely beaded and porcupine-quilled on front and rear flap. Among his tribe he was evidently a person of some distinction; but to me he was *just an Indian.*

When this band broke camp they struck northwest for Springer's. After they got over the divide the Mexican and I hooked up and loaded all our camp outfit, and what hides we could pull, and struck out for the head of Gageby, on the military trail. Pedro and Pinto with my new saddle lent considerable dignity to my outfit, he riding ahead, or off to one side, as fancy pleased him.

He called himself the scout. We camped near the head of the creek, and the next day went back for the rest of our hides. Here I made headquarters until the first of September, going as far east as we dared on account of the Indian Territory line, our camp being twelve miles west of this line, and about the same distance from Fort Elliott.

Some days we went west, taking our camp along. If we got a few hides by noon or a little after, we returned to camp; if not, we kept on, the Mexican scouting for water, which, when found, we camped by overnight.

Thus we put in the time until the first of September, when we pulled to Fort Elliott and Sweet Water. Here the Mexican fell in company with two of his race, and went with them to New Mexico.

In October I pulled south with two other outfits. We followed down the one-hundredth meridian line, keeping an average of about fifteen miles west on the Texas side to Red river, thence to the South fork of Pease river, where Willis Crawford and I went into camp for the winter.

I furnished everything and gave him a one-third interest in the hunt. We had fair success, and, all in all, as good a time as hunters could enjoy. We had fair hunting the most of the winter; but we did not rush matters as Hart did.

Freed's camp was five miles up the river from ours. Al. Waite and Frank Perry were three miles down the same stream; and north of us three miles, at some springs, was Dirty-face Jones.

Many times during the winter we visited each other's camps and passed many pleasant evenings in the buffalo-hide tepees or dugouts, as the case might be, exchanging experiences of the hunt; commenting upon the events occurring in the outside world when we occasionally heard of them. All this, interspersed with story-telling and song-singing, until the "wee sma' hours."

The turkeys in this region were just the opposite from those about our last winter's camp near the Salt Fork of the Brazos. Here they were tender, juicy and sweet; but not nearly so tame. But it would have been a very poor hunter indeed that in an hour or two's absence from camp could not bring in two or more of the big fat prizes.

This was a beautiful, mild winter, with the exception of two northers, one in November, the other in February, each lasting two or three days. On Christmas Day, and for several days before, the days were quite warm and the nights clear, with bright starlight, and pleasant. The sun usually rose from a perfectly clear sky, and passed down behind the horizon leaving a soft golden halo in its wake. This surely was the *American Hunters' Paradise*. And they were winning the Great Southwest. We hunters often talked about the future of this great, vast uninhabited region, with all its salt, gypsum, alkali and strongly impregnated sulphur waters, scattered over this vast expanse of territory 200 miles in width and 350 miles long, in western Texas alone. There were thousands of beautiful fresh-water springs of cool, pure water, and many babbling brooks where several varieties of fish abounded.

West of the pecan and oak shinnery ("cross-timber") belt, even on to the eastern escarpment of the Llano Estacado, were thousands of beautiful cottonwood groves, many wild plum bushes, and much mesquite.

CHAPTER VIII.

We hunters were optimistic enought to predict a wonderful future for a region of such delightful climate and such fertile soil. In March we sold our hides to Charles Rath, who sent his agent, George West, to follow up the hunters with two large freight trains to bring back the hides they got that winter. But a dozen such trains could not haul the hides that the hunters had in their many camps west from the one-hundredth meridian to the New Mexico line and south to the Brazos river. It was a red-letter killing and the slaughter reached its high-tide mark that winter and spring. The summer of 1876 I hunted with fair success in different parts of the Panhandle of Texas. But that year not many buffaloes went north to the Cimarron. They were giving ground. The terrible slaughter of the past two years had shortened their annual pilgrimage from the Cimarron to the Platte, 500 miles. In October I was back on the breaks of Red river. Army officers informed us that the Indians were restless. They had heard of Sitting Bull's annihilation of Custer's Seventh Cavalry, and it was in their hearts to emulate his and Gall's warriors. George Whitelaw with two men, Hank Campbell with two men, and Crawford and I, agreed to camp together for mutual protection. We found some excellent water-holes about three miles north of Red river, in rough ground.   Here we pitched camp and stayed until the last of November, getting all told 1600 hides from here.

Campbell's outfit and my own went west about six miles and camped at the head of a draw running through a large flat down to Red river.   Whitelaw went back to Fort Elliott.   There were, in this camp, Hank Campbell, Frank Lewis, "Crazy" Burns, Willis Crawford, and myself, the night of the 15th December, when a heavy blinding snow-storm came on.   This snow commenced falling as darkness set in; by daylight it had ceased, and there were seven inches of snow on the ground.

Sometime that night, while we were all wrapped in our warm beds and sound asleep, Old Nigger Horse, with 170 Comanche warriors, together with their families, passed by less than 200 feet feet from us, running away from Fort Sill.   They were being followed by two companies of soldiers that would have overtaken them if Miles, Custer, or Crook had been there.   This is my opinion.

The next morning "Crazy" Burns, as he was called, was the first one up, and while he was building the morning fire the soldiers appeared, and they told us they had abandoned the Indian trail on account of the weather. This act alone caused the loss of many lives of the hunters. These Indians kept on south and went into camp for the rest of the winter.   The place they selected was a pocket-cañon just south of the mouth of Thompson's cañon, and is so located on the old maps.

It was an excellent place for a defensive fight, being located as it was immediately under the escarpment of the Staked Plains.   They stayed here until the last of February.   Literally they were perfectly hidden.   But few hunters were that far south at the time, and none that

NIGGER HORSE (COMANCHE CHIEF) AND HIS HORSE.

far west. The fact developed afterward that the nearest hunter's camp was twelve miles from them. This was Billy Devins's, northeast of them. Five miles northeast of Devins's was the ill-fated Marshall Sewall's camp.

In the latter part of February these Indians began murdering and pillaging in earnest. But a few days before the first hunters were disturbed, they had evidently scouted the country well, for there were single Indians seen in different places far apart at the same time.

A few days after Nigger Horse and his band had passed by our camp, Rankin Moore came along with his outfit and told us he had not seen a buffalo since he had left Fort Elliott. We had not seen one for the last two days. So we agreed to pull south for the Brazos country. We crossed the Red river at the same place the Indians did, and followed their trail for ten miles, when it turned off more to the southwest; but we went on south. Moore had agreed to go to a certain place on the Salt Fork and camp there until Benson's outfit came along, Benson and he both having been at the place the winter before. This place was about ten miles up the river from where Arkansaw Jack's camp was the winter of my first hunt.

The evening we arrived at this place I took my horses down a broad ravine and hobbled them, nearly a quarter of a mile from camp, where there was better grass than at or near camp.

Just as I started with the horses Rankin Moore picked up his gun and said he would go up on the hill east of our camp. This draw that I went down ran eastward.

As I was going down the draw he was going up the hill on the south side of the draw. Just as I had hobbled the last horse, had picked up my gun and had taken perhaps five or six steps, when *zip!* went a bullet, and then the report of a gun which came from the hills south of me.

I had a cartridge in my gun. Raising it, and looking toward where the shot came from, *spat!* and the ground was struck by a bullet in front and to the left of me, the bullet passing between myself and the pinto pony.

Just at that moment *boom!* came the report of a bigger gun from the hills and also a considerable distance to the west of the shots coming toward me. Then came the strong audible voice of Moore, "Look out, Cook! There is an Injun trying to get you!"

When I first saw Moore he was running east toward the place the Indian was shooting at me from. I hurried out of the draw, running south to get under cover of the hills as soon as possible, thinking I was too much exposed in the draw.

As I ascended the hill, I peered cautiously as I went. I heard the report of Moore's gun again, this time not more than 200 yards from me, and nearly south, the direction I was going. I then hurried on up the hill and ran out to where Moore was then standing.

Looking intently southeast just a few rods from us we saw a succession of little knolls and hills with little basins in between them. The first thing Moore asked me was, "Are you hit?"

I answered, "Not a hit."

He said "Goody for you! I believe I got him. You keep to the left and I'll go around to the right."

We had not more than fairly started when Moore, who was great for off-hand shots, fired. I ran up close to him, and, looking off southwest nearly 400 yards, saw our Indian afoot. We both fired rapidly at him, he running like a quarter-horse for some breaks that he was then close to; but he got away.

Our rapid firing of six shots for Moore and five for me had brought every man and gun from camp, all believing it was an "Indian fight." After Moore had explained matters to the boys we all started for the little knolls, and soon found the Indian's horse breathing its last. We left everything just as we found them, viz.: saddle, bridle, lariat, and blanket. Moore had shot the horse in the left jugular vein, also grazed him along the spinal column with another bullet. We brought all our horses to camp, tied them to wagon-wheels, and took turns at night watch.

We now concluded to all stay together till Benson came, which was the third day after this event. We stood guard every night and kept close watch during the daytime; but did no hunting only for camp meat.

The next morning after the affair with the Indian, at breakfast, we were discussing the matter, and I remarked:

·"Well, Moore, I guess if you had not been where you were I would now be in the other hunting-ground."

He replied: "No; not unless he could shoot better, by practicing on you a while."

He said that when the Indian first fired at me he himself had not seen him until then, and he was almost sure the Indian had not seen him until he fired at him; and then his pony jumped, and as he turned to run he went in a staggering gait. Moore was 300 yards from him when he fired, which he did in a hurry before he could get his third shot at me. The Indian was over 250 yards from me when he fired. When Benson arrived he informed us that Charlie Rath himself was on his way down from Dodge City with a small train of supplies—lumber, nails, tools, and some extra men, to build a supply store somewhere east of Double Mountain, near the Double Mountain Fork of the Brazos; and that John Russell's train of fifty wagons,

drawn by six yoke of oxen to the wagon, was following
Rath, loaded with all kinds of hunters' supplies. So we
all decided to pull toward that point. When we got to the
McKinzie trail, looking south around the base of Double
Mountain, we could see that we were close to the *"main
herd"* of buffaloes, as the parlance went those days.

We had now been encamped and moving, and were
hardly making expenses; and this change decided us to
take chances. We held a council, at the close of which we
agreed to waive the former custom of conceding to each
camp a radius of a few miles, where they could hunt unmolested by one another, and to camp as close together as
we could.

We turned west and went up the trail to Stinking creek,
thence south in a rough broken country, and found camps
from a half-mile to a mile and a half apart, where we all
had good water. We were now a little south of west of
Double Mountain; the buffaloes were plentiful, and seemed
to be located and contented.

When we first reached this location Crawford and I were
camped at some water-holes fed by two springs. From
our camp the country sloped south to the Double Mountain Fork of the Brazos, which was some five or six miles
distant, our camp being west of the other outfits.

The evening of the day we came to this camp I killed
seventeen buffaloes about one mile north of camp, on the
eastern slope of a divide. I rode "Keno" on this occasion,
whereas heretofore I had hunted afoot nearly all the time.

As I was coming back from the killing to where I had
left "Keno," I noticed him looking intently to the west,
and on looking in that direction I saw a horseman approaching. Upon coming closer it proved to be Pat Garrett,
afterward better known as the slayer of "Billy the Kid"

in New Mexico, while he, Garrett, was sheriff of Lincoln county, New Mexico.

He accepted our invitation, rode to camp, and stayed all night with us. He was camped about eight miles northwest, near the Salt Fork. He seemed to think we were all doing wrong in taking the chances we were with the Indians. But we hunted away.

The next morning as we were driving out to skin the killing of the previous evening we heard steady, deliberate shooting close to where our carcasses lay; and on driving a little farther we came in sight of the hunter. We stopped and waited until he had quit shooting where he was. The buffaloes were moving off toward the west. He started to follow them, but at sight of us stopped and waited for us to come up.

He asked us if those were ours down there. I said, "Yes."

He said, "I did not know there was a soul within ten miles of here until last evening when I heard the shooting."

"Where is your camp?" I asked.

"Down by those trees," pointing to some cottonwoods about half a mile west.

"How long have you been there?"

"Three weeks."

"Any Indian signs?"

"Haven't seen any Indians; but heard there were some in the country."

I remarked, "You seem to be a new outfit to me."

"Yes; this is Bill Kress and Sol. Rees's outfit; I am Kress."

We told him where we were camped, and explained to him about the council the five outfits had had; who they were, as nearly as we could, and where they were encamped.

His next remark was a prophecy. "I'll tell you what, boys; we will fool around on this range a little too long; then what is left of us will have to get together and lick those Comanches. Reese and I are both of the oldest of hunters. We are from the Solomon river, in Kansas, and have been on the Kansas and Colorado border for many years. We have not hunted for two years until this winter. We went to Philadelphia last summer; attended the Centennial and blowed ourselves in; and we are out now for a stake. But in my opinion those Comanches will yet break out and give us trouble if we are here. April is generally the time up in Kansas to look out for Indians."

Garrett went on to his camp; Kress to his, and we to our work. For several days there was the sound of big guns to be heard in all directions. Finally, on the 20th of February, there came to our camp a runner, telling us that *"trouble had commenced."* Billy Devins's camp had been destroyed by the Indians; his horses taken, and he and his men barely escaped with their lives. Two Englishmen had both their wagons run up between two high stacks of hides and wood and brush thrown upon them; the torch was applied and several large cakes of tallow thrown on the fire to increase the heat. Their ammunition was all taken; their harness had all the best leather cut out of them and carried away, while they were out on foot hunting for buffaloes; that the hunters were concentrating at Rath's store. He had just come from Campbell's camp, and Campbell had told him where to find us; that Campbell himself had started for a camp south that he was sure he could find; while his boys were loading up to pull out for the McKinzie trail, and on to Rath's.

This runner was Louis Keyes. He was one-eighth-

breed Cherokee. He said, "Do you know of any camp
west of you?"

I replied, "Yes; and if you will help Crawford to load
the camp outfit and you two will strike for the trail, I'll
go and notify them. Don't take any hides; just the camp
outfit. Your horse seems to be a work-horse; hitch him
up by the side of the gray mare and I'll ride 'Keno.'"

Thus it was all arranged, and I was off in less time than
it takes to write it. I went to Kress and Reese and told
them what was going on; and while Kress and their helper
were loading their camp outfit, Reese and I were galloping
over the prairie and breaks hunting for Pat Garrett's
camp, which we found, with a card tacked up saying,
"Gone to Rath's store."

We rode back east and a little north to the McKinzie
trail; followed it down to the Stinking creek, where were
my own and eight other outfits. We were now twenty-
three men in number. We counted out in "reliefs," and
put out a guard at once of an entire relief; while when Reese
and I arrived they only had out one lookout or one guard.
Every one had eaten his supper when Reese and I got
there. We had had a hard ride for the time and distance.
Our horses were warm and hungry. We let them graze
until dark, when we all hooked up or saddled up and struck
down the trail. Every water-keg was full. We went
about four miles and turned to the left, traveling a mile
further. We corralled, tying up every animal known to
be a wanderer, and close-hobbled the rest, except four good
saddle-horses which were kept saddled. We used every
precaution that was thought to be necessary during Indian troubles. We built no fire; for sixty war-painted
bucks had been seen by Carr and Causey the morning of
this same day, between the McKinzie trail and the Double

Mountains. We were vigilant during the night. About an hour before daylight everybody was at his post of duty, so as to be ready in case of an attack, or an attempt to get the stock. But we were not molested.

After cooking and eating our breakfast, we hitched up and pulled on to the trail and followed down it several miles, where we came to a stake driven into the ground and several buffalo skulls piled around it. On this stake was a finger-board. Written on it was "RATH'S STORE."

Russell's big train had passed over this route, and had made a well-beaten trail to Rath's. Traveling over this trail, we soon entered a mesquite flat, almost a veritable thicket in places; and for twelve miles we traveled through this chapparal, mesquite, and live-oak mistletoed, dry-land region, to the Double Mountain Fork, before we could get water for our animals. We arrived at Rath's in the evening, and found nearly three hundred men, all on the *qui vive*. Water for cooking purposes was hauled a mile, in barrels; and the stock was all driven in a common herd to and from the creek, twice a day.

I met here several old acquaintances of the two winters and the spring before. Several were there that I had met in the Panhandle hunt. There was talk of organization. Remarks were made to the effect that we would give the buffaloes a rest and the Indians a chase. Rath's agent, West, knew every one of the northern hunters, all those from Kansas and Colorado down to the Red river country; but this last winter many new outfits were on the range from the settlements of Texas east of us, that had not yet been identified with the little army of northern hunters. West had a list of names of all that could be accounted for or their camps located.

Upon our arrival we were eagerly questioned, which questions ran something like the following:

"Do you boys know where Hi. Bickerdyke and the Deacon are?"

"Does anybody here know where Sewall's camp is?"

"Where are Al. Waite and Frank Perry?"

"Has anyone see Smoky Hill Thompson?"

Billy Devins said he knew about where Marshall Sewall was, and considered that he and the two men besides himself were on very dangerous ground, and ought to be looked after first; as all the others were believed to be back in the Pease river country. It was conceded, and so decided, that Devins was right.

And yet that night we organized a party of eighteen men to go to Sewall's camp. I was one of the number to go. We started early. West furnished Billy Devins, who was to be a guide, with a saddle-horse. We took one pack-mule, and we were to follow Devins.

He led out in a southwesterly direction, taking us out of the breaks of the Double Mountain Fork; then we kept as nearly due west as we could on account of the breaks.

We made a good 45-mile ride with hardly a halt. When we reached Billy Devins's destroyed camp, Billy ordered Joe Jackson and myself *on guard*. There were two good lookouts close to this camp; Jackson was sent to the one southeast, and I to the one west of the camp. We were about 200 yards apart.

The boys in camp were busy cooking, for we were all hungry. We had been on guard but a few minutes when Jackson called out: "Here comes a man afoot on our trail."

He came on into camp and dropped down onto the ground—tired, worn out, and hungry; saying, as he did so, "Thank God for this streak of luck!"

When the men had eaten, Joe Freed came out and relieved me, telling me that Marshall Sewall had been killed
two days before, about ten o'clock in the forenoon; that
the man who had come to our camp was Wild Skillet;
that he had struck our trail a mile or so back and knew
we were white men, and he had followed our trail to camp.
He was one of Sewall's men.

This news was important. I forgot my present hunger,
and listened to Freed relate the circumstances connected
with Sewall's death:

"Sewall had left his camp, the day he was killed, and
had found a large herd of buffaloes some two miles west,
and had killed several of them. Wild Skillet and Moccasin
Jim had started to drive out to skin them, when they saw
the Indians circling around Sewall and firing as they ran
around him. All at once they ran in to where he was,
some of them dismounting. That was all they could
tell about Sewall. They turned the team around, and
just as they started back toward the camp the Indians
discovered them and started for them. They thought
there were about fifty of the Indians. They saw they
were being pushed so rapidly that they would be soon
overtaken; then they headed the team for a brushy ravine
or a little cañon, in a rough, broken piece of ground that
came down from a plain and passed north of camp. The
boys drove as fast as they possibly could, running the
team over a steep bank to the edge of the brush. Here
they abandoned the wagon and took to the brush, going
down the little cañon; the Indians coming on and dividing, part taking each side, riding down to the edge of the
breaks and yelling that never-to-be-forgotten Comanche
war-whoop.

"But they did not get the men, and soon went away.

COMANCHE MEDICINE MAN.

The boys stayed in this brush cañon until dark, having followed it down a mile or so from where they first entered 'it. They had heard several shots in quick succession, several miles north of them, along toward evening, and presumed it was the same Indians attacking some other outfit."

At this point in the narrative, Devins called for me to "hurry to camp and eat."

After eating, we all saddled, packed up, and started for Sewall's camp, which Wild Skillet guided us to almost on a bee line. We reached our destination near midnight, and found the camp destroyed; ourselves tired and sleepy, and our horses needing rest and feed. We unsaddled and turned our horses loose, reasoning that we were perfectly safe for the night.

We were up at the first streak of dawn. The horse-guard brought in the horses. We ate our breakfast, and then rode out to where Sewall's body lay. We found it in such a condition that it could not be moved.

We all set to work with butcher-knives, cut and dug, and with our hands scalloped out a hole about two and one-half feet deep. We rolled the body into this grave, and after placing the dirt back we rode to some mesquite not far off, brought and piled it high over, around, and on the grave.

The Comanches had taken two scalp-locks from him; had stretched him straight out; had cut a gash in each temple and one at the navel; and had placed a point of his three-pronged rest-stick in each knife insertion and left the grewsome sight as we found it. There were 21 bloated unskinned buffalo carcasses lying from 60 to 200 yards from the body.

Our party was of the opinion that some of these Indians

had slipped up on Sewall while he was absorbed in his work of killing the buffaloes, and had given him a fatal shot from behind him; that the circle-riding that Wild Skillet spoke about was done after he had received his mortal wound. Sewall had a long-range 45 Creedmoor Sharp's, a nearly new gun, and he was known on the range as a *dead shot*. He was cool, level-headed, and a man of great nerve. We conjectured that they had sneaked up on him, as it was customary among all Indians to do so where the lay of the ground or circumstances permitted. For had Marshall Sewall had any chance at all, there would most undoubtedly have been one or more dead Indians.

Such could, and may have been the case, and their bodies carried away, as was the rule with the Indians, when they could obtain them. The Indians took Sewall's gun and also secured with it nearly seventy-five rounds of ammunition. They got the team the boys abandoned and Sewall's hunting-horse.

From where the wagon was abandoned we trailed the Indians back to where they killed Sewall and on toward the Staked Plains, which were in sight. After following the trail about three miles we halted on a hill. With the field-glasses we could see into the defile in which the Indians were encamped. But we did not know it at that time. We had lightened the pack-mule at Devins's camp, so as to give Wild Skillet a mount. From here we all went back to that place. Wild Skillet told us that Moccasin Jim had gone to the Englishmen's camp to warn them, they not having heard of their misfortune. And that he himself was hunting for Devins's camp, not knowing that it had been destroyed; that when he had found our trail, he was sure it was white men, and had followed it. It was decided at Devins's camp to send me back to Rath's over the route we came out on; to make the report, and get all who would to come and we would clean out the Comanches.

My instructions were to have West send a wagon-load of supplies to the Godey camp, which location was now generally known to the hunters. This camp was ten miles east of Devins's, but quite a distance south of the route we came out on. In addition, I was to inform the men at Rath's that the provisions would be expected to be at Godey's camp the next night. They further instructed me to say that they would stay in the danger region as an observation party, and would try to look up the English-men, and would watch for the Indians until the provisions came.

"Come back with the grub yourself, Cook, and bring as many of the boys along with you as you can," was the parting injunction.

I left them about four o'clock in the evening, taking the back trail. I rode a moderate gait until a little after sundown. I then dismounted, slipped the bridle-bits from Keno's mouth and let him graze. I had a cake of frying-pan bread and some fried hump-meat, which I ate. I then lay down a while, to give Keno time to eat a little longer. In spite of myself, I was soon sound asleep. I had intended to ride on to the Clear Fork trail yet that night.

When I awoke, it was very suddenly, Keno was lying down. The stars were shining brightly; and apparently there was no breeze. The very stillness made me rest-less. I had not unsaddled my horse, and when I lay down I was holding the end of the lariat in my right hand; the horse had not gone to the end of it. I went up to him, and patting him gently on the neck, said: "Well, Keno, let's be going." I was now about twenty-three miles from Rath's, and giving Keno a loose rein, with his long-reaching, flat-footed walk he stuck to the trail and with each step was shortening the distance; while I, never more wakeful, rode along and thought.

At first my mind went back to that lonely apology for a grave. I had met its occupant three different times at widely separated places on the range. He was an educated man, a native of Pennsylvania. He was a man who possessed a useful fund of information. He was not obtrusive, but was courteous and polite; respected others' opinions even where he differed from them. He neither drank nor used tobacco, and profanity never escaped his lips. He was not a professed Christian, but believed in the observance of the Golden Rule. He was a born politician, and would have been an excellent statesman. He was a man of hopeful, optimistic tendencies; and *why* should he have been taken when such men as Hurricane Bill, Dutch Henry, Squaw Johnny, and some others that I had in mind could roam these prairies, disregarding law and morality, with a price placed on some of their heads, as we hunters afterward learned? Then I thought of the rations, blankets, and clothing of all kinds which the Government was issuing to these very Indians at Fort Sill, when they stayed on their reservations; then I thought of the old map of Texas, this lone Star State, where was written across a great colored patch covering this very ground I was now riding over, "*Kiowa and Comanche Hunting Grounds.*"

Why did Texas ever concede that these were their hunting grounds? Did these Indians know that these grounds were conceded to them for hunting purposes?

INDIANS KILLING BUFFALO IN TEXAS.

STORY OF THE SOUTHWEST PLAINS.

If so, then the Comanche had some excuse. Then again I thought of what General Sheridan said, which every old-time army officer with whom I talked sanctioned: "Destroy the buffaloes and make a lasting peace," on this scalp-lock, blood-stained border.

Then I thought of the Boston man with his *sentimental gush* about "*Lo, the poor Indian!*" In my mind I would pilot him out to that lonely spot, and watch him as he gazed on the mutilated remains of one of the noblest specimens of American manhood between the two oceans; I would point out to him those two places, just in front of and above the temples, where the bare skull was showing; the places, too, where the two scalp-locks were taken from him, thus violating an unwritten law among the Indian race to "never take but one scalp from a white man."

Up to this time I had been imbued with the idea that wild Indians had some sense of justice, but none of mercy; but in this case they had neither.

Yes, Mr. Boston man, I would have you see one of the most horrible sights that mortal ever gazed upon, a part of which will not be printed in this book, on account of the blush it would bring to the cheeks of the reader.

Then, I want you to go back to Boston and *take a big think!*

Thus in silence I rode on, and when the Great Dipper, that ever-reliable timepiece of the firmament, revolving around the North Star, warned me that the early morning hour was approaching, I was still wakeful. Keno, walking at will, had carried me some little ways down the Clear Fork trail, when suddenly he filed to the left to a water-hole that I knew nothing of, but which he must have scented. After quenching his thirst, we returned to the trail and pressed on our journey.

Shortly after the sun had risen I was at Rath's, among the hunters. The crowd had augmented considerably during my two days' absence. The camps were numerous and close together. While riding in, I was observed from some distance, and when I dismounted, near the store, I was surrounded by an eager crowd, West being present.

After briefly stating the situation and delivering the instructions the boys had given me, many expressions were uttered, both of regret at Sewall's death and a willingness to help. I was told that arrangements would be made immediately to send provisions to Godey's camp, Godey having tendered a team and himself. West brought Keno a feed of oats and took me to the store, where his cook had breakfast ready. After I had eaten, West pointed to his bed and said: "Now, Cook, go to bed, and we boys will see that everything is in readiness by the time you get a good sleep."

But sleep was out of the question with me. I went outside. Just across the way about a good street's width was a saloon and restaurant, and coming out of it was my old friend Charlie Hart. He was about three sheets in the wind, but he recognized me at once, and gave me a hearty greeting. At the same time taking hold of me, he led me back with him to the saloon. There were about twenty men inside, but only three that I had met before. Hart called the crowd up to drink, after which I said: "Now, boys, how many of you are ready to go out and help hunt the Quohada Comanches?" And to my surprise, chagrin and disgust, only four declared themselves willing to go.

The temporary bar-tender at this time was Limpy Jim Smith, an ex-road-agent from Montana. I had heard a good deal about the man, but had never met him before.

As I started to leave the place, he came from behind the bar, and, taking me by the hand, said: "Wait a moment; I'll go with you, and we will organize." This man Smith had 2000 hides that he had taken since the last of November. He thought they were in a safe place, for they were on the big flat-top still east toward the settlements; "but," said he, "that is neither here nor there. We have just got to fight!"

Tom Lumpkins said: "Well, I have not lost any Indians and I don't propose to hunt any." This remark brought on some sharp words between Smith and Lumpkins, which ended in the death of Lumpkins a month later.

The regular bartender having come to his work of dealing out fishberries and rain-water for whisky, Smith and I went to where a big crowd were discussing the question of the hour. As we approached the crowd, big tall Hank Campbell came forward and shook hands with me, saying, "John, I'm going with you." Godey had now driven up in front of the store. West jumped up into the wagon and called for the crowd to assemble, after which he stated that "the company he represented would furnish any amount of supplies that the hunters wanted, now or hereafter, to use while defending themselves against the Indians and clearing the range of the Comanches." He added: "Here is a wagon and team ready to start for Godey's camp, by request of the eighteen men that found poor Sewall's body. Now, boys, let's have a general expression as to the best means to adopt after starting these supplies."

Smoky Hill Thompson, who was standing pretty well back in the crowd, commenced to talk, when he was interrupted by, "Louder! Come up here; get on the wagon and speak out!" And, suiting actions to words, the venerable old plainsman was picked up bodily by strong men and carried to the wagon. He was an old white-headed veteran of the frontier, one of the last of the Kit Carson type. He had hunted, trapped, and fought Indians from the Rocky Mountains to the Missouri river, and from the international boundary on the north to the Arkansas river on the south. He knew the habits, manners, customs, tricks, strategies and tactics of the Plains Indian as well as the Indian himself did. The vast country he had roamed over was on open book to him. His sobriquet was given to him on account of his last and longest residence in any one place, the Smoky Hill river, where Kansas and Colorado meet. "Boys," he said, in slow, deliberate words, "first start this outfit to Godey's; then organize two separate companies, one to go out and fight the Indians, the other to stay here to protect and defend this place and care for all the extra stock. Some of you hunters have from four to eight head of stock, and those that are not taken on the expedition must be taken out of the country, or well guarded. This place will most likely be the storm-center. Those Indians have seen those acres of hide-piles, and their revenge will be terrible; and this place, in my opinion, will be visited."

Smoky was right, as the sequel will show. His words were accepted by many of the hunters, and none dissented. I called Campbell, Carr, and Bill Kress into the store, where the clerks were getting the supplies ready which I was to take with me.

I said: "Now, Hank, you spoke to-day of going with me, but I believe you will do more good in the long run by staying here and helping in this organization; for you boys all know there has got to be some sifting done. There are men here to-day who will be in Fort Griffin, near the garrison, before to-morrow night. You, Carr, know of two men whom we do not want on the expedition; and there may be many others. But you, boys, go ahead and do the best you can. Joe Freed expects me to be at Godey's camp to-night; I'll tell the boys what you are doing."

"In that case," said Carr, "there is no need of more than four or five of the boys going with you to-day, is there? But we ought to keep in communication."

They agreed that they would proceed at once to effect an organization, and send two men to us as soon as it was completed, with a list of the names of the men who were to compose the field force.

"All right, then, boys; now get me the four or five men as you suggested and we will be off, for the time is passing. Get Squirrel-eye for one, if you can."

Hart lent me his hunting-horse for the occasion; I tied him behind the wagon, saddled and bridled. After the things were all put into the wagon, I spread some blankets over them and lay down. Soon Squirrel-eye, Billy Devins and three others whom I did not know, started, Godey himself driving the team. It was not long until I was asleep. I had come in there, and in less than three hours we were all on the road back. We had ample provisions, and besides this enough ammunition for two weeks, and oats enough to give each animal a moderate-sized feed for several days. We stopped a little after midday. I was sound asleep when Godey shook me, saying, "Hate to wake you, but we're camped for dinner."

After dinner we pulled on, and, seeing we would not make his camp before dark, Godey and I rode ahead. When we came in sight of the camp and a quarter of a mile from it, we saw men moving around the hide-piles.

They had the two Englishmen and Moccasin Jim with them, but had lost all of their horses but three. They got into a fight that day in the forenoon with the Indians, and dismounted to fight them on foot and advanced on the Indian camp. Nigger Horse had sent some of his warriors in a roundabout way, and they had got in the rear of the boys and got all of the horses but three head. One of the men, Spotted Jack, was badly wounded; and three others were slightly wounded. Their "long-range guns had done good work," they said; and when they were forced to retreat they kept the Indians so far away with their long-range guns that the Indians did poor execution with their short-range guns. They could distinguish the difference by the sound of Sewall's gun from the Indians' rim-and-center-fire Winchesters, models of '73, that they were mostly using. The boys were certain they had killed the Indian that was first using the Sewall gun. They were close to the Indians' stronghold, but they were in the rocks, broken fragments and disconnected slides that had fallen from the perpendicular escarpment of the Staked Plains.

The contour, or lay of the ground, was such that they deemed they had gone as close as was consistent with good judgment, against a natural fortress, and they just had to retreat.

Spotted Jack, regardless of the nature of the wound he had received, was able to walk in; and they were all there. But each one was censuring himself for his rashness.

Godey said: "Well, boys, this is no place to be to-night. Let's go back, meet the wagon, and I'll take you into a place where we can hold our own if they should come onto us."

We met the wagon, and went to the place designated. It was now after dark. Six of us immediately went on guard. Most of the rest got supper. They built a fire under a cliff in a little gorge.

When morning came we all pulled for Rath's, leaving nearly all the provisions and grain at Godey's. Squirrel-eye and Freed hurried on ahead, to report. After they had gone nearly half the way they met the two messengers who were to come to us at Godey's. The rest of us reached Rath's that evening. Two days later we left Rath's. There were now forty-five all told, of perhaps the best-armed and equipped outfit of men that ever went against Indians without artillery. I had bought a Creedmoor 45 Sharp's at Fort Elliott the fall before and most of the old hunters were now using that caliber. They were long-range guns, and by continuous practice most hunters had become good judges of distances and had learned to shoot pretty accurately by raising the muzzle of the gun, without raising or lowering the rear graduated sights.

As had been predicted, fully 125 men had left the range going east, northeast, and southeast, into the Henrietta, Phantom Hill, and Fort Griffin country. Eighty-five men had pledged themselves, the day we left Rath's to go to Godey's camp, *that they would go to the front*, and forty-five of us were now actually going. We started with three wagons, all loaded with provisions, horse feed, camp equipage, bedding, medicines, lints, and bandages.

All the other wagons were closely parked near the store. Smoky Hill Thompson was left in command and in charge of all the extra stock not required on the trip. West was his assistant in charge.

They had nearly 100 men at first, but the outfit gradually diminished in numbers until there were but forty-two faithfuls, when we returned on the 22d day of March.

Our party was commanded by Hank Campbell 1st, Jim

Smith 2d, and Joe Freed 3d in command. Thirty of us were to be mounted; fifteen footmen to be escort and wagon guard. There were from 100 to 250 rounds of ammunition to each man, beside bar lead, powder, primers, and reloading outfits. We took the route to the Sewall camp, going by the way of the Godey camp. We made short drives each day, keeping out advance and rear guards, and three scouts in advance of all.

We had with us Hosea, one of General McKinzie's scouts during the 1874 war. He knew the country thoroughly, from where we were to the Pecos river. He was a Mexican who could speak no English, and understand precious little.

The first night's camp demonstrated the fact that some things were overlooked in the organization of this independent little army. A quartermaster to issue grain was needed, and Ben Jackson was appointed to fill that office. The medical supplies ought to be in charge of some particular person, and that department was turned over to a former druggist, Shorty Woodson, the tallest, slimmest man on the range.

Then Campbell wanted an advisory board, five of whom he appointed rather at random, myself being included in the number. There was a roster kept by Powder-face Hudson. From this roster the guards were detailed in rotation. In fact, everything was done that could be done to promote order, discipline and harmony. There were several ex-Confederate soldiers and Union ex-soldiers who had joined issues in a common cause. There were three school-teachers. All the party were native-born Americans with the exception of the two Englishmen, whose camp had been destroyed.

When we had arrived within five miles of the Indian stronghold a reconnoissance was made, and the fact was apparent that the Indians had fled; they had gone up a narrow defile onto the Staked Plains proper.

We now had to send our wagons some distance south along the base of the escarpment, where, through and up a narrow, winding, steep incline, we managed, by doubling teams and pushing by hand, to get them on top.

We were now on the Llano Estacado, or "yarner," as the old Texans call it. We found that the Indians had burned two tepees in their camp. In Indian signification this meant they had had two deaths. The boys who were foolish enough to crowd onto them in their almost impregnable fortress had killed two of their number.

After the Indians had gotten on top of the plains they scattered like quails, some going up, some down the edge of the escarpment. They traveled in small parties over the short, thick, matted, curly mesquite grass, their different routes resembling the palm of the hand with the fingers spread out, they traveling from the wrist to the point or tips of the finger-ends.

We spent an entire day ferreting out these many dim trails to where they converged again far out on the plains. Not a lodge-pole had been dragged travois-fashion to here, but from here a travois trail started northeast toward Fort Sill. There had been a dry camp for night here.

Here the wily old Nigger Horse, reasonably expecting us to follow him, thought he would fool us by making us believe he was fleeing back to his reservation; and for another day, like the political fixers at a convention, he kept us guessing.

The pony signs at this camp indicated that they must have six or seven hundred head. Signs were scattered over more than a square mile; and here at this camp the old chief had played his ruse by starting a travois trail to-

wards Fort Sill, when as a matter of fact he had sent his
women and children on west to the extreme head of Thompson's Cañon, twenty miles east of the Casa Amarilla (Spanish for Yellow House), so called on account of a bold
rugged bluff with natural and excavated caverns dug out
by these Indians thirty years before. On top of this bluff
was a stone half-circle breastwork. This is the place
where, at the time mentioned, the entire Sioux nation came
down from their northern homes and fought the Cheyenne,
Arapahoe, Kiowa and Comanche alliance. We followed
the travois trail to Thompson's Cañon. There we found
a night camp, where they had held a scalp- and war-dance.
There was a circle thirty-five feet in diameter literally
tramped and padded down, where in their night orgies
they probably eulogized each other as big braves.

From this camp they continued their travois trail north
toward White Cañon, and after getting about six miles
out on a great plain, as level as a smooth sea, they commenced to scatter out again, dropping their lodge-poles
as they went. Then it was more guess-work, and this
time we guessed right, that the camp was up Thompson's
Cañon back of us and up the stream from where we crossed
it. We turned to the southwest.

I was ordered to go with and stay with the Mexican
scout and guide. I could now talk a little *Greaser* and
make understandable signs, and Hosea wanted me with
him. Here was where Commander Campbell's advisory
board assumed its first prerogative. At the request of
the guide we advised that the entire outfit should stop and
wait for a signal from us. That was Hosea, Louie Keyes,
and myself. We were to ride on to the cañon and follow
it up, looking for Indian signs, and if we thought that the
Indians were still above us, that one of us would ride back

in sight of the outfit and ride his horse in a circle until he was answered by a horseman; that Campbell would send out to one side and ride around in the same manner as the scout did. That would mean for the entire party to come on to the place where the scout was.

This being thoroughly understood, the three of us started and rode quite rapidly for about seven or eight miles. Then we were on the breaks of the cañon. Here we halted, and with our field-glasses we scanned the cañon up and down as far as the windings of the same would permit. Then we took the long-range view, and looking back to where we had left the boys we could see them as plainly as we could see them with the naked eye had they been close to us. There was a higher bluff on up the cañon nearly a mile, and upon looking to the south and west a distance of perhaps five or six miles we plainly saw five pack animals loaded with meat, and ten Indians, seven of which we made out to be squaws. They were all strung out in single file and were going west.

"Now," said the Mexican guide, "I know where their camp is." That was what every one wanted to know. We watched them for several minutes, they still going west until they passed over a rise in the ground and out of sight on the slope of the draw at the extreme head-waters of the Thompson Cañon, which Hosea told us was about eight miles from where we were.

Louie Keyes now rode back toward our boys for about two miles, and he rode the circle. Hosea and I looked until we saw one of the men ride from the outfit and he rode the circle in response. Then we saw the whole out-fit in motion, coming toward us. This was plains teleg-raphy. The man who invented long-visional binoculars was surely a benefactor. In this case they were a great economizer of horseflesh, and told us, as it were, where the Indians were encamped, though Hosea and I were eight miles from them. Upon looking again we saw several more Indians with pack-ponies going out from where the camp was supposed to be, traveling in the direction the loaded ones came from. This was evident proof, in my mind, that the camp was located where the guide had indicated.

Everyone who has followed up the Thompson Cañon of the Double Mountain Fork of the Brazos well remembers the grand, bold cold-water stream that comes flowing out of a nearly perpendicular bluff from the south side. Just below this place is a side draw with an overhanging cliff where the all-but level plain comes up to, and which is in the form of a crescent. "*Venga aca, Señor Cocinero!*" (Come here, Mr. Cook), said the Mexican, who had ridden some 200 yards farther up the cañon, while I was first looking at the Indians and back towards our approaching hunters. When I rode up to where he was he pointed down to this best of hiding-places and said: "*Esta bueno campo; Indio no le viese*" (This is a good camp; the Indians can't see it.) I told him to stay here and keep a good lookout until I returned.

I then rode back to where Louie Keyes was, and said, "Let's move so as to lead the boys into the cañon below here, then follow it up. Their camp is surely where Hosea said it was. And you know yesterday it was agreed in a general talk that we must try to surprise their camp, and open up on it just at the peep of day if we could do so. There is a splendid place to hide ourselves, horses, wagons and all, just a little way above where you left us; and if we can only get there without being seen by them I'll call it good luck."

"In that case," he said, "I will ride right to them and report to you all we have found." And at a good gallop he was off.

I rode south to, and a little down, the breaks of the cañon, and, finding a natural, easy descent into it, I dismounted and awaited the arrival of the outfit.

Before leaving Rath's Store I was offered the use of a large chestnut-sorrel horse that was noted for his speed and endurance. He was high-strung and of a rather nervous temperament, and his owner had become afraid of him, and was glad to have me accept him. I was glad to get him, for in case of a run I was sure of being well mounted.

When the expedition came up, Campbell left two men on top of the plain, who were to remain there and take observations until called into camp. He then sent Keyes and myself forward with orders to move lively and rejoin the Mexican, Hosea. We hurried up the cañon until we got nearly up to the place where we had seen the Indians from, when we slowed down, and rode up on top. Taking our glasses in hand, we looked the country well over and concluded we had not been seen.

Campbell had taken the precaution to tell the boys there would be no firing of guns, except at Indians. Hosea had left his horse in the cañon and was then crouched down on a high point above where the big spring on the opposite side of the cañon was. He was bareheaded, and with his field-glasses to his face he was looking on up the cañon. Louie said, "I'll bet he doesn't know we are here." He had just spoken the words, when Hosea crouched down lower and worked himself more downhill. Then he rose up and ran down, toward his horse as fast as he could, saying, "*Venga aca! venga aca!*" (Come here! Come here!)

We both plunged our horses off of the steep decline and were soon near his horse, with Hosea a close second. I will here omit the Mexican lingo; he said that "One Indian had crossed the cañon about a mile and a half above and was riding northeast, and he believed he was a scout out to see if they were being followed, and if he discovers us, and gets back to camp, they will break camp immediately, go to some of the lakes, and then it will be hard to catch them."

I said, "Wait a little," and dismounting, I handed Louie my horse's bridle-rein and ran up the hill, on the north side. As I neared the top, I took off my hat and with field-glasses in hand I looked and walked still higher until I was high enough to take in all the surroundings for a mile, and there, sure enough, not three-quarters of a mile from us was a Quohada Comanche warrior. Raising the glasses to my face, I could bring him closely to me. He was riding easterly down the cañon.

CHAPTER IX.

The Warrior's Last Ride.—Muffled Feet.—Bit Off More Than We
Could Chew.—The Cunning Warriors Tricked Us.—We Carried
Water in My Boots.—Captain Lee Captures Their Camp.—How
Lumpkins was Killed.—The Sewall Gun Hoodooed the Coman-
ches.—The Blood-curdling Yell, and We were Afoot.—They Sure
Waked Us Up.—Gathering the Clans.

I ran down the hill. Remounting, I said, "Come on,
boys." Down the cañon we went, meeting the expedition. After a brief report, Campbell said: "We must
get him, or he will ride on down, strike our trail, and give
the whole thing away." He added: "Say, Keyes, you
are an Injun. Can't you get that fellow?" Then he
ordered Freed "to go up on the hill and watch him."
When he got up on the hill, which was only a few rods
from us, he said to us, "Now, boys, keep perfectly quiet.
He is in a fox trot, going east, and he is coming in closer
to the cañon." One of the Englishmen, whose camp had
been plundered and destroyed, slipped off from a wagon,
ran up the hillside and said: "Where is the bloody cuss?
I want to kill him myself."

Keyes had ridden back down the cañon and had gone
up a side draw to intercept and kill him as he passed.
By this time two of the other boys had joined Freed, and,
all unconscious of his near approaching death, the Quohada
Comanche was nearing the breaks.

The Englishman was armed with an express rifle, which
he had brought from Europe. Keyes had daubed both of
his cheeks, demonstrating the fact that "blood is thicker
than water," and that the Indian blood in his veins had
cropped out in his actions.

(213)

On came the Quohada.   These Indians had sneaked up
and stolen Marshall Sewall's life, and perhaps this same
sign-rider was one of the party.   He was nearer the cañon.
His Winchester rifle was in a scabbard, fastened to the
trappings of his saddle.   The Englishman fired, and he
fell from his horse.   Al. Waite and I were side by side
facing each other at the time.   He whirled his horse and
started up, and I with him.   When we got up on the flat
the Indian was trying to get upon his feet, and, his pony
having bolted, was running on in the direction they had
been going.   We soon overtook him, but he would dodge
us, and in a zigzag he would keep angling in closer to the
breaks of the cañon.

The two trail-watchers whom Campbell left behind
when we came into the cañon now hurried on up to have
a hand in what was going on.   The four of us finally caught
the pony.   I was not afraid but what Waite or I either
could run ahead of him, but he was an artful dodger, and
simply did not wish to be caught.

By this time we were over a mile down the cañon from
the rest of the boys.   When we got back to them they
had taken the Indian's body down in the bottom, and left
it in some tall reeds near a water-hole, so it would be out
of sight for the present.

Keyes wanted to take the scalp.   But some of the boys
said, "No, no, Louie; we will kill them, but we must not
mutilate the bodies."

Every field-glass—and there were twelve in the crowd—
was now put to use.   Campbell now sent ten men ahead
with glasses.   He sent Jim Smith in charge.   They were
to put out guards above the camping-place, on both sides
of the cañon, and also below the same.   Hosea, the Mexican, went along with them.

At 3 P. M. we were in this quiet nook, safely hidden from prying eyes. What little breeze there was went directly down the cañon and under the projecting bluff. It being safe to do so, we made a camp-fire, cooked and ate. All hands were ravenously hungry. As soon as one appetite was appeased, the man who possessed it went to the relief of another man on guard, until all had been relieved from duty and fed.

Campbell, Smith and Freed withdrew from the crowd a short distance and held a council. While they were talking Bill Kress asked the question, which echo answered, "What did Campbell want an advisory board for? Look at him out there planning the whole thing himself." I did some thinking myself when he had appointed the five, Kress being one of the number; but I was charitable enough to think that he wanted as many of the party as possible to be distinguished by any glory that might accrue from the expedition. The council having ended, those three came in and Campbell addressed us in this way: "Now, boys, so far everything seems to be going right. We three, whom you have chosen to lead you, have the utmost confidence in your nerve; but it is one thing to talk about cleaning out a camp of 150 or 160 fighting Indians where they have their women and children along with them, for Indians will fight harder and better then under these circumstances than they will at any other time or place. We have decided to leave the wagons and camp outfit here. We will be in three divisions, and all act in concert. I will take one half of the mounted men, Smith the other half, and Freed here will have command of you foot men. Cook and Godey will go with Hosea to-night and locate their camp. We will follow up the cañon three or four miles and await their return.

If they find the camp they are to get the lay of the ground, so that we will know how to place our forces advantageously, in order to make an early-dawn attack. Smith and his men are to charge through the camp on a run, passing on to their pony herd, round it up, then circle around behind us; then if need be he can bring his men to our assistance. And, boys, don't kill any women or children if you can help it. After we have done all this, if we do do it, we will govern ourselves according to the circumstances then surrounding us." He closed his remarks by saying that he hoped and believed every man would do his whole duty.

For a moment there was profound silence, then Louie Keyes, the part Cherokee Indian, said that "it all sounded well, but how about that dead Indian down in the tules? He was a sign-rider. He was making a big circle around their camp to see if he could find any signs of approaching enemies. He won't go to their camp to-night. That will start them to wondering. They will then send scouts out in every direction, and if we are discovered the jig is up; for they will break for the sand-hills and get away from us."

"But," said Campbell, "that is one of the chances we will have to take."

Thus everything was planned. Hosea cut up two grain-sacks with which he could muffle his horse's feet, and he told Godey and me to do the same. We did so, but my horse got so nervous in trying to put them on him that it was deemed best to take a quieter horse, which I did for this occasion.

At good dark we three started up the cañon. It was thoroughly understood that shortly after our departure the whole party was to follow up about four miles, put out a guard, and wait for our return. Each man was to take one blanket and the boys were to get what sleep they could while we were gone.

After the three of us had gone about five miles, we came to the forks of the cañon, the north prong coming from near due west and the south prong from the south by a little east. Here we all dismounted. Godey held the three horses while the Mexican and I walked about fifty yards up the north prong. We were in a beaten trail which was made either by buffaloes or ponies.

Hosea got down upon his knees and after I spread a blanket over him he lit a match from time to time. He did this several times while he was examining the trail. He said there were pony-tracks in the trail, and they were coming down. We then came back, passed Godey, went a few steps up the south fork, and did the same. Here the tracks were going up. We proceeded up the south fork, riding very slowly, about a half-mile, and dismounted.

We again repeated the match-lighting as at the mouth of the cañon. Here the sides of the cañon were sloping and the breaks were lower. We proceeded still farther, and came to a dead horse lying across the well-beaten path over which we were passing. Here I put the blanket over the guide's head. He lit a match and examined the trail, after which he said in a whisper that he and I would go on afoot. I told Godey what he said. Then we went ahead.

We must have gone fully a mile, when we halted and sat down. He whispered, "Now let us listen."

After listening for some little time and hearing no unusual sound, he again whispered, saying, "There is a long deep water-hole just around the next bend a little above us;" and there was where he expected to find the camp.

APACHE FAMILY.

Any one who has attempted to crawl up close to a
hostile Indian camp on a dim, moonless, starlit night will
realize the necessity of using the utmost precaution, and
can imagine to what a tension the nerves are keyed. The
whir of a night-thrush, the flutter of a disturbed bird, a
misstep, a stumble, an involuntary cough or a sneeze, or
anything that would attract an alert ear which might be
in close proximity,—all these things must be taken into
account; and together, in a locality that had not been
seen in daylight, will produce a peculiar feeling.

We went a few steps farther; the path we were on ran
close up to the base of the hill at the bend, and we were
practically out of the cañon and right at the lower end
of the water-hole Hosea spoke about. We remained here
as much as five minutes, and could neither see nor hear
any sign of the camp.

We were lying down, side by side, trying to skylight the
surroundings. The Mexican reached over and gripped
my shoulder, arose, and then slowly started back down
the cañon, I following. We went at a snail's gait. Not
a word was uttered until we got back to Godey, when we
remounted our horses. The guide led the way and we
followed him up out of the cañon to the west, and when
well up out on the flat we halted, and Hosea said that he
was mistaken about the location of the camp; that it
must be on the North Fork at some water-holes which
he could find.

I said, "Well, lead out." And for an hour we rode northwest and came to the breaks of the North Fork, and here
for an hour and a half we cautiously reconnoitered, finding
the water-holes but no camp.

We watered our horses here.

The Mexican dismounted. Seating himself on the

ground, he placed both hands over his face and eyes, and there he sat in mute stillness for several minutes. More than a year later he told me at Fort Sill what then passed through his mind.

When he arose he said, "Now I am sure I can find them, but we can't do it and get back to the boys and get them there by daylight." He said they were surely around the next bend in the draw above the long water-hole we had visited on the South Fork; said he could take us all across a plain from where the boys were, and get there yet by daylight.

Back we went to where the crowd was. They were restless, and some were grumbling at our long absence. For it was now near morning. The wind was coming from the south, and several of the men declared they could smell a grease-smoke which emitted from all camps, more or less, where much meat or marrow-bones were roasted. I said nothing, as I could not smell a smoke, on account of a catarrh.

I made a full report of our trip, and told them that Hosea said if we would move quickly we could yet get there and surprise them. Campbell was outspoken in his belief that the Mexican was deceiving us on account of the Mexican meat-hunters who frequented this region from Fort Sumner on the Pecos river, in New Mexico, and that he believed some of them might be with these same Indians, and that Hosea wished to spare them. So Hosea, faithful Hosea, was under a cloud.

"Let us hurry," said Freed.

Out of the cavern we started; across the arm of the plain we went. When broad daylight of the 18th day of March, 1877, came, we were three miles from the camp and a hard fight.

Just as the dawn came, Hosea and I rode spiritedly ahead. I was now riding the large nervous chestnut-sorrel horse. When we were a mile and a half ahead of the advancing column we saw two Indians riding leisurely toward their ponies, which were southeast of their camp. They evidently had not discovered us. They went out of sight behind a rise in the ground.

We could now see a large band of horses and ponies on a higher plain of land beyond. To our right half a mile were the breaks of the head of the cañon the three of us were in the night before. The camp was straight ahead; off less than a mile and a half. We could see the tops of several tepees.

"To the canyone!" said the guide. "Go! Hurry! Tell the men to hurry to that white place!" (some white chalky breaks he pointed to).

I turned, let the sorrel out, and soon had the boys on the run for the breaks, which we all reached just as the sun had cleared the horizon. We entered the head of the cañon about 300 yards below the long water-hole that Hosea and I were at the night before.

Campbell got all the mounted men into line and took the fourteen to the right, as we were faced, and Smith took the left. We all dismounted, readjusted and cinched saddles, tied our hats behind our saddles, and remounted, Campbell filing his platoon, which I happened to be in, to the right and up the slope for the level of the plain. Smith did the same with his men to the left.

When we were well on top, the two mounted platoons were nearly 200 yards apart, and the infantry, as we now called it, were in the draw between us, with orders to stick to the draw. Joe Freed was ordered to get his men to within 200 yards of the camp as soon as he could, and put them in open skirmish line, but was not to go into the Indian camp.

When all was supposed to be in readiness, Campbell called out, "All right, Smith; go for them!"

Just as they started, Campbell, being on the extreme left of our platoon, rode past in the rear and said, "Boys, get about five paces apart; keep that way as much as you can, and keep as good an alignment as possible."

When he was well out to the right and about three paces in front, he gave the command, "FORWARD!"

Joe Jackson was next to me on my right, Billy Devins next to Joe on his right; to my left was Squirrel-eye. We were now facing due east and going at a moderate trot. Louie Keyes, on the extreme left, commenced the old Cherokee war-chant; his horse had raised a gallop. He was quite far out and ahead. That started Squirlie with his old Rebel yell; and soon we were all going at a rapid gait in an irregular line.

When we came in sight of the first row of tepees we saw the warriors running toward us, having poured out of their tepees, coming on afoot as fast as they could run. We began firing. The Indians got to the summit of a little rise between their camp and us, and dropping down on their bellies opened up a rapid fire on us at 200 yards.

Campbell, spurring his horse to its utmost speed, got in the lead of all, and riding down the front of the line said, "Back to the draw!" repeating it several times, but before half of us could turn our horses Joe Jackson fell from his saddle. Lee Grimes's horse was shot in the forehead, and in falling broke Lee's left wrist. Billy Devins dismounted, I following suit; we both ran to where Jackson was, letting our horses run back with the rest. Each of us took a good strong hold of Jackson and were dragging him back, when Billy's hold broke, he having been hit in the arm.

"For God's sake, boys," said Jackson, "drop flat upon the ground or they will get you both."

Lee Grimes crawled like a snake to where we were, and the three of us, one shot in the arm, another with a broken wrist, and I unhurt, lay in front of Jackson, and heard the bullets passing over us, but could not see the Indians that were shooting in our direction.

Presently, off to our front and left, we saw as many as one hundred Indians creeping up to the crest of a little hill on the north side of the draw, about 250 yards from us, and on the opposite side of that crest was Jim Smith and his men, dismounted, and firing on the ones on our side that we could not see. We all three began shooting at the ones we saw crawling up to the crest. Our work soon proved effective, for the rest of Campbell's platoon, after getting their horses to cover and leaving two men to hold and herd them, crawled forward on the flat, and getting sight of the same band we were shooting at made the place untenable.

Back down the hill and out of sight they went, dragging six of their number after them.

The firing in our direction having ceased, we took Jackson back to where our horses were, in a little side-draw of the main stream. Campbell brought the rest of his men back; and no sooner was this done than from the right and at the head of this draw there passed about twenty mounted Indians on the dead run, strung out at intervals of about six rods, shooting down the draw at us as they passed, and, circling to the right, crossed the main draw about 200 yards below us. At the same time another party of them were doing the same thing from the opposite side, running from near their camp along the plain on

POCKET CAÑON FIGHT BETWEEN HUNTERS AND COMANCHE WARRIORS, AT EASTERN EDGE OF STAKED PLAINS.

the north and crossing the main draw a little closer to us than the ones that were crossing from our side.

And for the next three hours, if one could have been where his vision could have taken in the entire field of operations, he would have witnessed one of the most spectacular dramas ever enacted, the head of Thompson's cañon being the stage. Five of us ran up the side-draw to near the crest and flattened out. Six of the boys ran northeast seventy-five yards to where the side-draw went off to the main ravine; and as the warriors came running down, crossing the draw from the north side, the six men worked their breech-blocks lively, and fired rapidly until they had all crossed the ravine, ascended the slope and passed out of sight of them onto the main flat.

Not all of them, for one of their number fell from his horse in the ravine; another had his horse killed as he ascended the slope. As they passed us that were near the head of this side-draw, they were a good 200 yards out from us, and we were firing away at them as they passed. In this run we killed two horses, and their riders ran for the sharp bend in the draw, south of their camp.

Squirrel-eye rose up and ran quite up onto the crest and said, "Here, boys, here!" We all hurried up to where he was. He had fired once, and was just taking aim again when we arrived. He was shooting at the Indian the other boys had killed the horse from under, and who was near 300 yards off and running for the same draw in the bend. The other one, too, had now got in, but, being farther out on the flat, was making a detour to keep out of the range of our long guns. He still lacked fully thirty rods of getting to cover. We all took a hand, and showered lead all around him.

All at once, he was flat upon the ground. Whether we

hit him or not, we never knew for sure. We crawled back
to our position as rapidly as we could, for we were now
being fired at from the direction in which we first advanced. We had barely got in place again when the
firing in the direction of where Smith and the infantry
were now together slackened, and for a few moments
there were only a few desultory shots.

Then all at once came the sound of a volley from the
main draw to our left and a little in front of us. Then,
pop! pop! a few more shots and Smith at the head of
his party came leading their horses down the main draw,
turned up the side-draw and joined our party.

We were called in and placed about a good wide pace
apart. Eighteen of us were ordered to crawl to the crest
and shoot at everything that showed up. Smith and
Campbell exchanged a few words when they met.

Campbell said, "Boys, we must leave this place. Smith
will take horses and wounded men down to the side ravine
that comes in at the long water-hole, while we will crawl
up on that crest and fire a few volleys at the camp, then
hold the position until Joe Freed and his footmen can get
out of the mess they are in."

When the eighteen of us got to the crest the Comanche
camp was in plain view, near 400 yards distant. There
was a large band of horses on the slope back of it, and
fifty or sixty ponies at the camp. Some were packed and
others were being packed. All this work was being done
by the squaws and children. Off to the left of the camp
was a red flag on a pole. To the right of the camp was
an Indian manipulating a looking-glass. A strong breeze
had sprung up, blowing from the direction of camp toward us down the draw. Estimating the distance, we

fired two volleys at the camp, when zip! spat! whirr! came a fusillade round and about us.

"Let the camp alone and mow the grass at the crest this side of it," said Campbell; and in a very short time three hundred rounds of ammunition had been fired, sweeping the crest for a hundred yards up and down it from where their position then was. Then some of the boys opened on the camp again with deliberate aim, while special targets were being picked out at the camp.

Freed and his men came marching up the side-draw that we were on the crest of. They were all present, and even jolly. Poor Hosea, who had gone in with them, had received a painful wound in the shoulder, but was wearing a grin on his face. Freed called to me to come down. Not having more than sixty feet to go, I was soon there. He said, "Now, you find out what the guide has been telling me. I can't understand him. In all his talk he keeps saying something about Apaches."

Hosea was holding his right shoulder lower than the other; had his right arm in a sling. Smith's men were now firing from the side-draw at the long water-hole. The boys on the crest were shooting pretty lively, too. Several of Freed's men were going up the slope to join Campbell's men on the crest.

I explained to Hosea what Freed wanted me to find out, and to my surprise he told us that we were fighting over 300 Indians; that the camp around the bend, which Campbell's men had not seen at all, were Staked Plains Apaches; and he was sure there must be 200 of them. I called Campbell down and told him what the scout had said. He laughed and said, "Maybe we have bit off more than we can chew." Then, addressing himself to those who immediately surrounded him and were present: "Well, boys, speak up; what do you think is best to do? Seeing what I did at the opening of this fight I thought I was taking my men into needless slaughter. That was why I fell back to this place; and I have felt badly about the whole affair; for I did not know what effect our falling back would have on the other two divisions."

We advised him to send Freed and his men to join Smith while we kept up a fusillade toward the camp.

The Indians having ceased firing, we were sure they were preparing some ruse. Freed started, after receiving instructions to rake, shoot up the main draw toward camp when he approached it, then pass on, join Smith, and from the top of the hill above the long water-hole open up a strong firing upon the camp. This would give us a chance to join them without being in danger of a rear attack or rush from the Indians.

The plan was carried out, and worked well. We were all soon concentrated, and holding a good position again. Smith informed us that his men had opened fire on about fifty Indians that had ridden down the cañon, keeping about a mile out on the plain.

Just then a thick smoke came down toward us from the Indian camp; and, just as the smoke was nearing us, a daring young Indian, dressed in war-bonnet and breech-clout, and riding a white horse that went like a streak, dashed across the draw below us not more than 200 yards away. He drew the fire of half our men, some shooting the second and third time, before his horse, which was on a dead run, *fell* and rolled over. Fully fifty more shots were fired before this painted, war-bonneted brave fell.

Then up the cañon came the party which had passed down; out onto the plain they came on a run, waving shields and uttering their wild, demoniac yell, once heard never to be forgotten. They were one-fourth of a mile from us when they suddenly halted.

Here Ben Jackson made his first remark since the fight began: "Keep your eyes towards their camp, boys; them fellers down in there have done that on purpose to draw our fire so that the main band of warriors can make a sneak on us down the draw, through that smoke."

'Twas a timely remark. Sure enough—here they came, pouring over the crest of the side-draw we had just vacated. But the smoke was not so thick as they wished it to be. For some were seen and must have been hit before they all got into it. The grass they had fired did not burn well, and soon the atmosphere was again clear.

But the cunning warriors had tricked us; and it was not until nearly a month later that we understood or knew the meaning of each of their moves in the fight, and the real execution our buffalo-guns had done. The party of warriors down the draw rode out upon the south side, and, making a wide detour, rode into the draw above camp.

There was now a complete lull. Joe Jackson, being wounded, had a burning thirst, and began calling for water. Not a canteen or cup of any kind in the crowd. I was wearing a pair of new boots which I had put on the day we left Rath's. It was nearly 100 yards out in the little valley to where the water was. Three different ones had started to crawl down to the water. I was really suffering from thirst myself. It was nearing noon, and my head was aching as if it would burst.

Ben Jackson said, "Boys, if you will shoot pretty lively at this edge of that side-draw, and up the main draw a little, Cook and I will crawl down and bring up a couple of bootfuls of water."

"All right," they said. And as the boys fired away we crawled down and both got a good drink of water, bathed our heads, then, taking off both of my boots and filling them with water, we crawled back, each of us holding a tight grip to the top of a boot-leg.

Joe Jackson quenched his thirst. Then we gave Grimes and Hosea the rest of the water. "Shorty," the druggist, had done what he could, which was not much, for the wounded men, Jackson and Hosea; but he bandaged Grimes's broken wrist, and gave each of them a drink of fourth-proof brandy from a bottle that had been put into Bill Kress's saddle-pockets.

We were in this place nearly an hour. Then the three commanders divided us into two parties, sending half of us on up this side-draw, with orders to crawl on our all-fours along the plain and get opposite the mouth of the draw that we of Campbell's men had vacated, and that we believed to be the one the main bodies of Indians were in. This party was in charge of Smith. They had been gone from us nearly half an hour, when their guns were heard; for the space of four or five minutes there was a general fusillade from both sides.

At last our boys drove them out up the draw; and as they went up over the crest going south they came into our view. They were running toward the sand-hills four miles away.

It was then we opened fire upon them at long range. After firing four or five times apiece, Campbell selected five men to remain with the wounded men and horses. Then he said, "Come on, boys; let's regain our old position. There goes Jim Smith and his men across the draw."

On the run we went, just as fast as we could go, and we were soon on the crest of the side-draw that we first fell back to. The tepees that we had had the view of then were down; not a sign of a living thing in sight.

"Have we licked them?"

"Yes," "No," would come the answer.

"Let's go into their camp now."

"No, don't do that; let's not get too far from those wounded men and our horses."

"I'm choking for water."

"I'm so hungry I could eat a raw coyote."

"Hello, Shorty; where is that war pony you said you was going to ride back, as you was walking up here last night?"

"Say, my dear Johnny Bull, you are chock-full of sand; that old blunderbuss of yourn scart 'em out of the country!"

"Shake, Deacon; I haven't had time to be sociable with you to-day; but no offense was meant."

"Pardon me, Carr; but you look worse than the devil."

And thus this good-natured, tired, thirsty, hungry crowd bandied one another while Campbell, Smith and Freed were in council.

"Back to the wagons, boys!" came the order. "Smith, you keep your men here until the rest of us cross the main draw."

Away we marched. After we had crossed the draw and were lined up facing toward the abandoned camp, Smith's men rejoined us, and down the draw we went to the long water-hole, previously putting out a guard on top of the plain. Everybody drank a sufficient amount of water. The horses were brought down and watered.

The ends of a blanket were laced together around two pieces of lodge-poles, several of which were lying around and near the watering-place. We made a stretcher for Joe Jackson. Squirrel-eye, George Cornett, Hi Bickerdyke and I rode back and got Grimes's saddle.

We now all felt that we were masters of the field since the Indians had fled. Then we followed down the plain and got the war-bonnet from the brave that rode to his death on the snow-white horse. Then we were off for the supply camp.

We got there an hour before sundown. We unsaddled and turned our horses loose. No fear of a raid for the present. The fires were built and a hurry-up supper prepared.

We opened two boxes of crackers; carved a big cheese; made two camp-kettles full of oyster-soup; opened peach cans by the dozen; set out a keg of pickles; opened a firkin of oleomargarine; made lots of strong coffee; and sat down to a feast. We had eaten nothing since four o'clock the day before.

After supper we attended all three of our worst wounded men the best we could. We probed Hosea's wound through the shoulder; washed it out clean; sprinkled it with iodoform and tied bandages around it as well as we could; made splints for Grimes's broken wrist, bound it up, and kept water handy for him to bathe it.

Poor Joe Jackson had been hit in the groin, by Sewall's gun, which was a 45, just as we turned, when we fell back the first time. The ball passed through, and lodged. He was hauled in a wagon 150 miles, to Fort Griffin, wheer the post surgeon extracted the bullet. But, poor fellow, after two months of suffering, although in the mean time he got up and went around after his surgical work was done, he took a relapse, and died.

The next morning we started back to Rath's. We arrived there on the 22d of the month. Just a week later, Captain Lee, of G Company, Tenth U. S. Cavalry, with five Tonkawa Indians for guides, scouts and trailers, and

STORY OF THE SOUTHWEST PLAINS.   233

his seventy-two colored troopers, took the field, under
orders from General Ord, who at that time was in command
of the Military Department of Texas, with his headquarters
at San Antonio.

Captain Lee's special mission was to find these Indians
and bring them in. From him we learned all that we did
not know already in regard to our fight with the Indians
on the 18th of March. It was now believed that, for a
time at least, we would be safe by going in small parties
to bring in the hides from the many camps in the Brazos
country.

Kress, Rees, Benson, Moore, Crawford and I went in a
body to our different camps for the hides we yet had on
the range. Rath sent freight teams to haul the hides
and bring them in. The work took nearly two weeks'
time in all. Some of the hunters went out ten to twenty
miles, selecting new camps, in hopes of getting a few hides
now and then.

Soon a general carelessness prevailed. The Indians
swept over the range again, coming to within five miles of
Rath's, killing three more hunters, destroying several
camps, and running off the stock.

Two days after this last raid, Tom Lumpkins, having
returned to Rath's, ran amuck. After making some
slighting remarks about our expedition against the Indians
and getting a reprimand from the hunter who had loaned
me the sorrel horse for the campaign, he deliberately drew
his pistol and shot, breaking the man's arm near the shoulder. At the time Lumpkins shot him, he (the man) was
sitting upon a chair, and my partner, Crawford, was cutting his hair. He was totally unarmed.

This all happened in the saloon. Crawford stepped in
front of Lumpkins and said, "What do you mean, Tom?"

"Get out of the way, Crawford; he has insulted me."

Just then Jim Smith pulled out his revolver, ran up, jerked Crawford to one side, and fired.

Tom then backed toward the door, shooting as he went, Smith following him up.

As Lumpkins came out of the door he turned to his left, still walking backward toward a wagon that John Godey and I were in, sacking up dried buffalo tongues. Smith kept following him up, shooting as he advanced.

Lumpkins fell about ten feet from the wagon. One of the bullets from Smith's revolver went through the pine wagon-box and lodged in the sack of dried tongues. Godey held the sack while I put the tongues into the sack.

The hunter whose arm was broken by Lumpkins, was an American-born Swede. He was not with us in the fight, but was enthusiastic in his praise of the manner in which the men conducted themselves who were there, and, being a rather impulsive man, he quickly rebuked the insult.

Jim Smith had previously come very near having trouble on this very same subject, with Lumpkins. This being the case, it was apparent to all that Smith was justifiable in what he did, under existing circumstances.

The wounded man and I had met several times during the past two and one-half years, and we had become quite intimate. At his special request I took him to Fort Griffin, that being the nearest place to a doctor or surgeon. As we were starting away, the boys were making arrangements to give Lumpkins as decent a burial as they could, Smith saying that he would defray all expenses of the burial.

Smith and several eye-witnesses of the killing all went to Fort Griffin also, where Smith surrendered himself to the civil authorities of Shackleford county. The record of his trial in April, 1877, says: "*Justifiable homicide.*"

While at Fort Griffin we learned that Captain Lee had found the Indians; had captured their camp, together with all their women and children.

The next day after returning from Fort Griffin, Crawford and I settled up all our affairs in regard to our partnership in the hunting business. After everything was settled satisfactorily between us, he took me aside and told me that "he never was so anxious to get to a peaceful, quiet, steady plodding place, in his life." Said his "nerves were not made for startling commotions." He said: "I have a mother, as I told you, who is dependent upon me; I have money enough now to buy a nice little place in Benton county, Arkansas, where I can make an excellent living, and make Mother as happy as she ever could be." He had before this told me of his father being killed at the siege of Vicksburg, and of their home in Missouri being broken up by the Federals. The ex-Confederates would call us "Unionists," ringing the changes to "Yanks."

After I had heard him through I took him by the hand and said: "Willis, I regret to part from you; but am glad you are so solicitous for your mother's welfare. Your idea of a good quiet home is an excellent one; and from this on I'll often think of you and imagine you contentedly situated."

The next day he started with a big hide-train for Fort Worth. I never met him again, but we kept track of each other for several years through the mails.

On the 25th of April there were some twenty-five or thirty of us lounging around the store and saloon at Rath's, when Captain Lee rode into the little place, bringing in most of the women and children of Nigger Horse's band. They all camped close by that night. This Captain Lee was one of the descendants of the famous "Light Horse

Harry," of Revolutionary fame, also a relative of the great Confederate general, "Marse" Robert E. Lee, the man who would not allow Gen. Grant to turn his right flank. Capt. Lee was a tall, square-shouldered, well-proportioned man, of great muscular strength, having a splendid voice and very distinct articulation. He was a fluent talker. He "would like to meet some of the hunters who had fought the Indians on the plains at the head of Thompson's cañon."

Just then Jim Harvey approached him and saluted, saying, "How do you do, Captain Lee?"

"Why, Jim Harvey, old Fourth Cavalry, ha! ha! Citizen Harvey now?"

"Yes, time expired at Fort Dodge three years ago; been hunting ever since."

"Were you at the hunters' fight?"

"Yes;" then looking over the crowd, now all at the store, "there are about half of the boys here now."

Then for an hour or more he entertained us with the details of his expedition and the Indians, and the Indians' story of our fight. We were sure we had killed a dozen Indians, but were surprised to learn that 31 had been killed outright, and 4 died the next day; that 22 more were wounded, and, when we were shooting lively at the camp, and the band of horses beyond, that we had killed 15 pack-horses already loaded; and the mounted warriors that were running and circling around us were only doing it to draw our fire so that the Indians could move camp without all being killed. We could now account for a good many things that happened that day.

And when we learned that the sand-hills to which they fled were honey-combed with caves and tunnels, shored and timbered up to keep them from caving in; and that

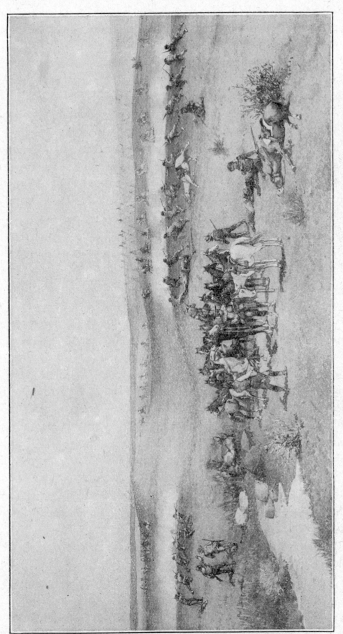

BUFFALO-HUNTERS FIGHTING COMANCHES AND APACHES, MARCH 18, 1877, ON THE STAKED PLAINS.

the Indians hoped that we would follow them there, where they could finally annihilate us, we thought our fight with them was a good day's work for us.

And we learned, also, that the Apaches from the Guadalupe Mountains, west of the Pecos river, had fled back to their own retreat more than 100 miles away; and that Captain Lee had been to our battle-ground. Tonkawa Johnson and his four tribesmen had trailed the Indians to these sand-hills, to find that they had left there after the Apaches had abandoned them, and they had gone on west to Laguna Plata, eight miles west of Casa Amarilla.

Then Captain Lee found them at a time when most of the warriors were out on raids; and his first duty sergeant had been killed by old Nigger Horse himself. At the same time the sergeant killed both Nigger Horse and his squaw, as they were trying to make their escape, both mounted upon one pony; five other warriors were killed, too.

It had been a running fight for eight miles toward the Blue sand-hills. Those who got away fled to them. He had destroyed near three tons of jerked meat; had melted nearly 300 pounds of bar lead and run it into a cake in a hole in the ground. His men carried fifteen parts of cans of Dupont powder up the margin of the lake from camp and blew it up, for three purposes:

First, To keep it from falling into the hand of the exasperated Indian raiders when they returned and found their chief dead, and most of their women and children captives.

Second, To show the captives that the white man had plenty more.

Third, Because he could not well carry it back to us.

The primers, some 10,000, he brought back with him; also a map he had made, showing where we could find the cake of lead. The lead, powder, and primers had been taken from the different hunters' camps, by Indian raiders, when they plundered and raided them. Captain Lee told us to look for a raid on this place at any time; complimented us, so far as he was personally concerned, for the manner in which we had "ginned them up"; hoped the buffaloes would soon be destroyed and the country made safe for the ranchman and home-builder.

Harvey, West and myself went out to his camp with him near a mile. We found the camp settled for the night, the captives on one side, near one hundred feet, with a strong guard around them; then the darky soldiers lounging and resting. Tonkawa Johnson and his friendly companions camped close by Captain Lee's quarters, which were now ready for him; and his cook was preparing his evening meal.

Harvey said: "Captain Lee, Tonkawa Johnson talks fairly good English; speaks good Spanish, and understands the Comanche language thoroughly. We would like to get your permission to have him go with us into the captive camp. We want to find out, if we can, how they liked the Sewall gun."

"Yes, certainly; go right in. Orderly, get Johnson and take him into their camp with these men." Harvey told Johnson what questions to ask. Lying upon an untanned buffalo-hide was a weazen-faced buck that had had his left eye shot out in our fight with them. Near him was another one, sitting up, with both arms broken, they having been broken in the fight with Lee.

When the talk which we had with them, through the interpreter, was ended, we had elicited many additional facts, to those already stated, in regard to our two encounters with them. The Sewall gun had been a hoodoo to them. Everyone who had used it had either been killed or been badly wounded.

When Freed heard this he was in high glee. For he had contended all the time that he had killed the first Indian who used the Sewall gun to shoot at the hunters, which was in the first encounter with them, in the stronghold at the edge of the Staked Plains. The second Indian who used the gun was badly wounded. Then Nigger Horse's son took it, and it was he that first used it, at our big fight, as we now called our 18th of March fight. And he too fell with the gun in his hands. Then Cinco Plumas, or Five Feathers, used it until near the close of the fight, when he too fell. The Indians said they left the Sewall gun in the tunneled sand-hills, wrapped up in a blanket with the two scalp-locks they had taken from Sewall. These superstitious creatures imagined the gun and scalp-locks were "bad medicine" for them; when, as a matter of fact, each one who used the gun placed himself in an exposed position in order to do effective work at long range. And, not being so well practiced in calculating distances as the hunters were, they laid all their misfortunes to the gun. We also learned that the looking-glass that Nigger Horse signaled with was smashed to smithereens by a bullet from one of our guns. A pappoose had been killed which was strapped to its mother's back. But this, of course, was because the pappoose happened to be where it was when the bullet passed along.

The next morning Captain Lee took up his march to Fort Griffin, where he was stationed, and the captives were sent on to Fort Sill.

On the 30th of April George Cornett came into Rath's and reported that John Sharp had been badly wounded the day before, near Double Mountain, and he wanted help to bring him in. The Indians had plundered his camp, cut the spokes out of his wagon, and run off his team. Louie Keyes, Cornett, Squirrel-eye, Hi. Bickerdyke, Joe Freed, Jim Harvey and myself took Rath's buggy team and went out after him. I drove the team; the others were on horseback.

We got to where Sharp was, in a brush thicket below his camp. We started back with him that night; came on back to the Double Mountain Fork; stopped to feed the horses and eat a cold lunch. We were now four miles from Rath. As the day-streaks were visible in the east on the morning of the first of May, 1877, we heard rapid firing in the direction of Rath's. We hooked the team to the buggy and all started for the place.

After going a mile or so, Harvey thought it best for some one to ride on rapidly to a high point about a mile ahead, and try to make out what it all meant. Squirlie, ever ready and ever present, fairly flew up the trail, and went to the summit of the high point where Rath's was in plain view, and much of the surrounding country also. One good, short look seemed to have satisfied him.

Back he came to us, on a dead run.

"Boys, they have tricked us. There are about seventy-five Injuns just over the hill," said he, as he pointed south. "They are going west to beat h—l, driving over 100 head of horses."

So, while we hurried on east as fast as we could go, Keno, the O Z mare and Pinto were all going west.

When we arrived at Rath's we met a cheap-looking crowd. There were about fifty men there, all told, and, with two exceptions, all flat afoot. The Indians had made a clean job of this raid.

There were night-watches out, it was true. But they

had taken all the horses northeast in the evening, about two miles, and let them loose to practically roam and graze at will. The herders must have been sound asleep. A general carelessness prevailed. Only two men were on guard at Rath's. Camp wagons were scattered here and there over forty acres of ground. Several men were sleeping at their camps. Some were sleeping in the store. Several had their beds made down in the aisles of the big hide-ricks.

The Indians were in two parties of about fifty each. One party rounded up and secured the horses in close herd and drove them around a half-mile south of the store. The store faced west, the saloon and restaurant east. The two were a street's width apart.

Just as daylight was dawning, fifty of these reckless thieves made a run between the buildings, shooting right and left and yelling as only Comanches can yell. They passed on to the bunch of horses, struck west with them, and kept moving. They had not injured a man in their run through camps and village. But, as one of the boys remarked, "They sure did wake us up."

It was during this same morning that the organization of what was afterwards known as "The Forlorn Hope" was talked of. We sent Sharp on to the hospital at Fort Griffin, and we put in the day "holding the empty sack" as the phrase went, and organized. There were thirty-eight men present who had lost all of their horses, mules, and ponies. Sam Carr was furious. Besides his two large fine mules, "Prince" was gone. He talked nearly the entire day about him; and when one of the boys said, "And you had a fine mule team, Sam," he replied, "Yes, but I can get more mules; but I can never get another 'Prince.'"

I am sure my readers love a noble horse. And Prince belonged in this category. He was a dapple-gray gelding, fifteen and three-fourths hands high; was seven years old; weighed eleven hundred pounds. His sire came from the Bluegrass region of Kentucky to near Topeka, Kansas, where Prince was foaled, and owned by Samuel Carr. He grew up on the Kansas farm a pet.

Sam was, and had been, his only trainer; and for performing many tricks, Prince was as perfect as horse could be. At the word of command he would go lame, and could scarcely hobble about. He would lie down and appear to be dead. He would hold his head sidewise with ears erect, at the command to "listen!" His master would have him lie down and hold his head erect. Then he would kneel on one knee, place his gun-muzzle on the crown of Prince's head between his ears, and fire the gun, and Prince would not even "bat" an eye. Carr would tell him to lie down; then he would lie down beside him, and, touching him on hip and wither, would say: "Now, cuddle up!" Then Prince would flatten out and bring all four of his legs up against Carr's body. He was fleet on foot; had great power of endurance, and was an excellent swimmer. He would follow his master anywhere he went, if told to do so. Carr would buy sugar in cubes, and nearly always kept a supply of cube cugar on hand for Prince. I heard Carr say to him once, "Oh, Prince, I found some sugar." The horse walked up and ate it from his hand.

Is it any wonder that big tears came coursing down the man's cheeks when he found out his faithful horse was gone? At first the boys were inclined to joke him about Prince. One of them said, "Well, Sam, if we don't get him back when we go out after the Quohada again we will get you a Dolly-Varden horse like that buzzard-headed pinto of Cook's that went off with him." But when the boys saw how Sam took the loss of Prince so much to heart, they ceased joking him.

After having a general talk about ways and means, and nearly all being of one mind, we all decided to practice Indian for the summer, if it took that long to accomplish what we now had resolved to do; which was: To take wagons as far as General McKenzie's supply camp of the '74 war; then pack our supplies, and roam the Staked Plains until we found the Indians' headquarters; then set them afoot as they did us, and fight them to a finish if they followed us.

Accordingly, we elected James Harvey to command us, all agreeing to obey implicitly, and execute the commands given us. Dick Wilkinson was made chief packer, to have regular detailed assistants. Sol. Rees was put in charge of the medical supplies. I was appointed Hosea's interpreter. He was to select anyone he chose to scout with him. Carr, Frank Perry and Bill Kress were sent to the cattle ranches, near Fort Griffin, to purchase saddle-horses and pack animals.

A new campaign was inaugurated. Powder-face Hudson and three other hunters came in that evening from Quirm's. The Indians had not gone there, so they had their horses. Hudson hitched up his team the next morning, and the three men who were to go after the horses threw their saddles into the wagon. West told them to come into the store and get anything they wanted; after which the four of them started for the settlements near Griffin.

The party that took Sharp to the hospital returned the fourth day, bringing the big chestnut-sorrel horse that I rode in the fight on the 18th of March. They also brought a letter from Oleson, the Swede, who loaned him to me for the March expedition. He was my horse now. I wish I had his letter to reproduce here. The horse was given to me as a gracious gift from a man whom I had befriended and who had learned that I was afoot.

When I took him to Griffin after Lumpkins had shot him, we took all his camp outfit and stock along. I had put a new cover on his wagon; and got Mr. Jackson's permission to back the wagon against his barn in the corral; and had taken Oleson's three horses to a pasture three miles down the Clear Fork; and I charged him nothing from the time I left Rath until my return; and so he remembered me in my present loss by making me a present of the horse.

Word now came to us that the entire border of the settlements was on the *qui vive*, from Fort Concho to Henrietta. From North Concho to the Brazos there was hardly a cattle ranch but had lost horses, the Indians having broken up into small parties; had stealthily slipped in and made a simultaneous raid for horses, taking them for a hundred miles up and down the border, and had closed, for the present, by gathering the clans together and setting the hunters afoot by their raid on Rath.

CHAPTER X.

When the ranchmen heard of our predicament, they
would not sell us horses, but would give every man a mount
who had lost stock. Besides this, they wrote out and
presented us with a "bill of sale" for every horse we could
get from the Indians bearing their brands. In addition
to all this, they made us a tender of money for supplies.

This they did for a two-fold reason: one was their time-
honored generosity; the other was because so long as
we were roaming the Plains, seeking the opportunity
we so much desired, we were acting as a buffer between
the Indians and the settlements. For they thought the
red-skins would have all they could do to dodge us and
keep what they had already stolen, without bothering
them. When we finally got started there were just twenty-
four of us in the party, afterward known as the "Forlorn
Hope."

After the supply camp was reached, we packed ten
head of animals and we were off to the "Yarner," as the
old Texans called the Staked Plains. Going to the head
of White cañon we ran on to a Mexican meat-hunting
outfit, and through our interpreter, Hosea, we told them
to pull back to the Pecos, and for them to get word to all
the Mexicans as soon as they could, to steer clear of the
Llano Estacado during that summer. We gave them to
understand that "a word to the wise" should be sufficient. From where we met the Mexicans, we went south

to our old battle-field. This time we could approach the place in a free-and-easy manner. Flowers were everywhere in full bloom. There were several different varieties; though none of us were good enough botanists to classify and name them. But we could smell the sweet perfume from them and admire their beauty; and for the next six weeks, wherever we roamed, the air was fragrant with their sweet odor. But we did not see "The Yellow Rose of Texas."

From here we went to, and explored, the tunneled sand-hills. There we found the Sewall gun, as had been told us.

We could find no water anywhere in this region, although we were in three parties and rode the country for miles around.

This must have been one of their last-resort retreats, when closely pushed for a temporary refuge. Some thought this place was where the Comanches and Apaches met to exchange horses and stolen goods; and it was a well-surmised fact that horses taken from the settlements of Texas were exchanged for horses stolen in New Mexico or on these plains; then, by the time the Indians had returned to their respective reservations, each exchanged horse was a long way from its original home, and in a strange land was seldom ever regained by the lawful owner.

From these sand-hills we returned to the battle-ground and made our second night's camp, near the long water-hole. From here we went to the Casa Amarilla by way of the North Fork of the Thompson cañon; from here to the Laguna Plata, where Captain Lee had captured the camp; thence marching south from the sand-hills, we struck a trail crossing ours at a left-angle, going towards the Laguna Sabinas, in nearly an easterly course. This we surmised must be a pretty strong party of Indians. Harvey now sent the pack train back to the Casa Amarilla with Dick Wilkinson and five men. The eighteen of us now took up the trail and followed it till dark. We were now about fifteen miles southeast of the point to which our pack train had gone, all of us as hungry as bears.

The trail we had followed was another fool's trail. The Indians knew we were in the country, and they thought to delay and puzzle us so they would get us as far away from their real hiding-place as possible. At one time the trail turned north, then northwest, then it would strike out northeast, and we kept twisting around on the trail until darkness overtook us. Harvey then told me to tell Hosea to guide us to the Casa Amarilla.

As we were approaching the camp a clear voice rang out, "Halt! Who are you?"

"Harvey's men," we replied.

"All right, boys; come ahead!"

We were camped on top of the edge of the bluff above the natural and excavated caves. From our position the next morning, we had a fine view through our glasses to the north, east, and south. Looking eastward for many miles, several bunches of wild horses were in sight. Small bands of buffalo and antelope could be seen, too. We lay over here all day; and when darkness set in we made a twenty-five mile march to Lake Sabinas. No Indian was there. Thence we marched to the Double Lakes, and to the big springs of the Colorado; thence we skirted the edge of the Llano Estacado north to near where Sewall was killed; thence back on the Staked Plains, visiting every place where water could be found that we knew of or could find.

Three different times we arrived at places the Indians had recently left. But they were elusive, and were cunning enough to send us on two fool's errands.

Thus our time was occupied, marching and counter-marching from place to place, until the 18th of July, where we were encamped on the head-waters of a tributary of the Colorado river, when it was deemed best to send out three different scouting parties by twos.

Harvey sent Al. Waite and me toward the head-waters of the North Concho; Hosea and Sol Rees were sent west toward the Blue sand-hills; Squirrel-eye and George Cornett were ordered to make a night ride in the direction of the Double Lakes. Waite and I left camp on the morning of the 19th, going south along the eastern edge of the Staked Plains. When we were some four miles from camp we saw to our left, and about two miles from us, moving animals. Focusing upon them with our glasses, three mules and five head of horses could be plainly seen.

"Now," said Waite, "let's get as close as we can to that stock and see what it means."

By turning east down a sag we kept out of sight of them. We traveled nearly a mile when we got a good-sized hill between us and where we had seen the animals. Then we headed for the hill. Its north side was steeply gullied. In one of these gullies I held the horses while Waite ascended the hill to get a good searching view of the surrounding country. It was about sixty-five yards from where I was holding the horses to where Waite was taking his observations.

After he had taken in the surroundings a short time, he said: "John, fasten the horses and come up here! I see Prince, George Williams's saddle-horse, and Billy Devins's mules, as sure as the world!"

I was soon on the hill at his side, and there, sure enough, not over a quarter of a mile distant, was Prince and seven other head of stock. Three were mules. They seemed to be contented. Some were grazing, one was lying down, and the others were standing. We both now used our glasses, taking in the dips, draws and points of land far and near. For an hour or so we talked and looked. Finally we decided that the horses and mules must have been lost by the Indians, after they had made the raid on Rath, and that they were there alone, and no hostile camp near; and that we would get them now and go back to camp, *which we did.*

We rode straight out to them, after we had remounted and got out of the gullies. Al. had been in the camp with Prince all of the fall and winter before. He rode up to them, while I stopped a few rods back to look for any decoy that might have been placed by the Indians.

He said "Hello, Prince!" and rode quite up to him. I am sure the horse recognized him; for he neighed and came up to Waite, who circled around the rest of the stock and started with them toward our camp.

After they had been driven to within a mile or so of camp we stopped, and went up on a hill, whence we looked the country over good again. Then, before going on to camp, Waite put his saddle on Prince. We drove the band into camp. Waite dismounted a few steps from where the boys were. They were all up and expectant.

Samuel Carr was greatly rejoiced at sight of Prince. The mules belonged to the two Moore brothers, who were known on the range far and near as both hide- and meat-hunters. They dried tons and tons of meat for a St. Louis firm. The horses belonged to different hunters. All had undoubtedly dropped out of the big band without being missed by the Indians, when taking them through the breaks, on the trip to the Plains.

The next morning Waite was ill, and Carr was sent with me toward the head of the North Concho. After getting as far south as where we had seen the stock from the day before, we turned due southwest and kept a steady walking gait for six hours. We came in sight of a slightly broken tract of ground about two miles away and to the left of the course we were traveling. We halted and brought our field-glasses into use. We noticed antelope were coming from the west towards the breaks. We thought we saw, many miles to the west, a band of horses. But the atmosphere at that time of day was slightly hazy; we could not determine for sure what the objects were. We decided to reconnoiter the country the antelope were traveling toward first.

Turning our horses to the left, we rode to the breaks and came to some sulphur springs. There were several of them, and it was a great watering-place. As we came close to them a band of wild horses scented us and went in a wild, mad rush out of the breaks. Galloping out upon the plains the clatter of their hoofs made a noise that we could hear when they were over a mile from us.

The big gray wolf was here and the coyote; also ravens, the blackest of black species of the crow family. A tremendously large eagle soared above us for a while, then took its flight toward the south prong of the Colorado. Some of these springs were strongly impregnated with sulphur. Two of them were splendid drinking-water. We found no sign of any Indians.

We felt comparatively safe, but we were ever vigilant. We were riding the best of horses. Each one of us car-

ried a canteen and a six-pound powder-can of water.
After watering our horses we rode west about three miles
and dismounted, to graze the horses and make some
coffee for ourselves. After building our fire of buffalo-
chips we made the coffee, sat down facing each other,
and placed our cooked meat and bread between us, I facing
west and Carr east. After eating and resting a while we
proceeded on west toward the objects that we had failed
to make out. It was now about four o'clock in the afternoon of the 20th of July. We were in a region that neither
of us had ever been in before. We thought we must be
west of the head of the North Concho, and yet a long
way north of it.

The objects that had attracted our attention were yet
a mystery to us, and as we were not satisfied without
further investigation we rode on west until near sundown. We had ascended a rise in the plain where we had
an excellent view for many miles around in all directions—
and there on west and southwest, scattered over many
thousands of acres of land, were bands of wild horses.
They were ranging in unmolested freedom and in perfect
quiet. No Indians near here, we reasoned, or these watch-
ful, quick-fleeing animals would not be so quietly and
contentedly grazing. As evening came on, young colts
came running and frisking around in reckless abandon in
their wild unfettered freedom. No other wild animal
will run from man's presence, be he white or red, quicker
than the American wild horse. How did these majestic-
looking creatures happen to be in this country? Some
historians tell us that their ancestry dates back to the
conquest of Mexico by the Spanish under Cortez, who
brought the original stock from old Spain, no horses being
in the country prior to the Aztec rule; and that from the

horses Cortez brought over the sea the wild horse of the old Southwest originated.

There were different methods by which these wild animals were captured, but one which I witnessed I will describe:

Early in the spring of 1878, a Mexican outfit came from San Miguel, New Mexico, to the Laguna Rica, bringing with them twenty head of saddle-horses and eight men, for the purpose of capturing wild horses. He wanted nothing but females, for breeding purposes.

I was camped at the Casa Amarilla, eight miles from Laguna Rica, where the Mexican found me the next day after his arrival. This was a great wild-horse region at the time. I had noticed that morning an unusual, continued, rapid movement among all the bands of wild horses that were in sight, but could not account for it at the time. In the evening the Mexican rode into my camp. His name was Valdez. He could speak good English; told me his business in the country and his method of securing the animals. He would single out a certain band of the animals and start two men on horseback toward them, their horses walking. When they got close enough for the band to scent or see them the wild animals would be on the *qui vive*, while the stallion that was master of the herd would trot and walk a short way towards the approaching horsemen, raise his head high, and look steadily at them. When assured of danger he would whirl around and run back toward the band, biting and squealing at them until he had them all on the run; then he would forge ahead and take the lead. Away they would all go, generally from three to five miles without stopping. Then he would come back a way on the trail, acting as rear guard.

In the mean time the two horsemen followed them up, still walking their horses, and when the now vigilant stallion saw that they were still coming he would start his band again.   Wild horses always run in a big circle; hence they would, on the second run, go from fifteen to twenty miles before stopping, but slowing down by degrees.

When the direction of the circle was determined, two other riders would start out and cross an arc of the circle. Another would do the same outside the circle; then one man would take two extra horses, hurry across the circle and intercept the first riders with fresh horses and a supply of tortillas, carne and agua (bread, meat and water). Another would station himself, with four extra horses, as near to the circle as caution and convenience would allow.

As the circle had once been completed, the horsemen adjusted themselves accordingly.   The wild horses were kept on the move as much as possible, both day and night.

The horsemen would drop in behind the wild animals at intervals; but they were always in a walk.   Thus it was called "walking them down."

On the third day the very old and weaker ones dropped out of the circle; by the fourth day the best of the herd were tired and leg-weary, so much so that the men could now close in on them and would have to drive them to keep them moving.

Sometimes an enraged stallion would turn on the pursuers and have to be shot.   The afternoon of the fourth day on which Valdez and his men had been following a mixed band of some eighty-odd head of these untamed steeds of the Llano Estacado, I by previous arrangement joined in the walk-down.   I did this for curiosity and observation.

The band at the time I left my camp was about six

miles southeast of me, and was then being driven by the Mexicans toward the Laguna Rica. When I got to where the horses were I actually felt sorry for the poor captive creatures. Some would lie down; then the stinging raw-hide end of a lariat would be snapped at them and strike unerringly where the vaquero intended it to. Up they would get, and reel ahead. It was night when the men got them to camp, and they kept those that were not literally fagged out on the move nearly all night—moving backward, then forward.

The next morning the Mexicans were all on hand with lariats. They roped and threw the mares down. They then took a knife and cut under each front knee-cap. This severed a ligament and let the joint-water out at the same time. Then they would brand them and turn them loose. In this way they got thirty-five mares, from yearlings up.

Using the knife the way they did stiffened both front legs. After getting all they cared for out of this band, they drove the ones they had crippled and branded to the margin of the lake; and with one herder to stay with them they were no trouble to handle afterward.

In a few days, after resting, regular water and grazing, they were in a condition to be driven to the ranch in San Miguel. They moved along as any horse would that was badly chest-foundered.

Coming back to the time and place Carr and I were watching the wild horses, and looking the country over with our glasses, we waited until dusk, and then started back in the direction we had approached the place from. Going a mile or so, we turned and traveled for an hour toward the North Star, and dismounted for the night, feeling sure, if we had possibly been seen during the day by Indians, that we had eluded them.

The day had been excessively warm. As darkness spread its canopy over the plain, not a breath of air seemed to be stirring, and the stars were shining brightly. Unsaddling our horses, we placed the saddles cantle to cantle and spread a blanket upon the ground. We could not help but note the silence. We ate our lunch, consisting of cold meat and bread, drank water from our canteens, and then lay down for the night upon our blankets, our saddles for pillows and the firmament for a quilt.

We lay stretched out talking in a low tone for hours before we could go to sleep. After our horses had finished grazing both lay down some fifty feet from us. When our conservation had ceased for a time the utmost stillness and silence prevailed. The buffaloes were nowhere in this vast solitude. We were so far from water that even the birds were not here, and Carr remarked that the *very stillness* was noisy.

I said "stillness," but we could hear a low murmur like m—m—mum—um—um. What caused this? Philosophers have told us that it was the last and least audible sound coming from a long distance. Being wafted along the earth's surface made us imagine that we thought we really heard something. After some time, Carr asked me how far from the Bender place, in Kansas, I had formerly lived. After answering him, he asked me: "Did you see a novel that is going the rounds claiming that the Benders left Kansas, crossed the Indian Territory, and were seen somewhere in western Texas on their way to Old Mexico?"

I said, "No; but Al. Waite told me that he had read such a story."

"Yes," said he, "he read it last winter, in my camp. Now," said he, "I don't think those Montgomery county people did right in misleading the public about the Benders."

"What do you mean, Sam?"   I asked.

"Well," he said, "they killed all of the Benders just below the mouth of Onion creek, in Montgomery county, Kansas, close to the Indian Territory line."

I said, "Well, that is a new one.   What will we hear next?"

"Now, John, I'll tell you that after the Independence crowd had gone over to the Bender country, dragged the creeks, and searched the country over for Dr. York's body, and when they started back after their fruitless search, that Senator York asked Kate Bender, the pretended clairvoyant, to go into a trance and tell him where his brother was.   She told him there were too many men present at the time, but if he would come back the next Friday night and bring but one man along she would go into a trance and reveal to him where his brother was."   Carr continued by saying that a member of the party had told him that while Kate and the Senator were talking he had occasion to go to the Bender stable; and while he was there he saw John and the old man Bender at the pig-pen and they were engaged in an animated talk, in a low tone of voice, which talk was in German; that the old man acted in an excited manner; and that he then suspected that the Benders believed or thought that they were under suspicion.   "Now," said Carr, "that was only conjecture by the man that told me; but, two days later, when this man saw Kate, John, the old woman and the old man in that same wagon, drawn by that same team, that was found tied to the blackjack tree at Thayer; met them in the early morning eighteen miles from where they committed their murders, and west of the Verdigris river, going southwest with trunks and rolls of bedding in the wagon, his suspicions were thoroughly aroused, and he put in a good portion of the day gathering a party to follow and overtake them, to bring them back for a full investigation; that fifteen men did follow and overtook them about nine o'clock at night; that they were all more or less intoxicated; that they, the Benders, were encamped by the side of a large sycamore log on the bank of the Verdigris river; that when the party told them they had come to take them back, John Bender started on a run for a brush thicket close by, when they shot him. Kate grabbed up a butcher-knife, and, screaming like a maniac, started to slashing at them, and did give one man quite a bad gash in the hand. And they had to shoot her to save themselves. Then they made a clean job of it and killed the old man and the old woman, after which they sunk all the dead bodies in the Verdigris river; then they each drank considerable liquor; swore themselves to secrecy; searched the contents of the wagon; found $800 in money in the wagon; $130 was in the old man's pocket, and there was $30 in John's pockets. These men divided the money equally between themselves. They burned up most of the things in the wagon; then entered into a contract with one of their party to take the team back to Thayer and leave it where it was found. As it was not their intention at first to kill the Benders, they each and all entered into a solemn compact not to divulge the secret. And each having his share of the money, even after the graves in the Bender garden gave up their dead, they thought best to remain silent still."

I asked him, "When did you hear all this?"

He replied: "Two years ago, up in the Panhandle. The man who told me was drinking at the time. And as the old saying goes, little children and drunken men sometimes tell the truth."

The next morning he came to me and asked me not to say anything about it. I promised him if I did I would not mention his name. I asked him: "Did you know anything of the man who told you that story?"

"Yes; his word to me is as good as any man's on the range; if he had been a man whose word I doubted I would tell you who it was."

The above is the story of what became of the Benders, as told to me that night.

About noon of the 20th of July our camp guard from his lookout notified us that he saw a column of soldiers to the southeast, heading for the Bull Creek Mountain. Their course would take them east of where we were camped. Harvey ordered James Foley, an ex-regular soldier, to intercept them and find out what their mission was.

We were now all agog. Every man who had field-glasses was up on the lookout. It was a level plain, where Foley had intercepted the soldiers. We could see the column halt and dismount; could plainly see two men and Foley a few steps in front of the soldiers. Soon we saw them remount their horses. Then they turned, and started straight toward our camp. When they arrived it proved to be Captain Nicholas Nolan and Lieutenant Charles Cooper with Company A, Tenth U. S. Cavalry. The Tenth was a colored regiment; the Indians called them "buffano" (buffalo) soldiers, on account of their color being dark, like the buffaloes. The company went into camp on the opposite side of the little branch from us, and facing us. They had a twenty-mule pack train. After their camp was in order, and the captain had eaten his dinner, he crossed the little branch to our camp and asked, "Who is in command of you hunters?" James

Harvey stepped toward him, but before-he could speak the Captain spoke, saying, "Well, the saints deliver us! Jim Harvey! And are you with this Forlorn Hope?" The two men were well acquainted, having campaigned together during the 1868 Indian war.

When the captain learned that Harvey was our leader, he asked him how many men he had. After being told, he looked the crowd over, his eyes going from man to man. He would look us over, look us individually up and down.

"Where are your other two men? I see but 22 here."

"They are out on a scout; I keep two men out all the time," said Harvey.

The custom and force of habit brought the military rules to the front, and poor old Nick Nolan forgot for the moment that he was in the presence of twenty-two American citizens that were under no obligations to obey military orders. Turning to Harvey he addressed him, saying:

"Captain Harvey, order your men into line, while I read my orders from General Ord."

We were standing and lounging in a group all close enough to hear distinctly.

Harvey evaded the order by saying: "Captain, the men will all pay strict attention to the reading of the orders."

Captain Nolan had taken the orders from his pocket and stood waiting a moment. Seeing that we made no movement whatever, he said:

"Oh, I see; that's all right, men; I have been twenty-five years in the regular army and am used to discipline. I forgot for the instant that I was in the presence of civilians."

At that we all arose to our feet and formed a semicircle near him. His orders were in substance that he would ration his company for a sixty-day campaign and proceed from Fort Concho to the region in the Staked Plains; find the hostile renegade Indians, and make his report. If possible, find the hunters who are out against the Indians; render them any assistance they may need in the way of supplies, medicine, etc.; and to form a junction with them if agreeable to them.

After reading his orders, he said:

"Now, men, perhaps I have a bit of news for you. The Governor of this State was on the point of sending the frontier battalion of rangers out here to disperse you on account of your not being a legalized body of armed men. But better counsel prevailed, and from higher authority than from the State of Texas, you are now recognized as being within your rights. Congress ought to pass a memorial in your behalf, for you are making future Indian wars an impossibility by the destruction of the buffaloes; and if you will show me those Indians, that is all I ask. I do not want you to help fight them. In fact, I should prefer that you would be merely spectators, and for the following reason: Three years ago, north of here in the Red river country, I was unfortunate enough to be placed in a position to have to stand a court-martial trial for cowardice; and nothing but my record during the war of our Rebellion saved me from disgrace and the loss of my commission. Colonel Shafter caused me my trouble. The facts in my case were that three years ago I had a company of fresh, new, raw recruits, just from Virginia. They had never been under fire, were not drilled in horsemanship, scarcely knew the manual of arms, and I could not get my men to go against Satanta and his warriors, which were some four to one. But now I have a company of fighters. And I wish to vindicate myself by going against the Indians you are hunting. Captain Lee has left Fort Griffin under orders the same as mine. Now, will you agree to take me to water once every twenty-four hours, and assist me to locate the Quohadas?"

Harvey told him the story of our travels in detail; described all of the watering-places, and closed by saying that we believed the Indians' headquarters were in the Blue sand-hills, about fifty miles west of the Double Lakes, and that we would take him to water every twenty-four hours if we could so so without jeopardizing our common interest, which was to find the Indians for him and to recover our stock that they had taken. These conditions were perfectly understood, regardless of Captain Nolan's report to the Secretary of War afterward.

I wish that I could write the story of the happenings of the next few days, as we all hoped and planned that the results might be. But as this book is written by an actual participant in the events and incidents already related and those yet to come, I will write them as they occurred from my personal observation, and from witnesses present.

Early on the morning of the 24th, Hosea and Hudson, who had gone on a scout the day before, came in and reported the finding of a trail going from the north prong of the Colorado in the direction of a chain of surface lakes that were between the Double Lakes and the Casa Amarilla. There had been a cloud-burst in that region the latter part of June, and so tremendous an amount of water fell in an amazing short time that it had filled the depressions to overflowing, and the waters had spread over a large area at first; and when we found this place early in July, we could see the outside water-line by the buffalo-chips and grass-blades that made a drift-line around the flood

margin; but absorption and evaporation had caused the
waters to recede until they were confined in the lower
basins. One of these yet had a surface of about ten
acres when we found it.

After the scouts had reported, the captain ordered his
bugler to sound "boots and saddles." We were soon
en route for the head of the extreme north prong of the
Colorado. Here we lay in camp all of the 22d. At night
we marched to the Double Lakes; lay over next day at
that place; and after night we marched to the chain of
surface lakes, but found no Indians. This day, the 23d, we
lay over at the largest of these lakes until evening, when
we took up the Indian trail for Laguna Sabinas, following a plain fresh trail. This surface lake, whose waters
were from the June waterspout or cloud-burst, now covered
a surface of about five acres of ground. Lieutenant
Cooper's measurement in the center of the basin showed
a depth of thirty-three inches.

Here we witnessed a remarkable sight: At one time
during the day could be seen horses, mules, buffaloes,
antelopes, coyotes, wolves, a sand-hill crane, negro soldiers,
white men, our part-Cherokee Indian and the Mexican
guide, all drinking and bathing at one and the same time
from this lake. Lieutenant Cooper first called attention
to the fact; and remarked that outside of a tented circus,
it was one of the greatest aggregations of the animal
kingdom ever witnessed on as small a space of land and
water.

One can imagine what kind of water this must have been
when taking into account that nearly a month previous
it had suddenly fallen from the clouds upon a dry, sun-
parched soil, with a hard-pan bottom; and being exposed to a broiling hot sun about sixteen hours of every

twenty-four, while the thermometer in midday was far above 100 degrees Fahrenheit, an occasional herd of buffalo standing and wallowing in it, the ever-coming and going antelope, the wolves, snipes, curlews, cranes, the wild mustang, all of which frequented the place for many miles around. And yet we mixed bread, made coffee, and filled our canteens from it. And yet again there were men in our party who in six more days, like Esau, would have sold their birthright for the privilege of drinking and bathing in this same decoction.

We arrived at Laguna Sabinas at midnight, secreting ourselves in a gully at the north end of the lake.

About 7 A. M. we saw a signal-smoke at the south end of the lake, six miles away. We had been seen, and their spies were sending the word, how far away we knew not; then back toward the Double Lakes up went a signal. We had been deceived nearly a month before by the high ascending spiral whirlwinds that the Llano Estacado was noted for, but these signs were unmistakable.

"Indios! Indios! yo les veo!" (Indians! Indians! I see them!) said Hosea; and riding out of a draw of the lake nearly three miles away, going east toward the head of the Red Fork of the Colorado, were thirty-odd Quohadas.

At Captain Nolan's command the darky bugler's blast for boots and saddles sent its vibrations down the lake; and away he ran for his horse, blowing as he ran.

Harvey ordered Carr and me to get out and keep in sight of the Indians. We were two miles from the lake when the troops got in motion with their pack train. The Indians turned south when Carr and I got within a mile of them, and away they went as fast as they could go. Carr and I followed on about two miles farther, and looking back saw that our party had stopped and were signaling to us. We rode back to learn that Nolan and Harry believed that when the Indians turned south it was a ruse, and that they believed the camp was on the Red Fork of the Colorado, and there is where we went, Nolan arguing that the camp was trying to get back to Fort Sill, being tired of being hounded around by both the soldiers and hunters, and that the devils were trying to mislead us as to their real intent. He said if he was mistaken, when we got to the Colorado he would go anywhere we said afterwards. Hosea insisted that the Indian camp must be in the Blue sand-hills; but we went with Nolan.

The next morning, the 25th, about 8 A. M., our out-guards sent in word that five or six Indians were coming straight for camp from the south, bearing a white flag. When they arrived at our camp it proved to be Quinnie or Quana, a half-breed Comanche, two oldish bucks and two squaws. Quinnie handed Nolan a large official envelope, which contained a commission from Gen. McKenzie, post commander at Fort Sill, to Quinnie to hunt up the Indians and bring them in.

The document was on heavy crisp paper, and was addressed to whom it might concern. It stated that the Indians wanted to give themselves up to him at Fort Sill, but they did not want to fall into the hands of the Texas authorities. The document cautioned people against molesting Quinnie in his mission. Captain Nolan swore as only a regular army officer of those days could. "Here," he said, "I had orders from my department commander to find them blanketed, breech-clouted devils, and make my own report; which practically means, by reading between the lines, to annihilate them if I want to. Then here comes a paper from a garrison commandant, delegating a half-breed tribesman to come out here and bring the renegades in; then winds up with a covert threat if they are molested."

Quinnie passed on down the edge of the plains, going south, intimating that he was going to the Mustang Springs country.

At noon we saddled up and went to the Double Lakes, northwest, arriving there after midnight. Hosea and Cornett were sent on six miles toward Laguna Rica, where they could have an early morning observation of the plains westward. Cornett came running into camp while we were eating breakfast, saying they had seen a large band of warriors going northwest from Laguna Rica, heading toward the Casa Amarilla. Boots and saddles again came the clear notes from the bugle; and away we went.

Every soldier had a canteen; every citizen had a canteen or a six-pound powder-can covered with blanketing, and a strap to sling over the shoulder; but the fact developed that some of these soldiers left this camp with empty canteens. I myself came near doing so. Many left with partially filled canteens. I was ordered to hurry to Hosea, who was following the Indians, to keep in good field-glass sight of them. I was told to have him wait until we all caught up with him. When I overtook him he was three miles northwest of Laguna Rica. The command came to us on a cut-off, missing the lake. It was 10 A. M. on the 27th, and furiously hot. The soldiers were out of water, and our boys dividing with them. We followed the trail until the middle of the afternoon, when it turned sharply to the southwest, and as we followed it along its size increased by trails coming into it from the east and southeast. It was now so plain that it could be seen some distance ahead. We lost sight of the Indians before the trail turned to the southwest. When dark-

ness set in we dismounted, but made no pretensions for
camping; not a drop of water in the party. The horses
were not unsaddled, neither were the packs removed.
At break of day we were following the trail; at 9 A. M. it
turned west; at noon it turned northwest; by 3 P. M. it
had turned to the west. They were giving us a dry trail;
they would finish us with thirst. The darky soldiers
commenced dropping out one by one and dismounting;
one fell from his horse, and soon another; a detail was
put behind to goad on the stragglers; the head of the
column marched on, and more soldiers were falling out of
line to lie prostrate. A stronger man was left with each
prostrate one; and so it went on until near five o'clock.

I was ahead on the trail with Hosea; we were both
suffering physical torture. My system rejected tobacco;
the saliva in my throat and mouth had dried up; my
jaws would not stay closed. We looked back; the column
was halted. A negro soldier was coming toward us; we
waited for him to come up. "The captain wishes you to
wait for the command," he said. We dismounted. The
soldier said he was afraid some of the troops would get
ugly; they were complaining bitterly about the thirst
and heat. The command came on, but it was demoralized. The Blue sand-hills were in plain view. We could
see the outlines of them with the scattered shrubbery
along their slopes.

We had been traveling along north of these hills for
several miles. The trail was turning southwest again.
Captain Nolan told me to ask Hosea if he could find the
Laguna Plata. Hosea said he could. Ask him when he
could get back from there by going now. Hosea studied
a moment and counted on his fingers. His answer was,
"midnight." Then Hosea asked what the captain meant.

"Captain Nolan," said Harvey, "I will pick out ten of my strongest men and take all the canteens and start them for Laguna Plata for water. We will follow the course for there to-night, and they, returning with water, will meet us and end this horrible feeling that we all have. When the sun goes down those prostrate men in the rear will revive. I can then get them together. I'll send my best horses with the men and they will bring us water in the night. Otherwise we will all perish. Will you send the guide with my men?"

Harvey was resting in what little shade his horse could furnish him. He called me to him. He said: "What do you think of it?"

I said Hosea told me we could get plenty of water in the sand-hills not over eight miles from here.

Harvey straightened up, and, addressing Nolan, said: "Hosea has never disappointed us. He says that eight miles from here in the sand-hills is plenty of water. We may have to fight the Indians first for it, but we will shoot them away from the water."

"Look," said Nolan, "I have twenty-five men prostrated. Look at your own men, suffering the tortures of the d—d. We are all suffering this minute, and if this keeps up much longer we will each be dethroned of his reason, and be a wandering lot of maniacs until a merciful death relieves us."

Tears were coursing down his cheeks. He was nearly sixty-five years of age, and was ready for the retired list. He had crossed the plains to Utah in 1857, being a sergeant in the First United States Dragoons, that were sent to Salt Lake during the Mormon troubles; had been in twenty-two fights and battles during the Rebellion, and had campaigned on the Indian frontier ever since. He was now too old for such arduous duty. He captured our sympathy at once, Union and Confederate ex-soldiers alike, and for the fraternal, soldierly feeling we gave way, and consented to his plan, thereby doing him and ourselves an injustice, and adding more horrors to our Forlorn Hope.

The soldiers detailed, and were placed in charge of a mulatto sergeant, and they, together with a boy, a citizen of Boston, Mass., who was on a visit to Fort Concho and who had accompanied Nolan, filed out toward the Laguna Plata, taking a northeast course.

In looking over my own party, I missed Samuel Carr and Al. Waite. Upon inquiry I was informed that Carr had become prostrated about a mile back from where we were, and Waite was staying with him until he revived. Each soldier who had been overcome along our trail had been left with a comrade to watch and care for him.

As the sun was sinking, the order to mount came. All those who could or did obey the order started toward Laguna Plata, thus reversing the direction we had traveled for a long way, southwest to northeast. I rode back to Carr and Waite and told them of the plan for the future, and by vigorous fanning and coaxing we managed to get him on his horse, Prince, which he was now riding.

Then we started north toward the command, cutting off the angle. After going a mile or so, Carr feebly dismounted, and said he could go no farther. He was inclined to stoutness, and was the only fleshy man in our party. Waite and I were slim as greyhounds. We waited this time fully an hour before we could get Carr on his horse again. But this time we came up to where the command was, being the last of the stragglers to come in.

We were now all together. Captain Nolan was lying

upon the ground, and said that he was too much exhausted to proceed any farther until he could get some sleep. It was every fellow for himself. We were all lying around on the plain, without any semblance of order, not even a guard out. I was lying on the eastern outskirts of the entire party, where I noticed several packmules pass me. I called out to the soldiers that their pack train was wandering off.

Men were snoring. Some were talking in low tones. Jim Harvey and Dick Wilkinson were nearest to me. My horse was reined up so that he could not get his head to the ground, and I was lying on the coil of the lariat, the end tied around the horse's neck. I fell asleep, and slept soundly until long after midnight, when we were awakened by the firing of guns. First a shot, then pop! pop! pop! and soon fully 100 shots had been fired. The muzzles of the guns were pointed upward.

Everyone was soon awake, and speculation was rife, the prevailing opinion being that Hosea and the soldiers were returning with water from the Laguna. But we waited and waited. Dick Wilkinson was missing, and did not answer our call. It was now the darkest part of the night. Objects could not be distinguished at 100 feet. The sky was somewhat overcast with a film of cloud, and all we could do was to await the coming of day.

When daylight came on, and the water party was nowhere in sight, Nolan told his lieutenant to set his compass for the Double Lakes. Now we knew that they must be at least fifty miles to the southeast. We insisted that if we kept on the northeast course we would all get water that day. He was lying on the ground with a talma over him, when I said, "Yes, captain, follow us now and we will lead you to water."

He threw the talma to one side, and, getting upon his feet, said: "If you men are thinking of going to the Laguna Plata, you are going to your destruction. You don't know where it is, nor how far. If it were within my authority I would prevent your going, only with me."

At that we parted company—we hunters for the Laguna Plata, the soldiers for the Double Lakes. We went northeast, and they east by south ten degrees.

Jim Harvey, Frank Perry, and Williams had lost their horses, as they had wandered off during the previous night, and were nowhere to be seen. Besides this, Dick Wilkerson had wandered away and he could not be seen. Carr had revived and seemed hopeful. We all started, and after going about two miles, Benson said, "Boys, I would like to go and stay with the soldiers." And he turned southeast and started to rejoin them. We resumed our journey, and after going a short distance we halted again. Thanks to the elements, the sun was obscured, and we thought we would not have to contend with the oppressive heat of the two preceding days. At this halt the boys who were afoot requested us to go ahead, and if we found water to return. Pint and quart cups were the only vessels we had to bring the water back in. We bade them good-by, promising to return as soon as possible. We saw Benson reach the Government troops, and on we went, some four miles, without a stop, when the sun burst out with its intense heat, and we were in a deplorable condition. Our pack train with two exceptions, had wandered off in the night.

At this halt Rees said, "Boys, we have our medicine kit on the black mule, and if you will let me have my way about it I will help you all go ahead."

"We will do anything to get rid of this horrible feeling," said Squirrel-eye. At this stage of our suffering our eyes

had sunken back in their sockets; the saliva had dried in
our mouths and throats; we were physically weak, and
rapidly growing weaker.

Rees opened the pack on the black mule and took from
it a quart bottle of high-proof brandy.   He opened the bottle
(we had two of them), cut a piece out of his shirt-sleeve,
saturated the rag with brandy, moistened each man's lips,
and had him inhale it through his nostrils.   It acted like
magic for a short time.   It inspirited us, and, while we
were in this condition, we got over as much ground as possible until the exhausted feeling returned again.   Then
Rees repeated the operation.

At the halt where the brandy was first used the second
bottle was left.   Two gun-wiping sticks were stuck in the
ground on our trail that our four footmen said they would
follow.   A blanket was fastened to the wiping-rods, and
Rees wrote out directions how to use the bottle of brandy,
adding, "For God's sake, boys, don't drink it."   He left
another piece of his shirt-sleeve, tying it and the directions
around the neck of the bottle.   About 12 o'clock we had
used up all the contents of our bottle, and the heat was
more intense than it had been at any time during that summer.   Rees told Waite and me to ride on ahead and signal back when we saw any favorable signs that we were
nearing water.

We told the boys that we would shoot four times in quick
succession if we had good news for them; Al. saying,
"That will be encouraging; then we will go on, get a
drink, water our horses and return to you with the truth
that we have found water and that we know where it is."

This being understood and assented to, we went on.
Our horses, which had been touchy and very spirited animals, would barely raise a trot by our using the quirt pretty

sharply. We kept moving steadily. While our party would make short moves and halt, some would dismount and try to get a little shade from their horses.

About three o'clock in the afternoon, when we were about two miles in advance, I said, "There, Al, are the breaks of the Casa Amarilla, straight ahead of us."

"Yes," he said, "I believe you are right."

Looking back toward our party we saw they had halted and some were yet back of them. Going on a little farther, to satisfy ourselves that we were nearing the Casa Amarilla, we halted again, and looking again we saw three men leave the advance, going nearly east. I unfastened my gun from the scabbard and fired the four shots. We noticed the three men turn toward us, and the others start on. We now rode on a half-mile or more, when Waite said: "John, I have my doubts about that being the Casa country."

CHAPTER XI.

Water At Last.—"Yes, Sah, Take Him, Sah."—Drinking Horse-
blood.—They Had Given Up to Die.—Rees said, "Find Carr."—
He was Lying in the Shade of His Horse.—It was Rees and the
Three Men.—We Ignited Soap-balls.—Twenty Years in Prison.—
We are All Here.—We Gathered Up Some Horses.—Last Great
Slaughter of the Buffalo.—Our Kangaroo Court, Always in Ses-
sion.—Judge ("Wild Bill") Kress On the Bench.

"Yes, Al, we are all right."

Soon we came to where we could see down into the depression where the briny salt lake was in front and two
miles east of the Casa Amarilla proper.

"Well," said Al, "if my tongue was not so thick I'd
whistle and sing a song." Turning his horse to the left he
said, "Let's go this way and strike the upper water-hole."
I said "No." The Casa Amarilla and the upper water-
hole were less than a mile apart, but I was afraid we might
miss the upper one by going too far west, and we parted.
We were then three miles from water. After I had ridden
down from the plateau into the basin and had rounded a
little point ahead, our stone pyramid and flag came into
view on the bluff above the spring.

As I rounded the point my horse worked his ears and
gave vent to a low whinny. He had scented the water,
and he started into a trot, and finally broke into a gallop
of his own accord. He was a headstrong animal, and
when we were near the water-hole, which was about twelve
feet over, I did not have strength enough to stop him. He
surged into the water, groaning as if he were dying. I dismounted in the water to loosen the cinches. He had been

so long without water and was so gaunt, he looked like a wasp. As he got more hollow, from time to time, I would tighten the rear cinch to keep the saddle from chafing his back.

Loosening both cinches entirely, and taking off the bridle, when I had to jerk with what strength I had to get his mouth out of the water, I let him drink until I thought he should have no more at that time; but I had to strike him over the head with the bridle-bits before I could drive him out of and away from the water.

As he turned suddenly the saddle fell off into the water and splashed water up into my face. I think no mortal ever experienced more sudden relief from intense suffering, both in body and mind, than I did at that time. I drank moderately of the water, and bathed my face and hands. The horse came back into the water and drank till he was tight as a drum. Then he went out a little way and began nibbling the grass, what little grass there was, near by, when a negro soldier came out of the draw from the upper water-hole. He had seven canteens full of water. He was one of the party that had started for the Laguna Plata the evening before, and getting lost from the others during the night, his horse had brought him to the upper water-hole, where he arrived about noon that day.

He told me there were two other white men at the water-hole, or big Dripping Spring proper. One got there a little after he did, and the other one had just come. I was quite sure the last one must be Al Waite.

I asked him if he had heard the first one's name?

"Yes; the man who just came called him Dick." So that accounted for Dick Wilkinson.

I said to the darky: "You give me that big U. S. horse; I'll take those canteens and go back on the trail."

He said, "Yes, sah! Take him, sah!" Which I would
have done anyway.

Taking off my belt and pointing to my Creedmoor, I
said, "I'll take your carbine. Give me your belt," which
he did. Then I was immediately off on the back track.

I had barely started when I saw two men approaching
from the salt lake. Turning and meeting them, I found
it was Rees and Foley. They had struck too far east,
and were coming back. They told me to hurry to Louie
Keyes, Cornett and Squirrel-eye. They had given up the
struggle.

I hurried ahead, and about a mile and a half from there
I met John Mathias afoot. I offered him water. He said:
"No, I know where the water is. Go on; hurry to the
other boys; Carr has wandered off. You get to Keyes,
Cornett, and Emery first. They are east of the route,
about two and one-half miles back."

Hurrying on a half-mile, I met the rest, except the
three or four alluded to. I left three canteens of water
with them. They said: "Burn the earth, Cook, to reach
Keyes, Cornett and Squirrel-eye. You will see their
horses, two of them, by going this way," they pointing
out the course.

I did not take time to hear all the truth, but made my
horse fairly fly, and soon I was beside them. They were
lying down, side by side, having been very methodical
about it. They were lying on their backs, facing the
east. They had written their names and had them fastened to their saddles. I dismounted and tied my horse
to the neck-rope of Cornett's horse, which stood there,
a melancholy wreck of what I knew he had been. Each
man had his face covered with a towel.

Charles Emery's horse had been killed and its blood

drank by the three men. They had severed his jugular
vein and used their tin-cup in which to catch the blood.
The dead horse was lying about twenty feet from the men.
I got down upon my knees at their heads and lifted the
towel from Cornett's face. His eyes were closed, apparently in death. Then I opened a canteen of water; saturated one of the towels, and began rubbing their faces
alternately.

Squirrel-eye was in the middle, and was the first to re-
spond. Dried blood was on their lips and mustaches.
Their lower jaws had dropped. Louie's tongue was
swollen and protruding. It was not death. They were
all in a comatose condition. The first murmur came·
from Emery; but it was only a mutter. I opened all
their shirt collars, took off their cartridge-belts, pulled
off two pairs of boots and took off the other one's shoes.
I began to talk loudly to them. I said anything and
everything I thought would arouse them.

Now, let the infidel laugh; but, feeling my utter help-
lessness, I said, "Oh, God, help me to save these men's
lives." I dashed water in their faces and on their chests.
I raised Keyes up to a sitting posture; but his head
dropped to one side, and I began to think he was a
"goner," sure.

Just then Emery raised himself up of his own accord
and said, "Where am I?" I placed Keyes back into a
reclining position, and, holding the canteen to Emery's
mouth, said, "Squirrel-eye, *drink!* there is lots of water;
we must hurry." I talked loudly. At the first swallow
he clutched the canteen with both hands, and would have
drained it of all the water had I allowed him to do so.
His consciousness came to him when I said, "Now, help
me with the other boys."

Just then Rees came to us, and asked: "Did you find Carr?"

I said, "No, Sol.; I've not had time yet."

Just then Cornett arose to his full height and said, "Oh! God, how long is this to last?"

Rees got him to drink some water.

Two of the canteens were nearly exhausted, when Rees said: "John, for God's sake try to find Carr; my own horse is about done up and that Government horse will carry you like the wind." I'll attend to the boys and get them to the water-hole."

Anticipating where Carr was from what Mathias had told me about where he last saw him, I rode west for several miles around the Casa Amarilla.

The plains were wavy or slightly undulating or rolling. I hurried on. After going some three miles I saw to my right, and about one mile west of the upper water-hole, a riderless horse. Having left my glasses on my own saddle, that was all I could make out. I hurried on to the horse, and on near approach I saw that it was "Prince."

Carr was lying on the shady side of him, but the sun was nearly down. I dismounted, threw the rein of the horse I was riding over the saddle-horn on Prince, went around to the side Carr was on, and said to him: "Well, you're making it into camp, I see." I was holding the canteen in my hand. He raised himself up to a sitting position and said, "It's Cook's voice, but I can't see you." I put one hand upon his brow and the canteen to his lips, when he, too, with the first swallow, seized the canteen with both hands.

After a good long drink, I took it from him, he letting go reluctantly. I wet his head, washed his face, trickled some water down his neck, and gave him another drink from the canteen. I saturated Sam's pocket-handker-chief with the little water that remained and moistened Prince's nostrils and lips with it; then said: "Now, Sam, get on your horse and let's go to camp, for there is lots to do."

I helped him to mount and got him to the upper water-hole. To my great surprise there were our pack animals, except the two head we had with us in the morning.

The absence of Wilkinson the night before was now accounted for. He had awakened before the shooting in the night, and, missing the pack-mules and his own horse, he went out away from the main crowd, and, lying flat upon his belly, he skylighted one of the mules moving off toward the Casa Amarilla; and he followed, passed by it looking for more, until he got to the lead of all, ex-cept his own horse, which he could not get up to, nor would his horse stop at his call. Knowing what animal instinct was, and as they were all going the same direction, one after another, he waited until the last one had passed him, when he followed in the rear. That took him to the big Dripping Spring at the Casa Amarilla.

He had killed a large buck antelope, and skinned him shot-pouch fashion. Turning the hide back like a stock-ing, he had tight-laced up both ends, and, filling the hide full of water through the opening of one of the front legs, closed it by tying a rawhide thong around it. He got forty-two quarts of water. While he was filling the hide, Waite went down to where I had struck the water, and finding Mathias, Foley, and the darky soldier there, and the rest of the party except Rees and the three men who had "thrown up the sponge," he explained to them about the pack outfit, and that he and Dick would start imme-diately for the relief of Harvey and those who were with him.

Mathias and the darky went back up to the Dripping Springs, leaving Foley to state matters to the others upon their arrival. It was now dark. Dick and Al. started across the country to find the footmen if possible. I rode down the draw to the Casa water-hole, where the main party had arrived. Getting the three canteens, I started for Rees and the three other men.

Soon it began to thunder in the southwest. The lightning was flashing in the south and west near the horizon. After I had gone some distance, it became quite dark. Fearing I would miss finding the men, I fired the carbine. I soon saw the flash and heard the report of a gun a half-mile or so to my left. Turning that way, I would fire now and again, and get an answer.

It was Rees and the three men, Rees walking and Emery riding Rees's horse. They were all burning with thirst; and soon the four men had drank the contents of the canteens.

The deep rumbling, muttering thunder was now almost continuous. The sky was overcast with heavy black clouds. The vivid, forked lightning was "cavorting" high above the horizon. We necessarily moved very slowly between lightning intervals, on account of the inky darkness.

On top of the Casa bluff, at short intervals, a streak of blaze would go up thirty or forty feet high and fall back to the ground. "Soap-balls," said Squirrel-eye, who had been raised in Texas. And so they were. There was a soap-root growing profusely in all this region, with which the Mexicans washed their clothes. From the top of its stalk grew a round, fuzzy ball about four inches in diameter, which would ignite at the touch of a burning match. They were something like the turpentine balls,

which the boys of my generation used to sport with on
Fourth of July nights.' And this lurid blaze could be seen
for many miles at night.

When we got within speaking distance that, well-known
clarion voice of John Mathias told us with vim, to "follow up the draw." He added: "We've got a coon cook,
and he has a supper ready of antelope, bread and coffee."

Mathias was a man whose countenance had but one
expression. It never changed. He always looked as if
dire misfortune had suddenly overtaken him. Yet withal
he was the most affable, sociable, and humorous man in
our company. He was always turning the sublime to
the ridiculous. But when others were in distress he was
tender-hearted. His help was free, and he was kind and
generous. We had no sooner reached camp when his
solicitation for the welfare of Harvey, Kress, Perry, and
Williams cropped out.

The violent thunder had abated, and the air was perfectly still, when Mathias said: "Now, boys, after you all
eat, let's all string out from here southwest toward where
we left the boys, those in front with the canteens keeping
within speaking distance of one another, and we will
throw up burning soap-balls to signal them in if they are
on the move."

Some, of the men could not eat at all. Those who did,
were not ravenously hungry. It was water, *water*, WATER,
they wanted first. Leaving the darky soldier and Louie
Keyes, whose vitality was at a low ebb, we all filed out on
the yarner, and with two men holding the four corners of a
blanket, to hold soap-balls in, dark though it was we gathered many a one, over a hundred, by shuffling and scuffling
our feet along and around.

All the while we were busily gathering them, one man

would light and toss the blazing ball as high as he could
throw it, and in the light of a blazing ball as it was ascending and descending, we would see others and skip toward
them by this light. We kept from one to as many as five
soap-balls in the air at once. These brightly burning
blazing balls were fine night signals.

Loud thunder and bright lightning could be heard and
seen, then continuous, deep roaring thunder like the sound
of artillery which was not far distant, could be distinctly
heard. Then to the south and southwest we heard a deaf-
ening and I may say an appalling roar that lasted, it seemed,
for at least three minutes. The sound was like the rushing
of a mighty torrent.

When it ceased the stillness of the tomb prevailed for
a while. We all returned to camp, and *to sleep*.

Not a drop of rain fell where we were. But the next
morning when the second relief party went out they found
the earth deluged six miles south of our camp, and rode
through one basin where the water was belly-deep to their
horses. They said the rain strip was two miles wide; and
one mile south of it they found our boys; Waite and Wilkinson had found them early in the morning. They had
traveled on about seven miles after they had found the
bottle of brandy, and they were in earnest when they declared that had it not been for that stimulant they would
have succumbed.

Another thing helped them: they held a bullet in their
mouths, which caused the saliva to flow, which kept the
mouth moist and they did not experience that dry, hot,
hacking sensation in their throats that we did.

But when found they were very weak. Hudson was delirious. On the evening of the 30th of July they arrived
in camp, where we remained three days resting and recu-

perating from this disaster. Benson was the only man of our party not present.

Hosea and the negro soldiers that went with him to Laguna Plata, with the exception of the colored soldier with us, found the lake near morning of the 29th.

At this lake occurred an act on the part of the mulatto sergeant which was a disgrace to manhood, and purchased the sergeant a home in the military prison at Fort Leavenworth, Kansas, for a period of twenty years at hard labor, when he should have been shot, as Mathias said, with all the buffalo-guns on the range. This sergeant refused to go back to the relief of his officers and comrades, and ordered his squad *not to return.* But one did disobey him, and followed Hosea with forty-four canteens full of water, and they struck the back track.

Faithful Hosea returned to where he found the previous night's halt; found that the soldiers had taken one course, we another. He followed the soldiers until he felt assured they would get to the Double Lakes or Laguna Sabinas. He thought they could not miss both, as they were nearly in sight of them then. Hosea turned and crossed that thirty miles of trackless waste to the Casa Amarilla, and found us the morning of the 31st.

The sergeant and his men put back to Fort Concho; and we hunters went east to our old battle-ground at the head of Thompson's cañon, where we found Benson, who had left the soldiers, after traveling half the day of the 29th, and when night came on he lost his horse and had walked the rest of the way, he being ninety-six hours without water. When we came to where he was he was as crazy as a bug. It was three weeks before his mind was thoroughly restored.

Here we found our missing pack-mules. Now we were

all together, not losing a man, after undergoing one of the most horrifying experiences that ever fell to mortals' lot on land. We read of horrors of the sea, where castaways resorted to cannibalism when they became frenzied, where seemingly there was nothing else could be done and live. But here in this great "Lone Star State," with water all around us, was a party of strong men who became demoralized by thirst, which, together with intense heat, will weaken the body and impair the mental faculties far quicker than hunger or any other calamity that can happen to man.

The soldiers first found Laguna Rica, then the Double Lakes, where Captain Lee was encamped at the time; but in covering the vast distance from where they left us they had killed and drank the blood from twenty-two of their horses; and yet five of them died on the route. So Lieutenant Ward told us when he went out from Fort Concho afterward, with a part of his company, and buried the dead.

For twenty miles this route was strewn with carbines, cartridge-belts, blankets, hats, blouses, pants, and cooking utensils, dead horses and mules, so that one object or a number of objects could be seen from one to another.

With those two officers and their colored soldiers was big raw-boned Barney Howard, black as a crow, and as kinky-wooled as his Congo Basin progenitors. He was the true *hero* of the occasion. After his own horse had been sacrificed, he said to the officers and men, "It would take worser dan dis for me to drap." And when Lieutenant Cooper handed him his watch and money that he had with him he asked Barney to give them to his (Cooper's) wife, if he (Barney) got through. Barney tied them up in the silk handkerchief that Mrs. Cooper had monogrammed, and said:

"I'll carry dese for you, sah, till we git to watah, for you isn't gwine to peter out and worry dat pooh little black-eyed woman, is you? No, sah, dat talk am all nonsense."

He threw military discipline aside and told Captain Nolan he ought to be ashamed of himself to set a whining patten (pattern) befo' his men. He would walk around among his weak, discouraged comrades, and tell them of the good things in store for them in the future. I had a long talk with this ebony-colored child of Ham, afterward, at Fort Concho. He was cut out for a regular, and it is but fair to presume that he climbed the San Juan hill, doing his duty in his capacity equally as well as Theodore Roosevelt did in his.

After recuperating, the soldiers went to Concho, and Captain Lee back to Fort Griffin.

What about the Indians?

That is another story, part of which was a revelation to us. They knew where we hunters were from day to day, and through an interpreter at Fort Sill, the next June, I listened to Cuatro Plumas's (Four Feathers) statement. He was born at the Big Springs of the Colorado.

They knew that Quinnie was coming to them. He was born at the south end of Laguna Sabinas, on the Staked Plains. One of the runners met Quinnie at the old camp they were in when they killed Sewall, and they told him where we were. After we had killed and wounded so many of them in March, they said they would never fight the hunters again, in a body. The lesson of the Adobe Walls, and that of the Casa Amarilla, as they called the place where we fought them in March, had taught them to not go up against the long-range guns that the hunters carried;

and that they would just dodge and elude us until we got weary of the chase.

Quinnie knew perfectly well, when he was observed coming straight to us, where we were, soldiers and all. He also knew where the Indians were camped, which was in the Blue sand-hills, not to exceed seven miles from where we finally abandoned the trail. He would never have thought of coming to our camp if the soldiers had not been with us, fearing we would seize him and under penalty of death make him take us to the Indians, which we surely would have done had it not been for Captain Nolan.

Quinnie expected us to follow him when he left our camp at the head of the Colorado. He would accomplish two purposes in coming out of his way some forty miles in all, to reach our camp and then get back again to the Indians: one was, "To show his commission and orders, thus hoping to allay the vengeance of the hunters, and check the movement of the soldiers against their camp;" the other was, "To get us as far south as possible, when he would, under cover of night, turn and hurry to the sand-hills and get the hostile Indians moving for Fort Sill, with us too far away to overtake them."

But we did not follow him. In the end we really did worse. Quinnie was supplied with a pair of army field-glasses from Fort Sill, and from their point of observance in the sand-hills they noted our approach on the 28th; and in the early evening they were all moving east, keeping in the basins of the sand-hills. When they saw our command turn toward the Laguna Plata, following the water party, they halted and camped. They saw as separate the morning of the 29th, and watched us all the forenoon. Then, on the evening of the 29th, they started to run the guantlet between us, and, some of them know-

ing these plains from childhood, they could safely antici-
pate where each party was that night; and keeping a
course as far from us hunters as possible, and crossing
Nolan's trail well in his rear, they got through to the
eastern breaks of the Staked Plains without being seen,
and hurried on to Fort Sill as fast as they could.

They left nearly 200 head of horses and mules in the
sand-hills. They camped one day, the 30th, in the rough
broken country northeast, a little way from the old first
camp, where Freed and his party first fought them. They
left more than one hundred head of stock here in these
breaks. They were so scared and in such a hurry they
were afraid to take time to gather them up. In fact,
they lost more or less stock until they got across Red
river into the Indian Territory.

After leaving the old battle-ground, where we found
Benson, we followed down Thompson's cañon at easy
stages, and when we were near the mouth of the cañon
we ran onto a large surveying party. At sight of us they
fortified in a hurry, the best they could. When we were
within a quarter of a mile of them, we sent a truce ahead,
and soon there were joyful greetings. They saw the Indians during the 30th, and were about to leave for Fort
Griffin, on account of their close proximity, but seeing
the next morning that they were gone and their horses
scattered in every direction, they concluded to remain
close in camp, awaiting developments. And when they
first saw us coming down the valley of the Thompson
Fork of the Brazos, they thought and feared we were
Indians.

Their story of the Indians' scattered horses interested
us considerably. We passed on out into the region where
they were to be found. We went into camp below where

the Indians had stopped over on the 30th, and went to work scouring the country over for horses. The next day we gathered in 136 head. Poor old Keno was there! His back on each side was raw and swollen, the top of his withers was bruised and chafed raw. When John Mathias saw him, and as I was using a lot of words about it, which I refrain from using here, he said: "It just makes a fellow feel like he wanted to scalp the Chairman of the Indian Rights Association."

None of us had ever seen the most of this stock. The big spotted horse belonging to George Williams, that one of the Indian warriors had caught, mounted, and rode through Rath, when the Rath raid was made, was even in worse condition than Keno. Billy Devins's, Freed's, and the two Englishmen's stock were all here, and some belonging to other hunters, who were not members of the Forlorn Hope, were also identified.

That evening we held a council. We looked over the descriptions in the "bills of sale" the ranchmen had given us. It was decided to divide the party, one-half taking the Indians' back trail for the sand-hills, the other half to take the stock, follow the Indians' trail to the north prong of the Salt Fork of the Brazos, thereby hoping to pick up more stock that the Indians might have left behind them, then turn and go to Rath and there await the return of the party that would go back to the sand-hills. Some of us were eager to go back, more from curiosity than otherwise; and we did so.

The next morning we were up by daylight. Breakfast was over and the division of the party about to be made. Harvey said:

"Now, boys, fix it up among yourselves which end of the trail you will take. I won't make the division. Some of you want to go back to the sand-hills. For myself, I am feeling badly. The last few days' work have been hard on me. You boys have readily performed every duty I have imposed upon you ever since we left Rath, and I now hand the responsibility over to you for the future."

"No, no," we told him, one and all of the same voice; "you make the detail. We will stay organized until the stock question is settled. You take one-third of the men then and go to Rath's Store. Take all the extra stock along and wait for us to come in."

He took Carr, Keyes, Cornett, Squirrel-eye, the two Englishmen, the negro soldier, the Boston boy, and poor Benson, whom we had to watch to keep him from wandering off; as he would keep saying, "I must go and find the boys." Had he suffered during his ninety-six hours of thirst?

I was one of the party who went to the sand-hills.

We separated, all three parties leaving camp at once, with "So-long to you," and "So-long to you," calling back to each other by name. "Don't let the Quohadas get those horses again." "Yes, and look out for the pale-face rustlers, too, Harvey." This last was an admonition with a meaning. For the cattle-men along the border had given us the names of a few professional horsethieves.

We were two days going back to the sand-hills. We followed the trail the Indians had made in their flight for Fort Sill. When we got fairly out of the breaks and on top of the "yarner," we met Tonkawa Johnson and his five scouts. From him we learned the condition of Nolan's command. Johnson had been sent out to hunt for that part of Nolan's missing pack train which was finally found at Laguna Rica.

We entered the Blue sand-hills where the Indians left them. After following the trail about seven miles we came to the place where they had lived since Captain Lee captured their camp at Laguna Plata. We passed by horses, mules and ponies for two miles before we came to the camp. We stayed in these sand-hills for three days. We went out to where we had abandoned the trail on the evening of the 28th of July. Seven miles on an air line would have led us to their camp. Twice that distance was the trail we abandoned, the trail leading past their camp on the north some five miles, and looping back again. We could not but admire their strategy. We rounded up in these sand-hills 107 head of stock, and drove them to Rath, where the other boys who had followed the Indian trail to the Brazos had arrived two days before us.

We placed all the stock in one herd, and sent out word in every direction for the hunters to come and get their stock. Rath boarded us at the restaurant until we got our outfits rigged up for the fall and winter hunt. In September we scattered over the range from the South Concho to the Pease river, as secure in our camps as if we were in a quiet and peaceful Quaker neighborhood, so far as Indians were concerned.

The summer of 1877 is on record as being the last of the Comanches in the rôle of raiders and scalpers; and we hunters were justly entitled to credit in winding up the Indian trouble in the great State of Texas, so far as the Kiowas and Comanches were concerned. Those Indians had been a standing menace to the settlement of 90,000 square miles of territory in Texas and New Mexico.

And to-day, 1907, it is a pleasing thought to the few surviving hunters of the old Southwest to know that the entire country of the then vast unsettled region is now dotted over with thousands of peaceful, prosperous homes.

I pulled out of Rath September 21st for the head of North Concho; and that winter hunted along the eastern edge of, and on, the Staked Plains.

The last great slaughter of the buffaloes was during the months of December, 1877, and January, 1878, more than one hundred thousand buffalo-hides being taken by the army of hunters during that fall and winter. That winter and spring many families came onto the range and selected their future homes, and killed buffaloes for hides and meat. More meat was cured that winter than the three previous years all put together.

In the spring of 1877 but few buffalo went north of Red river. The last big band of these fast-diminishing animals that I ever saw was ten miles south of the Mustang Spring, going southwest. They never came north again. And I afterward learned that the remnant of the main herd that were not killed crossed the Rio Grande and took to the hills of Chihuahua in old Mexico. This last view was in February, 1878. During the rest of the time that I was on the range, the hunters could only see a few isolated bands of buffaloes. And if one heard of a herd which contained fifty head he would not only look, but be surprised.

In May the hunters were leaving the range. Some went to the San Juan mines, some to the Black Hills, and some "back to the States," as they would say.

Many picked out one of the many fine locations that he had had an eye on for a year, two years, or three years, as the case might be, and he would settle down to ranching. In a few years, personally I lost track of them. *But in memory, never.*

Speaking of the members who took part in the battle of

March 18th, 1877, and were also members of the Forlorn Hope: I can now look back in my evening of life, with very many pleasant recollections. It was the most democratic body of men imaginable. Different in religious views, politics, financial standing, and in the social scale of life, yet, as the phrase goes, all "common as old boots." There were men with a classical education; some there were who could not read, write, or cipher; but they could name the brands and could tell you the peculiarities of the owners from the Rio Grande to the Red river. One of the Englishmen, as we called the two whose camp was literally destroyed, and who were with us in the Casa Amarilla fight, also a member of the "Forlorn Hope," was not wholly English, for Scotch blood flowed in his veins. He was a poet. He never told the author, but it came to him second-hand, that Harry Burns, the Scotch-Englishman, was a descendant of Bobbie Burns, the famous Scotch poet. His verses composed and published in the Dodge City *Times*, addressed to the "hunters" after the ninety days' scout, and which are reproduced in this book, are timely, and surely will be appreciated by the hunters of those days.

Another hunter, a "Prodigal Son," also composed a few verses when he was leaving western Kansas to hunt in Texas. The words were sung all over the range with as much vim as the old-time "John Brown's Body." It had a very catchy tune, and with the melody from the hunters' voices it was beautiful and soul-inspiring to me. One stanza and the chorus is all that I can now recall of it. It ran thus:

> "I love these wild flowers, in this fair land of ours,
>   I love to hear the wild curlew scream
> On the cliffs of white rock, where the antelope flock,
>   To graze on the herbage so green.

CHORUS.

"O, give me a home, where the buffalo roam,
Where the deer and the antelope play,
Where seldom is heard a discouraging word
And the sky is not cloudy all day.

We were camped at the Casa Amarilla on the Fourth of July. We made a flag from a part of a blue shirt; the red stripes from a red shirt, the white stripes from a flour-sack. We used the tin-foil from around our plug tobacco for stars. Our standard was a tepee-pole. We planted it on top of the pyramid which we made, twelve feet high, from the stones from the old Indian fort. After the flag was hoisted, it floated about twenty-five feet above the ground.

One of the boys said, "It's a little trick, aint it?" Then he added, "But it's got a mighty big meaning."

"Yes," said another; "I fit agin it wunst, but it's sacred now; I love it. It's got a portion of my old red shirt in its folds."

We delivered patriotic orations; declaimed some of Daniel Webster's and Henry Clay's speeches to Congress. We belabored King George in particular, and Great Britain in general, much to the delight of the two Englishmen, whom we had told in advance that "present company was excepted"; but that all Englishmen not present would "catch fits."

We had a code of etiquette, and woe to the man that violated it. There was a kangaroo court always in session, with Judge Kress (Wild Bill) on the bench. Men were even tried for imaginary offenses, and always found "guilty." The sentence was to go out a given number of steps from camp and bring in buffalo-chips to cook with. All those dry hot days there was not the semblance of ill-feeling one toward another. Some had singular peculiarities, but they were all by common consent passed by.

I remained in Texas until the fall of 1879; helped to organize Wheeler county in the Panhandle, it being the first county organized in that part of Texas.   From Texas

ALICE V. COOK.

I went to Chautauqua county, Kansas, and from there to Fort Berthold, in the Dakota Territory; was in the U. S. Indian service, serving as Superintendent of Indian farming; was there during the Sioux Indian Messiah craze, the winter Sitting Bull was killed.

I first saw Sitting Bull, that crafty old Medicine-man, in the winter of 1885, when he came to visit the Mandan, Gros Ventre, and Arickaree Indians. He was then paving the way to get into their good graces in order to get those friendly tribes to violate their peace compact with the Government. While living in Dakota Mrs. Cook was one of the unfortunate victims of the great blizzard of January,

JOHN NELSON CRUMP.

WAYNE SOLOMON REES.

1888. She lay in a snow-drift two nights and one day, over forty hours, and from the effects of this experience, her feet were badly frozen, so much so that she had to undergo a partial amputation of both feet. And when the wounds healed she suffered so with chilblains that I was compelled to take her to the Cascade mountain region of Oregon, where we now reside.

Having no living children of our own, we took to raise,

as best we could, an orphan child of an Confederate ex-soldier. When we took him, he was four years old. He is now (1907) near fourteen years of age, a manly little man. His father had been one of Robert E. Lee's veterans, enlisting in Virginia in 1861, and surrendering at Appomattox in 1865, having been continuously in the service four years, fighting for the principles that *his* conscience told him were right. He has the distinction of being one of the victims of the "Petersburg Mine Explosion." He was thrown many feet into the air, and fell back into the crater unharmed.

And if I am the only Union ex-soldier who has cared as best we could for the baby-boy of one of General Lee's valiant soldiers, I will feel it is a distinction that Mrs. Cook and myself can take great consolation in.

John Crump was the name of the Confederate soldier spoken of. I never changed his son's name, but left it by his father's request—John Nelson Crump. The Crumps were a credit to the State of Virginia.

CHAPTER XII.

A PEN SKETCH OF SOL. REES,

As Taken From the Man's Lips by the Author, Who First
Met Him in the Panhandle of Texas, in 1876.

"I was born in Delaware county, Indiana, on the 21st
day of October, 1847. I enlisted in Co. E., 147th Indiana
Regiment, March 5th, 1865. But as that greatest of
modern wars was near its close, I did not even see the big
end of the last of it. I came to Kansas in 1866, stopping
for a time in the old Delaware Indian Reserve, southwest
of Fort Leavenworth. From among the Delawares I
went out to northwest Kansas, in 1872, and took up a
claim on the Prairie Dog, in Decatur county. I trapped,
and hunted buffalo, until the Indians stole my stock,
when I had to quit hunting long enough to get even, and
a little ahead, of the redskins. In summer-time I would
put in my time improving my homestead; in winter,
hunting and trapping. But when Kansas passed her
drastic "hunting law," concerning the buffalo-hide hunters,
I drifted to the Panhandle of Texas, in 1876 (after taking
in the Philadelphia Centennial); for the next three and
one-half years you have had a pretty good trail of me."

(297)

SOL REES.

To digress for the moment. This Sol. Rees was one of the Government scouts and guides in what is known as the "Dull Knife War" of 1878. Dull Knife was chief of a large band of northern Cheyenne warlike Indians.

Congress had passed an act moving all of the troublesome Indians from the so-called Cheyenne country north to the Indian Territory. Dull Knife and his band were taken to the Indian Territory, to near Fort Reno, on the North Fork of the Canadian river. Totally dissatisfied with the conditions as had been represented to him by the United States commissioners, he asked for, and was granted, a council. Robert Bent, a son of old Col. Bent, was a half-breed southern Cheyenne, and was the interpreter.

After the council was in sitting, Dull Knife arose and cited his wrongs. It has been said no more eloquence has ever come from the lips of an Indian orator. He said in brief: "I am going back to where my children were born; where my father and mother are buried according to Indian rites; where my forefathers followed the chase; where the snow-waters from the mountains run clear toward the white man's sea; yes, where the spreckled trout leaps the swift-running waters. You people have *lied* to us. Here your streams run slow and sluggish; the water is not good; our children sicken and die. My young warriors have been out for nearly two moons, and find no buffalo; you said there were plenty; they find only the skeletons; the white hunters have killed them for their hides. Take us back to the land of our fathers. I am done."

At this, Little Robe, head chief of the southern Cheyennes, knocked him down with a loaded quirt-handle. After regaining his feet, he shook the dust from his blanket, then, folding it around himself, walked out of the council lodge and said: "*I am going;*" and go he did.

Robert Bent said: "Little Robe, you have made a mistake." That same night his band was surrounded at their camp, by what effective troops there were at the fort; but, regardless of that, the band slipped past the cordon, Dull Knife at their lead, and for 800 miles, he whipped, eluded, and out-strategied the U. S. Army, and left a bloody trail of murder and rapine equal in atrocity to any in the annals of Indian warfare.

The author was on Gageby creek, in the Panhandle of Texas, twelve miles from Fort Elliott, sleeping soundly at midnight, when a runner came from Major Bankhead, in command, requesting me to report to him at once. And for two months I was in the saddle, but never north of the Arkansas river. I had lost track of Rees, early in the spring before the outbreak. Nor did I see or hear from him until the spring of 1907, only to find that he too had served as scout and and guide on the Dull Knife raid. I here copy two official documents, now in Reese's possession, given him at that time.

OFFICE ACTING ASST. QUARTERMASTER, U. S. A.,
FORT WALLACE, KANSAS, Nov. 4, 1878.

Sol. Rees, Citizen Scout, has this day presented to me a certificate, given him by Major Mock, Fourth U. S. Cavalry, for thirty-nine days' service as scout and guide, at $5 per day, amounting to one hundred and ninety-five dollars. This certificate I have forwarded to Department Headquarters, asking authority and funds to pay Rees's claim. On a favorable reply and funds being furnished, I will pay the claim.   GEORGE M. LOVE,
1st Lieut. 16th Inf., Acting Asst. Q. M.

OFFICE ACTING ASST. Q. M., U. S. A.,
FORT WALLACE, KANSAS, Nov. 26, 1878.

Mr. Sol. Rees, Slab City, Kan.—SIR: Enclosed please find my check, No. 59, on First National Bank of Leavenworth, Kansas, for $195,

in payment for your services as scout and guide, in October and November, 1878, and for which you signed Receipt Rolls, on your being
discharged. On this coming to hand, please acknowledge receipt.

I am, sir, very respectfully,

Your obedient servant,

GEORGE M. LOVE,

1st Lieut. 16th Inf., Acting A. Q. M.

The author now gives Rees's experiences and his observations as to the part he took in it. This is as he dictated
it to the author:

I was in Kirwin, Kansas, when I heard of the runaways.
It was on the 29th day of September, and anticipating
the route they would follow to the Platte river, on account
of water, I made a night ride, and got home just at daylight. I met settlers the next morning, and they told me
the Indians had camped that night on the Prairie Dog,
nine miles above my home. I saddled up and struck
that way. When I got about five miles, I met a party
of homeseekers, who were bringing in a wounded man toward my place. I went on, and after a while I found the
Indians had gone to the Sappa. I then went to Oberlin,
found the people badly excited, and there I organized a
party.

Poorly armed as they were, I started on the trail. We
went from there to Jake Kieffer's ranch. There the wounded began to come in, and the people that got away
from the Indians. Here we reorganized and I was elected
captain. Then we took the trail of the Indians, and just
as we got up the divide, we saw three Indians rise up out
of a draw,—man, woman, and boy about sixteen years
old. We headed them off to keep them from joining the
main band, and drove them to the timber on the Sappa.
Here we separated into three parties, one to go above,

another below, and the other to scare them out of the brush. The party I was with, when we came to the brush, did not want to go in close. So I saw it was up to me alone. I saw a squaw going up a little divide. I shot twice at her. Then I saw the buck slide down off of a bank and run into the brush, a patch of willows. I got on my horse and rode toward the willows. He rose up and shot at me. I was not more than twenty steps from him. I had been leaning over on the right side of my horse, at the time he shot. I wished to expose as little of my body as possible. I rose up and shot at him. We took shot about for five shots, when in trying to work the cylinder of my revolver, the last cartridge had slipped back, and the cylinder would not work. The warrior had fired his last shot, but I did not know it at the time.

I then went back to a man named Ingalls, and got a Colt's repeating rifle. When I came back to where I had left the Indian, he was gone. He had crossed the Sappa on a drift; and I can't, for the life of me, see how he could have done it. I dismounted and followed over, and found he was soon to be a good Injun. Taking out my knife, he signed to me, "not to scalp him until he was dead," but I had no time to spare; for there was much to do—it seemed to be a busy time of the year. So I took his scalp. I opened his shirt and found four bullet-holes in his chest, that you could cover with the palm of your hand.

After this we started back down the creek, and had gone only a short distance when we met Major Mock, with five companies of the Fourth U. S. Cavalry and two companies of the Nineteenth Infantry. The troops were all angry. Col. Lewis had been killed the day before. Here is where I met our old friend Hi. Bickerdyke. As soon as I met him, he said: "Major, here is my old friend

SOL REES'S FIGHT WITH INDIAN.

Sol. Rees, one of the hottest Indian trailers I ever met. I have been with him in Texas in tight places."

The major said, "Glad to see you, Rees. Will you go with us as scout and guide at $5 per day and rations, until this thing is ended? I understand you are an old northern Kansas buffalo hunter, and know the country well." I said: "Yes, Major, I'll go; but not so much for the five dollars as to have this thing settled, once for all, so that we settlers can develop our homes in peace." We struck the trail on a divide. "Take the lead, Reese, and everyone will follow you," he said. We followed the trail down on the Beaver; and there we got into a mess. We found where the Indians had butchered four men. They had been digging potatoes and had been literally hacked to pieces by the hoes they were using in their work. They were the old-fashioned, heavy "nigger" hoes, as they had been called in slavery days. Evidently, this had been done by squaws and small boys, for all of the moccasin-tracks indicated it. The hogpen had been opened, so that the hogs could eat the bodies. We did not have time to give the unfortunates decent burial, so the major ordered the soldiers to build a strong rail pen around the mutilated bodies, and we passed on rapidly, fearing the devils would do even worse; and the idea now was to crowd them.

From here the trail went up a divide. I said to Hi. Bickerdyke, "You take the left, I'll take the right, and Amos will lead the command up the divide." I had gone about a mile when I saw something moving toward a jut in the draw. I rode fast, and when I got up close instead of going around, as is usual in such cases, I rode straight to the object. It proved to be a white girl about sixteen years old. She was nude, her neck and shoulders

were lacerated with quirt (whip) marks. She was badly
frightened and threw up her hands in an appealing way.
I said: "Poor girl! Have they shot you?"

She answered: "No; but I suffer so with pain and
fright."

She was of foreign origin. It was hard for me to understand her, she talked so brokenly. All the humane
characteristics I ever possessed came to the front, and
I guess I shed tears. The sight of that poor helpless girl
so angered me that I then promised myself that as long
as there was a warpath Indian, I would camp on his trail.
When she saw me approaching her she sat down in the
grass.

I said: "Poor child; what can I do for you? Where
are your people?" She understood me, and said she
wanted something to cover her body. I dismounted,
unsaddled my horse, and tossed her my top saddle-blanket.
I turned my back, and she arose, wrapped the blanket
around her body, and walked toward me and said: "A
string." Turning toward her, I cut about four feet from
the end of my lariat. Unwinding the strands, I tied one
around her waist; then, folding the top of the blanket
over her head and shoulders, I cut holes in under where it
should fit around her neck. I ran one of the strands
through and tied it so as to keep the blanket from falling down over her shoulders. I then got her on behind
me and started for the troops. When I got up on the
divide I was nearly two miles behind the command. It
had halted upon noticing my approach from the rear.
I rode up, and turned the girl over to Major Mock. The
major got George Shoemaker to take her back, in hopes
of finding her people, or some women to care for her.

That night we went on to the Republican river, about

six miles below the forks. The Indians camped about three miles above, on a little stream sometimes called Deer creek. That night Major Mock wanted to know of me if I could find a cowboy who would carry a dispatch to Ogalalla, Nebraska. I told him I would try. I started at once to hunt one, and had gone but a little way until I met Bill Street. I asked him if he could get through to Ogalalla?

He said, "Yes."

"Well, come on to camp." I introduced him to Major Mock, and said: "Here is your man."

The major handed him the dispatch, saying, "Hurry to Ogalalla."

The next morning we went up the river and struck their last night's camp. And for a natural, fortified camp, they surely had it. I believe they expected to be attacked here. They had not been gone long, for there were live coals from the willow-brush fires, which was evidence that we were not far behind them. They struck for the breaks of the North Fork of the Republican. Across the divide, and coming up on the breaks to the north, we could see the Indians, and they us, at the same time. The Indians started to run. Mock started to a creek straight ahead, on the Frenchman's Fork of the Republican, to camp for noon.

I asked, "Major, are you not going to chase those Indians now, and stop these horrible murders of the helpless settlers?"

He said: "No, Rees, the men and horses are worn out, and must have a little rest and food."

We went to the creek, camped, but did not unsaddle. Ate a cold lunch, mounted, and took the trail, which was now easily followed. Packs were dropped; worn-out ponies left on the trail; and many garments carried from settlers' homes. Among others was a wedding dress that had been worn by Annie Pangle, who had been married in my house to a man named Bayliss. I passed on at the head of the command, and saw that Dull Knife and his band were running for their lives.

The famous Amos Chapman and I were now riding together, when we saw a pack ahead of us that looked peculiar. I dismounted to look at it. *It was a live Indian.* Pulling out my six-shooter I would have killed him, but Amos said: "Don't, Sol; here comes the major on a run; let's wait until he comes up." Amos was a good sign-talker, and tried to talk to him; but he was stoical and silent.

I put my 45 to his ear and said: "Ame, it's signs or death." He seemed to realize what would come, and sign-talk he did, a-plenty. He said he was tired out, and could not keep up, and his people had left him, not having time to stop and make a travois to take him along. Having lost so much time here, the Indians got out of sight. When the wagons came up this played-out warrior was loaded onto one, and hauled for two days, when some of the soldiers, who loved their dead Colonel Lewis, sent him to the "happy hunting-grounds" by the bullet route; and Major Mock never did find out who did it.

From where we loaded this warrior the trail was still easily followed.

About dusk the Major rode ahead again, and asked me, "How far is it to Ogalalla?"

I told him, "Six or seven miles northwest."

"Pull for there; for I have just got to have supplies."

We headed that way, and traveled to the South Platte, arriving there in the fore part of the night.

Here we remained until about 2 P. M. next day, waiting for supplies to come from Sidney. Mock thought
that the Indians would pass near Ogalalla. But a tele-
gram reached him from Fort Leavenworth, stating that
Major Thornburg would soon be on the ground, with fresh
troops and horses, and for him to follow Thornburg's trail.
Information having been received by Thornburg that
the Indians had crossed the Union Pacific Railroad, six
miles east of Ogalalla, instead of west of there, as Mock
had supposed they would, having killed a cowboy near
where they crossed. We then followed the military road
to the crossing of the North Platte. Here we found
Thornburg's supply train quicksanded. Here our quartermaster, Lieutenant Wood [whom the author well
knew], broke "red tape." Taking all the supplies we
needed and the best of Thornburg's mules, we moved on
north, and never did see him or his command of fresh
troops.

In moving north we came to a small creek and found
Thornburg's trail; also Dull Knife's trail. We followed
them to the head of the creek. From there Thornburg
turned west.

But we scouts were satisfied that an Indian ruse had
been played. Riding on ahead, north, I struck a trail
where some were afoot. This was evidently the squaw
and pappoose trail. About twenty miles farther the trail
gave out. By twos and fours they scattered like quails,
having agreed on some meeting-place farther on toward
their northern home; the warriors doing the same with
Thornburg, when he, too, found himself without a trail.
He started a dispatch across to Mock; the bearer was
wounded and lost his horse. But we got the dispatch.
The Indians got his horse, leaving his saddle. The dis-

patch was lying about twenty feet from the saddle. It seemed to me the soldier thought the dispatch might be found by some of Mock's scouts. The message called upon Mock to send him some practical scouts, as he had lost the warrior trail.

Mock could not get one of us to go. We all three thought we were pretty fair trailers and knew what Dull Knife was up to. He wanted to make us lose all the time possible, so that he and his band could concentrate many miles away toward the North Star, while we were picking up the broken threads of his trail. And he did it. Amos and Hi. reasoned the case with Mock, and I assented to all the two scouts said. So no trailers went to Thornburg.

Dull Knife and his band were finally surrounded near Fort Robinson, Nebraska; cut their way out; escaped to near Fort Keogh, Montana, where they were recaptured, and finally settled down to farming. Dull Knife died in 1885, at the age of 78 years.

While Mock, Hi., Amos and I were talking about the ruse Dull Knife had played Thornburg, a courier arrived from Fort Sidney, with a dispatch, ordering Mock's command to Sidney on the U. P. R. R. near South Platte. We lay over there a few days, and started back to the Indian Territory, with another band of disarmed northern Cheyennes, whose chief's name I do not now recall. But Dull Knife will forever ring in my ears.

There were about 300 of these Indians, men, women and children. We took a course for Wallace, Kansas. We crossed a trackless, unsettled region at the time; no roads or trails, except, at times, the evidences of the old buffalo trails, until we struck the head of Chief creek, a branch of the Republican. During the night's camp there came a heavy snow-storm; no timber, no brush

or wind-breaks, and nothing but buffalo-chips to cook
with. The next morning the major asked me if I could
take him to timber by noon. I told him I could, but
doubted if his command and wards could make it.

He asked me about the route. "For three miles to the
Republican, it was good; but from there to Dead Willow
over the sand-hills it was the devil's own route."

Arriving at Dead Willow we stayed three or four days,
I forget which. During this time Lieutenant Wood had a
bridge built, and a route laid out for crossing the Arickaree.
Then we went a southeast course to the South Republican,
one day's march.

Next morning Major Mock asked me if I could get a
dispatch to Fort Wallace that day? I told him I could if
I had a good mount. He said, "Take your pick from the
command." I took Harry Coon's mule. The reason for
that was I had noticed him on the entire trip. He was a
careful stepper; never stumbled. Harry never used
spurs or quirt on him. So I started with the message,
leading my own saddle-horse. This message was urgent,
and was addressed to the commanding officer at Fort
Leavenworth. I got to Wallace just at sundown, and
handed the message to the commanding officer at the fort.

He asked, "Where did you leave the command?"

I said, "On the Republican."

He seemed amazed. "Orderly, take this man's stock
to the corral, and see they are well cared for." He invited me to his quarters. The next morning, the poor
faithful mule could not walk out of the corral. I pitied
him; but I had to deliver that message.

I stayed at Wallace during the four days it took the command to arrive. Here I was discharged, at my own request, as I wanted to go home. The officers all said,

"Why not go on to the Indian Territory, as it amounts to $5 a day going and coming."

I said: "No; I told you before, it was not the five dollars a day I was after. It was the protection of settlers, and the love of adventure. This thing of herding Indians with no guns in their hands makes me feel cheap. But Amos and Hi. live down there, and that is all right."

After returning to my home on the Prairie Dog, I remained there, putting on improvements, until the fall of 1880. Now here on this creek, where you just had your swim, is forty-five miles to the Smoky, south, where our old friend Smoky Hill Thompson used to live; and ninety miles north is the Platte, where our leader in the Casa Amarilla battle, Hank Campbell, lived.

I liked this location and decided to keep it as my future home. But, like yourself, I am of a restless disposition. So I rented out my farm and went to New Mexico, and was gone three years. I was in business in Raton.

One day Jim Carson, a son of Kit, came into my place and said: "Mr. Rees, my mother is coming down from Taos to visit some of her Mexican friends. She has heard of you, and would be glad to see you."

You know Raton is the old Willow Springs you used to know before the Santa Fe was built down through Dick Hooten's pass, in the Raton Mountains. Well, just across the arroyo is a little Mexican hamlet, say 300 yards from Raton proper. At the time I speak of, I met the Spanish widow of the famous Kit Carson, the grand old scout, guide, and interpreter. [He was the man who piloted John C. Frémont to the Pacific Coast.] She was one of the best-preserved old ladies I ever saw, sixty-three years of age; she could talk both English and Spanish fluently, and was a perfect sign-talker. After nearly an hour's talk, she said she would like to stay there if she only had money enough to buy her a washtub, board, and some soap. (Poor soul! profligate Jim had squandered her last dollar!) I looked at her, and in silence I asked myself, "What has Kit Carson done for humanity?" I went across the arroyo and bought two washtubs, and boards, a box of soap, and several other articles. I think the bill amounted to twenty-odd dollars. I hired some Mexicans to take them to her. I had a log house with two rooms built for her. When told it was hers, she said: "Oh, I can never earn money enough to pay for this." I said: "Mrs. Carson, Kit has paid for this, through me, for what he has done to open up the West to settlers."

She moved in. In less than two months she had twelve washtubs busy; elderly Mexican women at work; all quiet and orderly; twenty-five cents apiece for washing a common woolen shirt; and every day all were as busy as could be. In three months she sent for me, and insisted that I should tell her how much money I had paid out for her. "I want to pay it and then tell you how grateful I feel toward you." I saw her meaning, for she *was a lady.* I put the price at a sum far under what I knew it had cost me. She opened a chest and handed me the money, saying: "Mr. Rees, only for you, I do not know what I should have done. I shall always feel so grateful."

Did she? Was she?

I was taken down with mountain fever. The second day I became delirious, and finally unconscious.

What did Mother Carson do? She sent four strong Mexicans to my room; came herself with them. A soft mattress was placed on a door for a litter, and I was carried to her house, placed on her own bed, and for five days and nights that angel of mercy, this simple, dignified widow of Kit's, nursed me back to life. And when consciousness was restored, she was lying across the foot of the bed, not having taken off her moccasins during that long vigil.

There is a beauty-spot picked out in the "Kingdom Come" for such noble, high-minded women.

And now, John, I guess I have told you about all there is to say. You see me now far different from what you knew me in the old days. Three years ago I had a stroke of paralysis. That accounts for my indistinct articulation, and you are one of the very few that I would talk to about the past. For, you know, you and I have gone through places that it seems incredible to this day and generation.

Yet *you* know the Story of the Plains, especially the old Southwest as we knew it for years.

———————

Reader, there is something more to be said. I found this man Rees at the town of Jennings, five miles down the Prairie Dog from his ranch. He is now a broken-down man in body, but has ample means. He is to-day less than sixty years of age; but he has been a man of iron. He has dared and done what the average man of to-day would shrink from. But here in the quiet of his home, where he is surrounded with the luxuries of life, he pines for buffalo-meat. He may not have a tablet of fame; yet he has a lovable wife, two interesting daughters, and three boys: John Rees, twenty-one years old, a manly man; his son Ray, a polite little fellow of twelve; and his prattling baby-boy, Wayne Solomon Rees, three years, who will some day emulate his father, and he is to-day the youngest child of an ex-soldier of the grand old Union army. His honest, open countenance, as shown in his picture in this chapter, could not help but excite the admiration of mankind.

The author congratulates himself that he has lived to see the day that he could trot this little tot on his knees, in the quiet of the Rees home, and while dancing him would think of the days that his father did deeds that were noble and courageous.

Reader, go into the quiet of this home, as I have done. Hear the girls play up-to-date music on a fine piano, that an indulgent father has purchased them. Look into John Rees's room and see the trophy of a Comanche warrior's beaded buckskin jacket that his father brought home from Texas ten years before John was born. Look at the painting on the wall of that ever-to-be-mysterious massacre.

The first night that I slept with John Rees and awoke in the morning at chicken-crow, I lay there thinking, while John was peacefully sleeping. My memory carried me back to days when his father, with a fortitude and courage born of heroes, saved the lives of eighteen men from a horrible death. Yet Mr. Seton says we were the dregs of the border towns.

I wish to speak of Georgia Rees: Her father loves the jingle of "Marching Through Georgia," the old war-song from "Atlanta to the Sea;" and as Georgia plays this inspiring song at her father's request, Sol. keeps time to the music, by thumping his cane on the floor. And that is why the author thinks he named the baby-girl Georgia.

CHAPTER XIII.

Mortimer N. Kress ("Wild Bill").—His Heroic Example at the Battle of Casa Amarilla.—His Unselfish Generosity.—His Sublime Fortitude in the Hour of Distress.—He Stood as a Buffer Between Savagery and Civilization—He is Geography Itself.

SOME OF "WILD BILL'S" RECOLLECTIONS.

The author visited him at his home in Nebraska, in the spring of 1907. The noted hunter, Indian fighter, and scout, Sol. Rees, took me from Jennings, Kansas, to the home of Kress, near Hastings, Nebr., generously defraying the expenses. The three of us separated in Texas in the spring of 1878; and after twenty-nine years of neither hearing from nor seeing each other, we held a reunion of the "Forlorn Hope;" and it did my heart good to once more meet this big, generous, warm-hearted plainsman of the old days. As I looked in the face of the man who stood as a buffer between the settlers and wild Indians on the frontier of Nebraska and the western border of Texas, my thoughts went back to two particular incidents of the many thrilling ones I had passed through in company with him.

The first was at the hunters' fight with the Indians on the 18th of March, 1877, already described. All through that fierce fight, he kept a level head and used a dangerous gun. He tore away the mask and showed the real mettle and fiber of his composition. When there would be a lull in the fight, or a change of base was made, Kress kept those within his hearing livened up by his dry humor and seemingly total indifference to his surroundings.

Then again on the 27th, 28th and 29th of July, already alluded to, he divided up a six-pound powder-can of water

MORTIMER N. KRESS.
(Wild Bill.)

as generously as though a river were flowing near by; and
men of his type suffered and moved on. How thankful
I felt while at his home, so beautifully located on the
banks of the sparkling waters of the Little Blue, to see my
comrade living in a manor-house, his cribs and granaries
groaning with the 1906 harvest, and surrounded by a
community that fairly pay him reverence. For they
know enough of his past life and the sacrifices he made,
to help make it possible for his neighbors to have the
peaceful, happy homes that surround this once "Wild
Bill." In the country where he resides he was the first
settler on the Little Blue, having homesteaded in 1869.
He has identified himself with that particular region for
thirty-nine years; and has seen the passing of the overland stage line, the Indian, and the buffalo.

And he is far better equipped to write "The Border and
the Buffalo," than myself. He is a native of Pennsylvania; soldiered four years during the Rebellion, in the
First Pennsylvania Cavalry. I was closely identified with
him from 1875 to 1878, in Texas, in a common cause,
viz., "The destruction of the buffalo, and settling the wild
Indian question," which had the approval of all frontier
army officers, regardless of the fact that Ernest Thompson Seton said "the hunters were the dregs of the border
towns."

While talking with Kress at his home in regard to his
experience on the 29th and 30th of July, 1877, when we
became demoralized for want of water, I learned that
he and Jim Harvey, our citizen captain, were in very
poor health when we left the Double Lakes on the 27th.
Here is his own statement:

"I dissent from your version of Captain Nolan setting
his compass for the Double Lakes. That is what he talked

ALENE KRESS.

of; but he tried to go northeast. I had quite a talk with
Lieutenant Cooper that morning. Their bugler had been
across there the summer before. There were four wagons
in the outfit; and that bugler convinced Cooper and Nolan
that he could strike the trail and follow it to the Casa
Amarilla, Yellow House Springs. I told the lieutenant it
would be impossible, as the new grass had grown since
then and the best of trailers would fail to find it. But
they started north of northeast, while the lieutenant and
I stood talking. I soon drew his attention to the bugler
circling to the east, and remarked that 'he could not follow any course; that his officers should pay no attention
to him, but strike a course of their own.' And I added:
'As for me, I am going northeast.' While we were yet
talking, the command was going due east. The lieutenant
remarked that they were 'like a lot of sheep without a
leader or herder.' During this time my horse started off
toward the troops, and I walked four miles before I overtook him. Benson caught him for me, as he had left you
boys and gone to the soldiers. By this time the soldiers
were going southeast. I tried to get Benson to go with
me toward the Casa Amarilla, but he said he was going
east. Poor fellow! He had a worse time than any of
us.

"I started back, cutting off the angle. When I met
Jim Harvey, about four miles from where I left Benson, he
told me that Perry and George Williams were back near
the place where we dry-camped the night before, and he
could not get them to walk. He asked me to go back with
him and we would try to get them through in the evening. So back we went. I led my horse. Harvey, Perry,
and George had each lost his horse during the night. We
made a shade for the boys by digging holes in the ground

with our butcher-knives, setting the stock of each big-fifty in the holes, then guying the muzzles with my lariat. We then put blankets on top and had a good shade for them. I think it was now near noon, and very hot.

"After a while George thought he could travel. So he and Harvey started on. I tried to get Perry on my horse, but he was too much played out to try to help himself. Great beads of cold sweat dropped from my brow while I was trying to lift him onto my horse. After Harvey and George had gone about a mile, George toppled over. Harvey went on, and met two negro soldiers, who were returning from the Laguna Plata with water. They gave Harvey one full canteen, rode on, and gave George one; then came onto Perry and me. The soldiers, who had several canteens, divided with us.

"About 3 P. M. we were all four together, the soldiers having passed on seeking their command. As the shades of night came on, we dropped to sleep. But it was a troubled one. Thirst ever haunted us. It was *thirst*, water, thirst and water, until it was all gone, and still we were all in a horrible condition. That same night along toward morning it rained some, where we were, but the rain was heavier north and east of us. We spread out the blanket and caught a few sips of water.

"At daylight I started on to look for water. I could hear a great roaring to the north, while it was sprinkling where we were. I went afoot, hoping to find a depression or lagoon containing water. I went much farther than I thought, or had intended to go, and was on the point of turning back, when I saw a lagoon with water in it about two hundred yards from me. As I started toward it I looked. While looking to the east a long way off I saw two men on horseback. I fired my big-fifty gun, and at

the same time, walked backward and forward. I fired
three shots before attracting their attention. I saw them
stop, then start toward me. When they came up it was
Dick Wilkinson and Al. Waite. They said: 'We could
not hear your gun, but saw the smoke, we are truly glad
to see you alive. How and where are Harvey and the
other boys? You and Harvey concerned us the most, as
you were both very sick men when we left the Double
Lakes.'

"I told them the others were O. K. They both dismounted, and we all went down to the lagoon. They
handed me a quart cup to drink from, and I drank a-plenty.
The boys emptied the water out of the green antelope-
hide they had been carrying all night, and refilled it with
rain-water, and we started back to where the other three
men were. We had not proceeded far when I said: 'Dick,
ride on, and we will stay here. There is no use of us all
going over the ground twice.' So on he went. Soon a
shot was fired by the boys, who had become uneasy about
me. Dick heard it, and had no trouble in riding to
them.

"When they got back to the lagoon and had quenched
their thirst, it commenced to rain, and there was quite a
shower. Perry began grumbling about getting so wet.
This exasperated me so much that, weak as I was, I threw
him into the lagoon. We made some coffee here, and ate
some bread and antelope-meat which the relief boys had
brought out. Then we started on. I told Perry to ride
my horse, and Jim Harvey and I walked along together.
As darkness was approaching we were nearing the Casa
Amarilla, when Perry, who was always in the rear, dismounted, and my horse wandered away from him, and I

never heard of him or the saddle again. But Perry did get to camp. Now, Cook, you know the rest."

Yes, the author feels that he knows something of the entire proceedings of the ninety days we were in that sun-baked region. And I then felt I was in the company of a brave man.

Reader, he is to-day a living example of human fortitude. Chivalrous, charitable, jovial, kind and considerate. He was geography itself, having roamed over the country from the Big Horn to southern Texas, and from the Missouri river to the Rocky Mountains.

The American Desert, as it was marked on the old maps, faded away and became the homes of multiplied thousands under his personal observation. Perhaps no man has seen a greater advance of civilization, in the same length of time, than this old plainsman, whose picture, together with his daughter Alene, will be found in this chapter.

BILL KRESS'S YEARNINGS FOR THE BUFFALO RANGE.

1. It comes to me often in silence,
    When the firelight glimmers low,
  And the black, uncertain shadows
    Seem wraiths of long ago.
  Always with a throb of heart-ache,
    That thrills each pulsive vein,
  Comes that old, unquiet longing,
    For the "Buffalo Range" again.

2. I am sick of the din of cities,
    And the faces cold and strange,
  I feel the warmth and welcome
    Where my yearning fancies range
  Back to the old border homestead.
    With an aching sense of pain,
  I dream of that old chasing
    On the Buffalo Range again.

3. Far out in the distant shadows
    Is the buffalo crash and din,
  And, slowly the cloudy shadows
    Come drifting, drifting in;
  Sobbing the night-wind murmurs
    To the splash of the Texas rain;
  Come back to me the memories
    Of the Buffalo Hunt again.

4. To me those memories, "thus Muse,"
    That never may die away.
  It seems the hands of angels,
    On a mystic harp at play,
  Have touched with a yearning sadness
    On a beautiful, broken strain,
  To which is my fond heart yearning
    For the Buffalo Chase again.

CHAPTER XIV.

M. V. DAILY,

SOLDIER, INDIAN FIGHTER, BUFFALO-HUNTER, AND HOMESTEADER.

His picture shows the loss of his trigger finger; done by Missouri bushwhackers. Yet he trained the middle finger to pull trigger, and told the author, in 1907, that he could shoot just as well as ever.

When the wild plains Indians, armed with lances, bows and arrows, attacked a stage-coach, in 1865, on the Arkansas river, this man Daily was driving the six mules drawing the coach, which had sixty arrows imbedded in it; and a lance that was thrust at him by a big Kiowa, went between his right arm and body, passing through into the coach. He got his coach into Larned, and himself unhurt.

He homesteaded in Thomas county, Kansas; hunted buffalo; built sod houses; broke prairie; went through the drought era; saw the country nearly depopulated on account of successive failures of crops; witnessed the change in climatic conditions; the hot winds abate; the coming of rainfall; and the return of starved-out settlers, bringing with them people and capital. And to-day the country is well settled with a happy, prosperous people.

MART DALEY.

MISCELLANEOUS STORIES

OF

BUFFALO LAND.

MISCELLANOUS STORIES.

STAMPEDE OF THE WHEEL-OXEN.

The month of February, 1875, when I was in the employ of Charles Hart, skinning buffaloes, I had an experience which was both amusing and embarrassing.

As we were *en route* down from the Panhandle of Texas to the Brazos hunting-grounds, we passed by an abandoned Government wagon. It was on a sandy stretch of ground between South Pease river and a prong of the Salt Fork of the Brazos. After we had arrived where we did our principal hunting that winter and spring, Hadley, the freighter (he who afterwards proved to be a disappointment) said to me one evening that he could skin as many buffalo as I could, and that if I would take his yoke of wheel-oxen, go back and bring in that wagon we had seen on our way down, he would skin the buffaloes in my stead, and have the number of hides accredited to me. I told him I would sleep over the proposition. I went to bed, and reasoned the matter out thus:

That it was not over fifteen miles back to where the wagon was. It had a good tongue in it. It stood up on four good wheels. When we passed it it looked as if it had been in that one place as much as a year. I could make the round trip in two days. Those oxen were large, very strong, in good flesh, well broken, and perfectly gentle. In view of all the facts, I decided to make the trip. Accordingly, the next morning I told Hadley to yoke up his oxen, give me a log-chain and a box of Frazer's axle-grease, and I would make the trip; would start as soon as breakfast was over.

I took three blankets and a wagon-sheet and folded them soldier-fashion, and placed a hatchet and frying-pan on the fold; also took a bag of salt, some ground coffee, about four pounds of bacon, three pones of bread, baked in a Dutch oven, a tin cup, a few extra cartridges; rolled the whole outfit up in the blankets, laid this roll on top of the yoke between the bows, wrapped the chain around the bundle, yoke and all; then with a lariat securely bound everything fast, tied on a coffee-pot, and was off to bring in that abandoned wagon.

Now there was not a settler's home within eighty miles of the camp I just left, except what was known as the Mathews Ranch, on California creek, sixty miles south-east of our camp. The morning being quite chilly, I wore a heavy short coat. I was leaving camp just as the sun appeared above the horizon.

As the early forenoon wore away, it became quite warm. I stopped the oxen, took off my coat, and fastened it to the pack on the yoke. Starting again, I walked behind the patient, plodding old oxen for an hour or more, when we approached some breaks. At this time I judged I was much more than half the distance from camp to where I was going. Presently the oxen raised their heads, sniffing the air; they turned a little to the left and increased their speed. I knew at once they had winded water. I followed after them, but upon going a few rods farther the oxen broke into a trot, and about the time they did so we were on the brink of a downward slope, and close to a large pool of water, just west of us, with a bald low butte on the west side of the water. As the oxen trotted faster, I decreased my gait to a slow walk. I saw the oxen rush into the water, belly-deep, stop, and commence drinking. I was nearly 200 yards behind them. My cartridge-belt was chafing my hips. I stopped to buckle the belt another hole tighter, when all at once about 100 buffaloes came thundering down the slope from the northeast, in a mad rush for the water. Seemingly I was not noticed at all by them, but before they got fairly into the water the old "whoa-haws" (as the Indians called oxen) bolted and whirled to the southwest,—and away they went, out of the water, up the steep slope which joined onto the butte jutting down to the water. It seemed that at the same instant the oxen stampeded, the buffalo whirled around towards a northwest direction; and off they went, up the slope, on the north end of the square bluff butte, but not until I had noticed that the velocity of motion of the rear of the herd, by their sudden impact, had knocked down several of their number at the edge of the water. I stood looking at this spectacular scene in amused wonderment. It all occurred so suddenly that I remember laughing outright.

But the fun was gone almost as soon as oxen and buffaloes. I hurried to the top of the slope, up which the oxen ran, and saw they were fully three-quarters of a mile away, still running, and headed toward a band of buffaloes that were feeding about a mile beyond them. I followed the oxen, and soon got into a depression of the ground where I could see out but a short distance. When I came out upon higher ground, I saw the oxen and three separate small herds of buffalo all running west,—by which time the oxen were fully two miles ahead of me.

I slowed down to a moderately good walking gait, and set in for a siege. I was very thirsty, and hungry, too.

To my left about one-fourth mile were some stunted brush and two cottonwood trees, in the head of a draw that put into the creek our camp was on. I went to this in hopes of finding water. Upon arriving there I found a little seepage spring. Using my hands, I dug the mud and trash all out until I had a hole some eight or ten inches deep and a foot in diameter. I then sat down with my back against one of the cottonwood trees and rested a few moments. When I saw the water-hole was full of water, I took a good long draught at it, such as it was, and started on after the oxen.

Wanting a chew of tobacco, it suddenly occurred to me that that hunter's luxury was in one of my coat pockets. I kept on west, heading for a hill in the direction the oxen had gone. When I reached the top of the hill the oxen were nowhere in sight. Here I had a good view of the country in general for several miles around. But there were many dips, spurs and ravines. I could neither see into nor behind them. I sat down to rest and range the country over with my eyes, hoping to catch a glimpse of the old oxen. I remained there until the sun was low.

Just southeast of this hill was the extreme head of the creek our camp was on, and its course was to the southeast, and, as I judged, about ten miles down. About three miles down the stream was quite a clump of cottonwood trees.

My thoughts were now to look for the oxen's trail, and judging from where I then was and where I had last seen the "whoa-haws," I thought I could go to near the place. I then started back that way, and after going a mile and a half or thereabouts, I commenced to describe a large circle, intently looking for the trail. But upon coming around to the starting-point I failed to find any sign of a trail.

By this time the sun was setting. Then I thought, "Down the creek our camp is on I will go." Accordingly, I started to the creek in a southeasterly direction from where I then was. I came to the creek almost a mile above the clump of cottonwoods before mentioned. It was then as dark as it would get, that beautiful February night. The sky was as clear as a bell, and the moon had just fulled. On my near approach to the trees I could hear the last quiet "quit" and flutter of wild turkeys settling themselves for the night's roost. Cautiously slipping up, with the roost between myself and the moon, I lay down and peered up at trees full of wild turkeys. The evening was calm and still. After watching them some little time I rose up and walked under some of the trees they were roosting upon. I could and would have shot one and broiled it, only for the reason that we had tried one in the very camp on this same creek that my companions were now camped upon, a few miles below. But that turkey was so bitter from eating china-berries that it was unpalatable; and I supposed that all turkeys were alike in that region. I disturbed them as I passed under the trees, for they started the alarm, and kept up that excited "quit! quit! quit!" uttering it more rapidly until it was answered back from one end of the roost to the other.

I passed on down the creek about a mile below the roost, on my way to camp and companions, whom I left the morning before, and was now pretty tired and hungry, and feeling very cheap to be compelled to go back and report that I did not find the wagon but lost the yoke of oxen. Suddenly I heard a noise to my right between myself and the creek. Upon stooping down I saw five buffaloes, not more than seventy-five yards from me. Three were lying down, the other two were standing, one just behind the other. The rear-most one was the smaller of the two. I sat flat upon the ground, pointed the gun at the hind one, and tried to draw a bead. But, bright as the night was, there was no accuracy. I would raise and lower the gun, and finally I fired. At this time I was west of them. They all broke and ran east down the creek. I rose up and pointed the gun in the direction they were going, and fired again. I then trotted on after them some 100 yards, stooped down and skylighted them, and saw, off to the right of the others and in their rear, that one had halted. I lay down flat, and soon the buffalo started to move off, but after reeling and staggering for a few rods it fell over; and then I was sure I had given it a mortal shot. Waiting some minutes, I crawled up close, with the carcass between the moon and myself, when I observed it was dead.

It must have been between 8 and 9 o'clock P. M. by this time. Now, I thought, I have good meat and will have a roast. So, laying my Sharp's 44 on the short buffalo-grass and taking my butcher-knife from the scabbard on the cartridge-belt, I cut out the hump that lay upper-most, and started for the creek. After coming to the stream proper, which stood in shallow pools, I followed down some distance and came to some stunted cotton-woods and hackberry. Here, too, was a wild-turkey roost. I stalked boldly along and came to a fallen dead cottonwood, laid the buffalo hump on the small log, and proceeded to build a fire. All the matches I left camp with were in a match-box in my inside coat pocket with the oxen. But I had a gun. Taking the bullet out of a shell with my teeth, I emptied all but a little of the powder out of the shell, and after cutting out a piece of my cotton handkerchief I proceeded to gather dry tinder from the lower side of the log. Then, after getting some dry twigs and putting all in shape of a rat's nest against the butt end of the log on the ground, I held the muzzle of the gun close to the cotton rag that lay in this tinder nest, and fired the charge. I got down on my knees, and soon I had fanned the ignited cotton into a blaze, and in a short time I had a fine fire to cook my buffalo-steak by.

As I approached the place I had waked up the turkeys, and when I began breaking the twigs and dead limbs they flew in every direction. They did all of their noisy "quit, quit, quit," and sputtering, before they flew, but after they left their perches all one could hear was the flapping of their wings. Then all was silence so far as the turkeys were concerned.

I now sharpened some long green sticks, and slicing the meat across the grain, I took those long slices and impaled them on the sticks, as one would take up long stitches, Then pushing the other end of the stick into the ground at an angle of about 45 degrees, close to the heat of the fire, I let the meat broil. When the main fire burned down, I gathered the hot embers in little heaps and placed slices of meat upon them to broil also; and had I been fortunate enough to have a little salt, 'twould have been a feast for a congressman,—yea, a President. As it was, the rich juicy broil and roast were simply delicious, very palatable and strengthening.

After eating I lay down and slept soundly at first, but *froze out* as the common expression is sometimes used. Then I got up and started on down the creek. I had not gone over a mile, until in front of me and on my left I noticed a peculiar-looking object. Lying down to sky-light it, to my great surprise and delight I saw it was the two old work-oxen. They were as innocent, docile and contented as if they were in some barnyard in eastern Kansas instead of sly old runaways. As I walked up to them they arose and stretched themselves just as if they had had an all-night's rest. They had turned in towards this creek east of the circle I had made the evening before, and I had walked over their trail the day before when going west towards the hill spoken of while I was going from where I scooped the mud out of the seepy spring. All of which accounts for my not finding them the previous day. Their animal instinct taught them where our camp was, and after getting over their stampede fright and terror they calmed down and turned for camp. And when in the early morning I accidentally ran across them, my surprise was great. I first untied my coat and put it on, and took a chew of tobacco. The pack on the yoke was yet taut and safe—thanks to my little experience in learning both the diamond and Texas hitch in the mountains of New Mexico. The only thing missing was the coffee-pot. It had been tied with a whang string to the outside of the pack, and had come loose and lost off somewhere.

I drove the oxen down to the creek, where there was a china-wood grove, unpacked my outfit, tied one end of the lariat around the near ox's horns, and snubbed them up to a china-wood tree. I then proceeded to build a fire and cook breakfast. By this time it was broad daylight. Unrolling my pack, I took out the bacon, sliced off some, took the frying-pan, went down to the bank of the creek to a water pool, scooped the pan full of water, came back to camp, and after filling the tin cup I put the slices of bacon in the pan and placed it on the fire to parboil. I now went to the water again and washed my face and hands thoroughly. When the bacon was parboiled and fried,

I split open one of the cakes of bread laid the slices of meat on one half and poured the meat-fryings on the other. Then, heating the frying-pan very hot, I poured the cold water from the tin cup into the pan, and rinced it out. Then filling the pan again with water from the pool, I soon had me some good strong coffee.

After eating my breakfast, I lay down a while on my bedding, and by the time the sun was an hour high was again on my way after the abandoned wagon. Looking down the creek our camp was on, after I had left the creek, and getting on a rise in the land, I could see very plainly a gypsum bluff near our camp, and not more than three miles down the creek. I now reasoned that from where I was it was twelve or fourteen miles to the wagon, and I would have to take a little east by north course, which I now did, and traveled until the sun had passed the meridian. When I finally came in sight of the wagon, about two miles off to the northwest of the way I was then going, there was a bunch of china-wood, straight north, and some water-holes by them, where we had nooned the day we passed the lone wagon. To this spot I went. Now I was little less than half a mile from the wagon. I took off the pack from the yoke, unyoked the oxen, watered them, lariatted the near ox near by, and got some dinner. I had killed a cottontail rabbit about the middle of the forenoon. This I stewed in the frying-pan, with some thin slices of bacon added.

After dinner I rested for an hour or more, then yoked up the oxen, and drove them out to bring the wagon to this place for the night. After getting there and hitching onto the wagon I found it hard to budge. The wheels were nearly all set. They were gummed. But I geed and hawed until I finally got all the wheels to rolling, and got back to my temporary camp all right. I stopped the wagon on solid ground; then with the hatchet I tapped the taps until I got them loose, and by jumping the wheels I greased the wagon. That night I slept in the wagon-box with one blanket and part of the wagon-sheet under me and the other two blankets and half the wagon-sheet over me, using my coat for a pillow. And there alone in that wild-game land I felt perfectly secure, for as yet we gave no thought to the Indians.

The next morning I made me a wagon-seat of china-wood poles, placed all my bedding upon it for a cushion, and that same evening I had rejoined my companions, with the wagon pulled in at last by my runaway oxen.

FAVORITE HUNTING-GROUNDS.

Many hunters had their favorite hunting-grounds when the killing was at its height; during the years 1876–7. Frequently, when several outfits would chance to meet at some regular camping-ground *en route* to and from the great game park, they would discuss the variety and quantity of game at such-and-such places. But what I saw in what are now Howard and Mitchell counties, in Texas, will ever be indelibly impressed upon my mind.

It was on the Red Fork of the Colorado and its tributaries. The time was the fall and early winter of 1877. For two months a man named Cox and myself hunted together. I did the killing, and roamed around a good deal on horseback. The first month the buffalo were scattering, and not very plentiful, the first three weeks; but during all this time wild turkeys were so numerous that no attention was paid to them at all. Bear were plentiful. Deer were in bands of from two to fifty. Here were the musk hog, beaver, otter, mink, polecat, coyote, and prairie wolves. Panther were very numerous, and one day I met a hunter with what he called a mountain lion hide. He had killed the animal early that morning in some rough breaks on the north side of the Red Fork. I called it a cougar-hide; and if there is any difference between the two, I never could distinguish it. This hunter told me he saw a large buck antelope kill a rattlesnake that morning. Said he watched the unequal fight from a distance of 150 yards.

He asked me if I had been at the Hackberry holes. I told him no.

"Well," he said, "you go there, and forever afterwards you can tell fish stories."

He told me where to find them after he had described the place to me; on that same day I rode to these holes. They were a wonderful sight—one link after another, like a chain of long, oblong, clear water-holes. Some were thirty feet in depth, as I learned afterwards.

I followed these holes up to the Divide between the Red Fork and North Concho Divide, and there near the summit were the famous Hackberry Springs. They boldly and strongly broke out of the hillside, and rushed down into the flat towards the Colorado river. It was clear cold water, and seemed to me to be non-mineralized. I was charmed with the spot, and wanted the satisfaction and pleasure of once camping upon the Hackberry.

I went back down the stream, passing by some five or six of the deep-blue oblong water-holes, and noticed that every one of them fairly teemed with fish. They were mostly the blue, forked-tail channel catfish.

I hurried to camp, some seven miles away and told a "fish story." Cox had an Irish Catholic brother-in-law with him in camp, who said: "Good! To-morrow is Friday. Let us pull for there and fish and feast."

Early the next morning we were on the route for that place. We reached our destination about 9 A. M., pitched our camp among some chittim-wood trees, and went to fishing,—each fellow fishing from a different water-hole. We used the liver from a large fat deer we had killed on our way to the fishing-grounds. I did not have a timepiece, but I don't think I had fished to exceed ten minutes when I quit and started for camp, about 200 yards away. I had caught five catfish. The smallest weighed 2½ pounds and the largest one 9 pounds.

I dressed the catch and was building the camp-fire, when
Cox came in with seven fish ranging from 1½ to 12 pounds
each. Soon Dennis Ryan came in with four of a nearly
uniform size, weighing at the top notch, all four of them,
24 pounds.

We camped here several days. On the third day after
coming to this camp I had ridden west some two miles
and sighted a band of buffalo, out of which I killed twelve,
—all good robe hides.

On coming into camp I observed the wagon and team
gone. My first thought was that Cox and Ryan had heard
my shooting, hitched up, and gone out to skin the buffaloes they thought I had killed. I saw the bedding all
rolled up and the ammunition-box on top of it, and a piece
of paper fastened to the box. Upon looking closely I
saw it was a note from Cox saying:

"We cilled threa barr. One old shee and two cubs
comin yearlins we gone arter the mete and hides don't be
frade.—J. Cox."

I got me some dinner. Took the label off a baking-
powder can and wrote on the blank side of it:

"Killed twelve buffaloes. Gone to skin them. Come
a due west course."

This note I attached to a fishing-pole and fastened the
pole to the ammunition-box, and struck out for my killing. I had skinned nine of the carcasses; the sun was
low, and I was nearly four miles from camp, when a man
rode up to me and notified me that I was on his range.

I asked him where his camp was.

He said, "At Agua Grande" (the big springs of the
Colorado).

I then told him that my camp was on Hackberry.
"Now," said I, "I have been to the Big Springs and you

are fully twelve miles from your camp. I am about three and a half or four miles from mine. It doesn't make any difference how long each of us has been encamped at each place; these buffaloes are nearer my camp than yours. Besides, I got to them first.''

Then I asked him if that was satisfactory. He was yet on his horse, about twenty feet from me. He ignored my question, but asked me who I was and where I came from. I told him my name and how long I had been on the Range. That I came from the Staked Plains trouble of the summer before to Fort Concho with Captain Nolan, to serve as a witness to Capt. Nolan's report to the War Department.

The man said, "Hold on! Hold on! That's enough. So you are one of the buffalo-hunters that were after the Injuns? Now, pardner, you can have the whole country. Kill 'em right in my own camp if you want to.''

He then dismounted and helped me skin the other three, and then went to camp with me and stayed all night. Cox and Ryan were preparing the supper when we came in sight of the camp-fire, for it had now grown dark.

This visitor's home was in eastern Tom Green county, and he was enthusiastic in praising the northern hunters who had come down on the Southern Range and "fit" (as he expressed it) the Indians. He declared that now the Indians were out of the way and the buffalo about gone the country would soon settle up. So General Sheridan was right! The hunters had actually made this possible. This visitor's name was Parker. He told us that a few days before a man in a camp at the Soda Springs had cut an artery in his left arm and would have bled to death, only he managed to tie a strong rawhide string around the arm above the wound, and by using the steel that he sharpened the knife with made a torniquet and stopped the flow of the blood. The man, he said, was alone, five miles from camp, skinning buffalo, and was afoot. After the accident he started for camp, and lost his way. When darkness came on he kept wandering around over the prairie and in the breaks until nearly exhausted, when he sat down on the edge of a worn buffalo-trail, and had been sitting there but a short time when he heard a noise, and, peering through the dim starlight, he saw three buffaloes coming down the trail he was sitting in. He pointed his gun in their direction and fired, and by accident killed an old stub-horned bull. The other two bolted, and ran as fast as they could. Some two or three minutes after he had fired at the buffalo he heard a big fifty boom out plainly and distinctly to the eastward, not far off from him. Thinking it to be an answer to a distress signal, he fired his gun in midair, and heard the ever-welcome, "Youpie way ho!" He answered back, and soon in the semi-darkness he was piloted into his own camp.

And this is just simply another of the many remarkable incidents that happened on the Range during the passing of the buffalo.

THE UNSEEN TRAGEDY.

The unseen tragedy occurred near the North Concho, where two brothers were encamped during the last winter of the big slaughter. The surviving brother's story was·

"We were sitting in our camp, loading ammunition. It was about 10 A. M. when my brother said:

"'There are two old stub-horned bulls going up the ravine that we found the Indian skeleton in. I'll take my gun and head them off at the top of the Divide, and kill them.'

"He cut across, trotting along afoot, about three-quarters of a mile, to intercept them.

"From camp I could not see the place where the report of the gun came from. I first heard one shot, then a short interval, then two shots in as quick succession as could be fired from a Sharp's lever gun. Then all was quiet. My brother not returning, after nearly an hour had elapsed I thought he must have killed both animals and was skinning them; hence I went to work and got dinner. After eating I hitched up the team and drove out after the hides. When I got on top of the hill I saw a dead buffalo in front of me about 200 yards away, and on beyond a little ways further I saw another dead one, and my brother lying on the ground about fifteen feet behind that dead animal. I hurried on to where George was lying, only to find him quite dead."

How did it happen? No one knows. His neck was broken, and his body badly bruised. Presumably, he, thinking the buffalo dead, or at least dying, walked up to

him, when the old denizen of the plains made his last fight
for life,—arose, and dealt George Bryan the blow that
broke his neck, and landed him where he lay when found.
This seems reasonable, from the fact that his gun was
lying quite close to the buffalo when found. He evidently fell dead after snuffing out the life of the hunter.
Yet this, like many other tragedies that occurred in the
destruction of the great herds that roamed from the Rio
Grande river to Manitoba, and then on farther, is a mystery.

BELLFIELD AND THE DRIED APPLES.

During the time that many of the camps banded together for mutual protection, and during the Indian raids
of 1877, George Bellfield, of Adobe Walls and Casa Ar-
marilla notoriety, was camped upon a tributary of the
Colorado river. Joe Hoard, Joe Rutledge and Frank
Lewis each joined him. They and George mutually agreed
to camp together. None of them having a camp helper at
the time, it was agreed among them to take "turn about"
in doing the cooking. It must be remembered that George
was of Teutonic origin, and talked very brokenly. As
they started in, George's was the fourth turn. As the
other three were leaving camp one morning for the day's
hunt, Frank Lewis called back:

"O, George! Cook some dried apples. We hain't had
any for a long time now."

George made no pretensions as a cook, but his main
hobby was to have a great plenty. There was a large
army camp kettle in camp, that held five gallons, bought
at a sale of condemned goods at Fort Elliott. He filled
this kettle nearly full of dried apples, poured water on until
the kettle was full, and placed it on hot coals to simmer.
Soon the apples began to swell and heave up above the
top of that camp-kettle. George scraped off a messpan
full from the top of the kettle, shoveled some more coals
around the bottom, and went ahead with his other duties.

Soon he noticed the kettle was again top-heavy. He
grabbed up a frying-pan, filled it, then got a Dutch oven
and baled it full. He thought strange of it, stopped, and
stood watching them still heaving up.

(346)

He then ran to the wagon nearest the fire, jerked a wagon-sheet from under his bed, drew it up alongside the kettle, and scooped and scraped apples off the top as fast as they would rise, until he had a windrow of partly swelled apples.

Then the swelling stopped, and the apples were cooking in a normal condition when the men came into camp. The first thing he said was:

"By shing! der vas a pig bargain in dem drite apples. Dey swell much as dree dimes. Ven I goes to Charley Rath's I puys me soom more yust like dem."

This is the same George Bellfield who came in to the Adobe Walls, after the Indians raised the siege in 1874, and seeing the prairie strewn with dead horses (for half a mile around were dead horses which the hunters had killed from under mounted warriors), asked the question:

"Vat kind of a disease is der matter mit de horses?'

He was told by Cranky McCabe, "They died of lead poison."

Bellfield was all unconscious that a fierce attack had been made, and a three-days siege had been laid upon a small band of bold buffalo-hunters, and this by as daring a combination of tribes as ever roamed the Southwest. At the time all this happened, Bellfield was in his camp, alone, eight miles up the Canadian river, while there were thousands of Indians roaming at will all over the country. Yet, somehow they missed him; otherwise the author would never have seen honest, whole-souled George Bellfield.

AN INCIDENT OF BEN JACKSON'S EXPERIENCE.

Most all the big-game hunters were men of adventure. They loved the wild, uninhabited region of the great Southwest. Nearly all of them had read of Daniel Boone wandering alone in the wilds of the then uninhabited lands east of the Mississippi. Most of these men had passed through the War of the Rebellion, on one side or the other. They were of necessity self-reliant, and could and did meet every emergency as a matter of course.

Take the incident of Ben Jackson. He left his lonely camp, 200 miles from Fort Worth, with a two-horse load of buffalo-hides. Twelve miles from his starting-point three Indians made a running attack on him. He killed one of them and the other two ran out of range of his gun. He was on the divide between North and South Pease rivers. After traveling a mile or so from the dead Indian, he noticed the other two, paralleling him,—one on each side of him and just out of range. All at once "kerchug!" and down went the left front wheel of the wagon. The sudden drop brought Ben to the ground; also gun, mess-kit, bedding, and ammunition-box.

He was nearly a mile from wood and water. The two Indians saw the predicament he was in, and they circled in between him and the South Pease river. He unhitched his team, hobbled them close to the wagon, laid down flat upon the ground, crawled like a snake towards a break to the right of him, and when 300 yards from his outfit he wriggled himself into a deep buffalo-wallow in the edge of a prairie-dog town. And here he lay, peeping out on the flat and waiting events.

The hill in the break towards which he had been crawling was less than 200 yards from him. While lying here, his quick, alert ear and steady eye taking everything around him, and his mind busy evolving a way out of his present predicament, a large diamond rattlesnake came crawling obliquely just in front of him from a near-by prairie-dog hole. Not wishing to disclose his position to the Indians by shooting the snake, he suddenly pressed the heavy gun-barrel down on the snake, about six inches back of its head. Pressing the gun down hard with his left hand, he took his wiping-stick in his right hand and played a tattoo on its head until he had killed it. All the time he was doing this the body was wriggling and writhing, while the rattlers kept the ever zee-zee-zz-z until death.

All that time two wild plains Indians were seeking Ben's life. The dead Indian's horse was grazing towards his wagon. Ben heard a horse whinny behind the breaks he had started for. Looking intently, he soon saw an Indian crawling around a point in the break towards him. Without being seen, Jackson had got into the wallow. He waited until the Indian's body was in full view. The warrior rose up in a sitting posture, when Ben, seeing this, drew a bead, fired, and sent him to the happy hunting-grounds.

After the Indian had rolled over, Ben, thinking perhaps he was "playing possum" on him, waited some little time, when he heard a loud halloo, the sound coming from the direction of the wagon. Upon looking around he saw "Limpy Jim" Smith. Looking again, and seeing the last Indian he shot still lying where he fell, he got up and walked out upon the flat and hailed the man at the wagon, saying:

"Glad you came, for with Injuns, snakes, and my wagon breaking down, I've got a good deal to do, and I want you to help me set my wagon-tire."

Smith, in relating the affair, said Jackson was cool and deliberate, and acted as if such things were of an every-day occurrence.

Smith was on his way north from the Double Mountain Fork of the Brazos to Fort Elliott. He was on horse-back, and, seeing Jackson's outfit from a distance, rode to it from sheer curiosity; for people were few and far apart in that region at that time of the year, this being early in the fall of 1876, and before the general outbreaks of the spring of 1877.

The rest of this story,—how the two men unloaded the hides, got the two dead Indians' ponies, went to the South Pease river, got a keg of water, cut some china-wood poles, brought all to the wagon, cooked and ate a hearty meal, then made false spokes for the wheel, wrapped the felloes with gunny-sacks, heated the tire with a buffalo-chip fire, reset the tire, put on the wheel, loaded everything onto the wagon, and drove that evening and night twenty-five miles, and at daylight next morning were in sight of the Kiowa Peak, where they felt they were perfectly safe,— is only one of the many incidents that happened on the buffalo range which illustrate the correctness of the say-ing that "truth is stranger than fiction."

MY KANSAS QUEEN.

1. My kingdom is the prairie,
   The grasses, and the flowers;
And listening to the summer wind
   I while away the hours.
My wealth is but the love of you,
   Who are so free from guile;
The only tribute that I ask
   Is the sunshine of your smile.

CHORUS.

My prairie princess,
   Give me your heart;
I'll be unhappy if we live apart;
   Transform this lonely life of mine
To gladsome summer shine;
   Be my sunny-haired sweetheart,
Be my Kansas queen.

3. No matter if the winter sky
   With clouds is overcast;
Your face holds all the sunshine
   Of the happy summer past;
And the morning star of boyhood
   Was never half so fair,
As when the tiny snowflakes
   Turn to diamonds in your hair.

CHORUS.

JOHN GUERINE, Author.

AT·THE·SPRING·OF·THE·SHINING·ROCK